Thank You!

Thank you for buying this book.

With over a hundred sketch charts, loads of information and many aerial photographs, we think you will find this book a bargain when you consider it is still about the price of a chart.

We sell far less of these books than we do of our guides to the Windwards and Leewards. This means we cannot update it with the same regularity. In addition the size of Venezuela makes getting everywhere hard.

Jeff Fisher, my partner in early versions, is in China building boats. So in this edition, the Venezuela part was updated by Oscar Hernandez, an old friend who is also a Venezuelan diplomat and at one time was the representing Venezuela in Grenada.

He visited all major marine centers and towns to get the latest information, however, for the most part he went by car, "roading" as he calls it; he would have preferred to sail. The down side of this is that he did not revisit many of the isolated anchorages. So do not be too surprised is you read a description of a bay with "one farmhouse" and find it to contain a fancy housing development we have missed.

We expect this edition to be on the shelves for some years, so the information will slowly get dated.

Keep this guide up to date via www.doyleguides.com

In order to get around this we publish updated information on our website: www.Doyleguides.com, check out the latest information on this site before you set sail. This site is not commercial in the sense we do not try to sell you anything and we do not charge people for links and there are no ads on it.

Unlike the other guide areas I do not make frequent visits to Venezuela or Bonaire, so the internet updates I give come from emails to me, news reports and occasional phone calls.

I very much welcome input from cruisers. I tried a system of direct posting from readers on the web site several times . Each time, within a month, it got taken over by machines just endlessly posting links to everything from airlines to porno sites. So we are back to regular email. I will try and post all your relevant comments as they come in. Please email them to me through www.doyleguides.com or sailorsguide@hotmail.com

Thank you, Chris Doyle

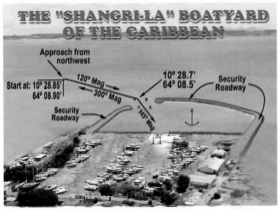

CRUISING GUIDE TO

Chris Doyle	Text, charts, layout
Oscar Hernández	Venezuela update
George DeSalvo	Bonaire update
Sally Erdle	Illustrations
Jeff Fisher	Photos

Oscar Hernández

Venezuela Ministry of Tourism,

Laura DeSalvo, Harry Terhorst,

Ellen Sanpere, Laura de Salvo,

Robert-Jan Richters, Chris Doyle

DISTRIBUTION

USA AND WORLDWIDE
Cruising Guide Publications
P.O. Box 1017, Dunedin, Florida
34697-1017, Tel: 727-733-5322
info@cruisingguides.com

VENEZUELA
Oscar Hernandez,
58 212 239-9197/ 412 234-8007
Oscar_Hernandez_ve@yahoo.com

TRINIDAD & TOBAGO
Boaters' Enterprises
Crews Inn, Chaguaramas, Trinidad
Tel: 868-634-2055
JackD@BoatersEnterprise.com

ST. VINCENT AND THE
GRENADINES
Frances Punnett, Box 17 St. Vincent
Tel: 784-458-4246

ST. LUCIA
Ted Bull, Box 125, Castries, St.
Lucia, Tel/Fax: 758-452-8177
E-mail: windshift@candw.lc

GRENADA
Alan Hooper,
Tel: 473-444-3622/409-9451
email: sark@caribsurf.com

AUTHOR'S NOTES

In the text we give a very rough price guide to the restaurants. This is an estimate of what you might spend to eat out and have a drink:

$A is $50 U.S. or over
$B is $25 to $50 U.S.
$C is $12 to $25 U.S.
$D is under $12 U.S.

We are happy to include advertising. It gives extra information and keeps the price of the book reasonable. If you wish to help us keep it that way, tell all the restaurateurs and shopkeepers, "I read about it in the Cruising Guide." It helps us no end.

Tell us about your experiences, good or bad. We will consider your comments when writing the next edition.
Please email your comments to:
sailorsguide@hotmail.com
If your information is by way of an update we may post it on our web site:
doyleguides.com

Printed in Trinidad

ACKNOWLEDGEMENTS

Many thanks to all those who helped. Especially for the emails I got from Venezuela. Elen Sanpere, Yousaf Butt, Larry Rudnick, Farrari, Catherine and Daniel Beauvois, Dick and Tricia Marx are among others who sent in helpful updates

Thank you all

Chris Doyle

VENEZUELA AND BONAIRE

PUBLISHED BY
CHRIS DOYLE PUBLISHING
in association with
CRUISING GUIDE PUBLICATIONS

ISBN 0-944428-78-9

First edition published in
Cruising guide to Trinidad & Tobago,
Venezuela and Bonaire 1994

Published as Cruising Guide to
Venezuela and Bonaire   1997
Second edition published   2002
This edition Published   2006

ANYONE reprinting ANYTHING from this book without the permission of the publishers is in BIG TROUBLE.

SKETCH CHART INFORMATION

Our sketch charts are interpretive and designed for yachts drawing about 6.5 feet. Deeper yachts should refer to the depths on their charts.

LAND	HILLS	ROADS PATHS

LAND HEIGHTS ARE IN FEET AND APPROXIMATE

WATER TOO SHALLOW FOR NAVIGATION OR DANGEROUS IN SOME CONDITIONS

 SURFACE REEF   +5 ROCKS, SHOALS, DRYING HEIGHTS AT LOW WATER

NAVIGABLE WATER   60 9 DEPTHS ARE IN FEET AND APPROXIMATE

1.5 KNOTS CURRENT   CHURCH    AERIAL

MANGROVES   ANCHORAGE   PICK UP MOORING ONLY

WRECKS   DAY STOP ANCHORAGE

GREEN BEACON
GREEN BUOYS (PORT)

RED BEACON
RED BUOYS (STARBOARD)

 IALA B MARKS SHOWING DIRECTION OF DANGER (BUOYS & BEACONS)

ISOLATED SHOAL BEACONS & BUOYS

YELLOW BUOYS

RED & GREEN DIVIDED CHANNEL BUOYS   MOORING OR OTHER BUOY

SECTOR   **LIGHTS**
WHITE (W)   FL = FLASHING, F = FIXED, L = LONG,
GREEN (G)   Q = QUICK, M = MILES
YELLOW (Y)   LIGHT EXPLANATION:
RED (R)   FL (2) 4S, 6M
                 LIGHT GROUP FLASHING 2 EVERY
                 FOUR SECONDS, VISIBLE 6 MILES

 SNORKELING SITE   SCUBA DIVING SITE
ONLY THOSE SITES THAT ARE EASILY ACCESSIBLE ARE SHOWN

CRUISING GUIDE TO

VENEZUELA
& BONAIRE

by Chris Doyle

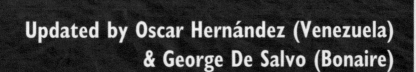

Updated by Oscar Hernández (Venezuela)
& George De Salvo (Bonaire)

TABLE OF CONTENTS

MARGARITA TO ARAYA (cont)

CUMANA AND GOLFO DE CARIACO 118

MOCHIMA TO PUERTO LA CRUZ 145

VENEZUELA'S OFFSHORE ISLANDS 229

PLANNING & CRUISING

Introduction

*V*enezuela covers the northeastern part of South America. It is a beautiful country, large enough to offer all kinds of landscapes and climates. A country of rainforests, deserts, idyllic islands, and Andean mountains so tall they are capped in snow. There are immense areas of mangroves and savannas with table mountains. Here you find the world's tallest waterfall, Angel Falls.

Venezuelan society has been influenced by Indian civilizations, Spanish conquest, and a long, hard struggle for independence. Today it is an independent country with a Spanish tradition. Oil is a major resource, and Venezuelans are technologically advanced. There have been both economic and political problems in the last few years, but the country has vast resources, both human and material, and there is hope that things will turn around at some point.

Many yachtspeople visit Venezuela to haul out and refit their vessels. One of the big advantages of hauling here is that the coastal area around Puerto la Cruz and Cumaná is extremely dry, excellent for both drying out hulls and getting work done.

Venezuela offers superb cruising. You can get away from it all and find deserted or uncrowded anchorages. There are idyllic beaches and mangrove islands where you can watch parrots and scarlet ibis.

When you run out of time on your immigration card, it is sometimes more fun to sail to Bonaire than to deal with the officials to get an extension. Also, for those heading west, Bonaire is the gateway to the ABC islands.

Bonaire lies to the west of Venezuela's offshore islands and is part of the Netherlands Antilles. Bonaire is small; you can drive right round it in a day with time to spare, but it is also delightful, with a sparkling clean town and clear water. It would take weeks to explore Bonaire's dive sites, which are so good and plentiful that this diminutive island is a world-class diving center. Bonaire produces salt and is also known for the delicate pink flamingos that come from Venezuela to feed on the salt flats.

While many boats visit Venezuela and Bonaire, it is still enough off the beaten track to bring out the adventurer in all of us.

Welcome to Venezuela and Bonaire!

Page 14-15:
Juangirego with insets
of Cariaquita and the
Bonaire salt ponds

Opposite:
Table mountain

Planning your Cruise

Cruising comfort

The water temperature throughout this cruising area is a few degrees colder than in the Eastern Caribbean. This makes for pleasant swimming and a refreshing plunge in the heat of the day. Scuba divers and snorkelers who are sensitive to the cold might find a wetsuit jacket helpful.

The wind often dies at night along the coast of Venezuela. This can make it warm for sleeping below, especially in marinas. Windscoops or efficient 12-volt fans are useful luxuries.

Many interesting anchorages along Venezuela's coast are in mangrove lagoons or very close to shore. Considering this, they are far less buggy than one might expect. However, the odd whining mosquito often manages to find your ear in the middle of the night. Screening the cabins with mosquito netting, while not essential, may save you some aggravation. Screens are not necessary for sitting out in the cockpit. For those who do not have screens, a can of bug repellent and a pack of mosquito coils should suffice for the occasional buggy anchorage.

Fishing

Fishing is excellent throughout this region. The westerly setting equatorial current hits the continental shelf, causing colder, nutrient-rich water to rise from the sea bed. That old lure and line that has been hanging unsuccessfully over the stern of your yacht for hundreds of miles is likely to jump into action and surprise you.

In Venezuela, spear fishing is forbidden in all park areas, which includes most of the best anchorages. In addition, when you are in some parks, officials may hold your spear gun till you depart, which can be a hassle. My suggestion is to trade your spear gun for a light casting rod. A trip out at daybreak or sunset will often bring in a tasty little barracuda or snapper. If you don't have any luck casting, troll behind the dinghy going close to mangroves and reefs with a small lure. If this fails, trade or buy from the fishermen.

From our questioning of locals, ciguatera poisoning seems to be extremely rare throughout this region. However, to ensure your own safety, avoid really big barracudas and jacks.

Planning & Cruising

Swimming

Water clarity varies a lot with location. In the outer islands, visibility can be fantastic, as can the snorkeling. Closer to shore, some places are clear, others murky. The abundance of Christmas tree worms and fan worms makes for brightly colored underwater landscapes.

I have heard of no shark attacks or unusual aquatic dangers in Venezuela or Bonaire. Caimans and small crocodiles exist in some areas, but they prefer the muddy backwaters you are unlikely to swim in. Be aware of currents, watch where you put your feet, and enjoy the swimming and snorkeling.

Money matters

The currency in Venezuela is the Bolívar, and in Bonaire they use NA guilders. (See details in our *Island at a glance* sections.)

U.S. dollars are welcome in Bonaire and can be used much the same as local currency.

Venezuela now has strict new currency rules. Historically, artificial exchange rates have had problems, so expect that regulations and the exchange rate may change anytime. The official exchange rate is now 1$US to 2150 Bs or 100 Bs to 0.04651$US (www.doyleguides.com links to an exchange rate calculator). You can get cash at the of-ficial rate from Cambios and with your credit or debit cards from street-side ATMs. On entry, you have to declare the origin of large quantities of US cash ($10,000 as we go to press). Changing money back into U.S. dollars is going to be hard, so don't get a huge surplus. In this kind of system there is always a black market. Dabbling in this will likely lead you to a long jail term. You might want to check out their accommodations before you go this route.

Credit/debit cards work well for goods and services throughout the region, though there have been occasional problems in Venezuela because of very high credit card charges. There have also been occasional credit card frauds, where money has been drawn from a credit card account. Keep track of your transactions, never leave a carbon copy of a transaction around, and keep an eye on your account to make sure all is OK.

Language

Spanish is spoken in Venezuela, and English is understood by only a small number of people. If you have a chance to learn some Spanish before you arrive, so much the better. If not, pack along some Spanish books or tapes and study as you go. It doesn't take much to pick up the basics necessary for shopping, traveling, and going to restaurants.

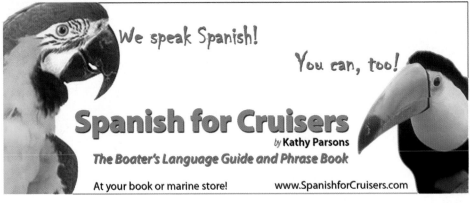

Planning & Cruising

The people in Venezuela are generally very patient and kind to those struggling with their language. We have added some Spanish words and phrases in the back of this guide to help you along.

You should also get Spanish for Cruisers by Kathy Parsons: it is exceptionally useful and user-friendly.

In Bonaire, they speak Papiamento and Dutch. Luckily, both English and Spanish are also spoken.

Communications

The best way to stay in touch is to pick up a mobile phone. You can get a phone ready to go for about 40$US, or if you have a phone you might just get a SIM which is very inexpensive, either one for pre-paid cards, or a post-paid plan where you pay by credit card.

The best companies are Digitel, Digicel, Telcel, Movilnet and Movistar. Digitel, and Digicel which use GSM technology is probably the best way to go. Digitel is based in Caracas so most calls in outlaying areas are roaming, which can be expensive.

Digicel has offices in Puerto la Cruz on Av. Principal de Lecherias near Calle Pampatar, across from the Centro Com. Anna. (0281 262-6060 www.digicel.com.ve.) Like the other providers, the charges for outgoing calls are calculated by the second, and can add up, so many people use text messages.

Photography

If you are using a digital camera, you will probably not need too much in the way of supplies.

For traditionalists, photographic supplies are available in the large towns in Venezuela and in Bonaire. Film is usually reasonably priced, and there are first-rate facilities for developing and printing your print film. Slide film can also be developed fast and well, but it has to be the E6 process type (Fujichrome, Ektachrome).

When you are leaving a major town to go cruising, buy plenty of film, because nothing will be available in smaller towns and villages. For aquatic shots, a polarizing filter brings out the water colors and clouds.

Medical care

Medical care in Venezuela is excellent. Many people without insurance visit Venezuela for medical services, as the cost is only a fraction of what it is in the U.A. Venezuela has top-quality, up-to-date equipment even for highly specialized medical procedures. This includes advanced eye surgery, both for the removal of growths and cataracts and for correction of lens shape. Venezuela's dentists are also highly trained, modern and reasonably priced.

We have listed some of the most useful facilities in our directory section.

Bonaire is too small to have really extensive medical facilities, but you can easily fly to neighboring Curacao.

Dangers

Venezuela has abundant wildlife, including poisonous snakes such as the fer-de-lance, bushmaster, and coral snake. There are also scorpions and centipedes. Most of these stay in the wilder regions and don't

present much danger, as long as you keep your eyes open and tread carefully. Small ticks and biting insects can be more annoying. The liberal use of repellent or long pants and shoes and socks is advisable when you go exploring in the forest. Insect repellent can also be handy ashore in the evenings.

Vampire bats

Sooner or later you will hear tales about vampire bats. These make wonderful after-dinner stories as you sit out in the cockpit: the quiet flutter of wings as you sleep; the tiny, furry body that cuddles up ever so gently to your toes so as not to wake you; a small incision carefully made with razor-sharp teeth; and then the bat gently licks away the blood while you sweetly dream. As an actual threat, they rank very low. They are unknown in Bonaire. In Venezuela, bats have been known to feed on yachtspeople, but this is quite rare.

Before 1987, when only a few hundred foreign yachts would cruise these waters annually, I didn't hear of any attacks. I suspect the chances of being bitten are so small that there were just not enough yachts to make it likely. With an increasing number of yachts, more attacks have been reported over a larger area. Locals also are occasional victims, though they tend to ignore the bites.

Isla Borracha has had more reported bat attacks than elsewhere. It lies a few miles off Puerto la Cruz, and there is a small fishing village in the anchorage. Villagers say that a few of them have been bitten by bats. Bat attacks have also been reported in Laguna Grande in Golfo de Cariaco and in several anchorages along the northern coast of the Península de Paria. The chances of getting bitten by a bat are very low unless you anchor in Isla Borracha. However, it is very easy to protect yourself. As far as I know, bats have not yet figured out how to cut through mosquito net, so screen in and sleep tight.

When a bat bites you, it adds an anticoagulant so you will keep bleeding. This can make for a mess, but is not usually medically too serious. More threatening is the chance of contracting rabies. If you are the unlucky one who gets bitten, then rabies shots are essential. It is not worth taking chances with this.

Hepatitis and cholera

We have not heard of any yachtsperson getting cholera. We have heard of a few cases of hepatitis. To be on the safe side, wash everything well and do not eat raw oysters or fish.

Security

Bonaire has had a few incidents over the last few years, so you don't want to relax your vigilance completely, despite the peaceful nature of the place.

Venezuela appears to have more problems per visiting yacht than the Eastern Caribbean. This is not only true of

El Oculto view

Opposite:
Iguana in Chimana
Secunda

Planning & Cruising

Margarita - Oscar Hernandez photos

yachts getting robbed but also of robbery in general, including pickpockets and muggers ashore. Those from yachts are targeted, but not particularly, Venezuelans get robbed, too.

Life is not-risk free; there is no way to guarantee nothing will happen, but with the right mindset, you do not need to take unnecessary risks, and many people cruise in Venezuela without any problem.

Ashore, be very careful when you come out of a bank, as street people know you have gone there to get money.

When you go ashore in Venezuela, be streetwise. It is unwise to wear flashy jewelry. Pickpockets do exist, so stay aware of what is going on around you. Don't set your handbag or briefcase down somewhere and move away. Take taxis at night if going through doubtful areas, and if you are renting a car, do not leave anything, even in the trunk. Always park it in a guarded area, or you may come back and find the spark plugs or wheels gone. It is also advisable to use a wheel-locking device if it is supplied. Do not keep large stashes of cash on board; use travelers checks and credit cards.

Thefts of outboards, dinghies, and odds and ends may happen anywhere. You need to keep things locked up tight.

Accept that if you have a fancy inflatable with a good outboard, you should look after it very carefully. If you visit Venezuela

with an old, solid dinghy and ratty-looking, two-horse outboard, you probably won't have a problem, but I would still hoist and lock it, and go into marinas in places like Puerto la Cruz and Cumaná.

Recent moves and increased patrols by officials have cut back a bit on yacht theft, which is good news, and recent reports are that the coast guard has been very helpful.

More worrying is a significant incidence of armed robbery and attack in some areas of Venezuela, sometimes with loss of life or physical damage to the victims. For a current take on the situation, communicate with the security net on SSB: 8104.0 at 0815 local time, before the marine weather forecast. This can give you an idea of how things are. If this is not possible, you can go online. My website, www.doyleguides.com, gives links both to the caribcruisers net, which lists all the crimes reported to them in the last few years, and Onsa.org the website of the Venezuelan association which has a map of danger areas.

Onsa gives a risk map. You should check out the current version. As we went to press, the safest areas were the offshore islands, the marinas around Caracas, and Morrocoy national park to Chichiriviche. The worst area is the eastern end of the Península de Paria. Also in the bad area are Puerto la Cruz, and Margarita. Puerto Cabello and the Golfo de Cariaco, are not so bad, but be alert.

My personal recommendation is to stay well clear of Araya and the north coast of the Península de Paria (especially east of Carúpano) and use marinas in Cumaná and Puerto La Cruz. I would treat the Mochima National Park with some caution, either sailing in company or returning to a safe haven at night.

I would not tell people exactly when I was leaving or what route I was taking.

However, things change rapidly for better or worse, so check with those websites.

You need to be able to hoist your dinghy at night, and even then, if you have an attractive rig, it is going to be hard to keep it. Locals seem to be adept at cutting through wire and chain and removing your dinghy while you sleep. You are clearly at higher risk if you hang out for a long time in a major town anchorage. Do not leave anything on deck, including scuba tanks, snorkeling gear, or washing hanging from the lifelines.

Be especially careful in large towns like Puerto la Cruz and Cumaná. Ask other yachts in the area how things are and leave someone on board at all times if necessary, or go into a marina that has good security.

Before venturing into isolated areas, get local information on whether there have been any recent problems. You can ask other cruisers or request information on one of the cruisers' nets that sometimes operate on the VHF. Try to get information from people who have recently cruised where you are going. If you anchor in an area that may be risky, then figure a way to lock yourself in for the night. If anyone boards, use the VHF, and if you cannot raise anyone, pretend that you have got through and speak loudly. Keep a fog horn and spotlight handy, and you may have a chance of scaring a prowler away.

Punch the Guadacosta phone numbers into your phone (see our directory).

Keep in mind that most people cruise without having significant problems, and places where others fear to drop anchor are often some of the best.

Drugs

Illegal drugs are taken very seriously by law enforcement officers throughout this area. Anyone getting caught even with one joint can expect confiscation of the yacht, a monster fine, and a long jail term.

STAR

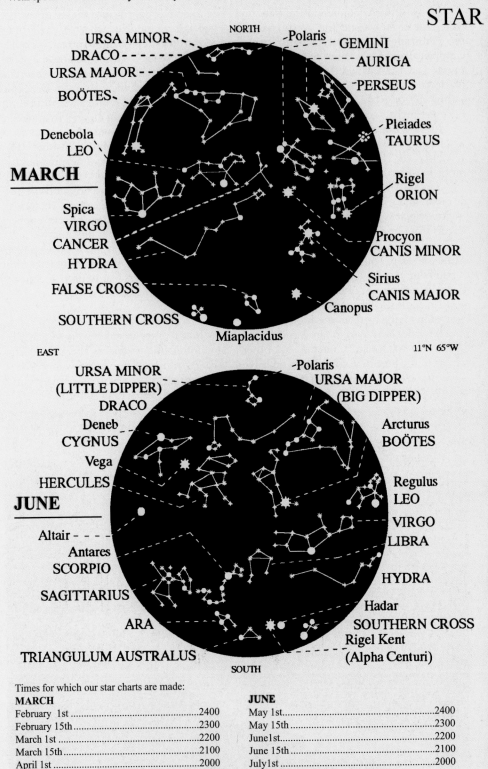

NORTH

URSA MINOR
DRACO
URSA MAJOR
BOÖTES

Polaris   GEMINI
AURIGA
PERSEUS

Denebola
LEO

MARCH

Pleiades
TAURUS

Rigel
ORION

Spica
VIRGO
CANCER
HYDRA
FALSE CROSS
SOUTHERN CROSS

Procyon
CANIS MINOR

Sirius
CANIS MAJOR

Canopus

Miaplacidus

EAST   11°N 65°W

URSA MINOR
(LITTLE DIPPER)
DRACO

Polaris
URSA MAJOR
(BIG DIPPER)

Deneb
CYGNUS
Vega
HERCULES

Arcturus
BOÖTES

JUNE

Regulus
LEO

VIRGO
LIBRA

Altair
Antares
SCORPIO
SAGITTARIUS
ARA
TRIANGULUM AUSTRALUS

HYDRA

Hadar
SOUTHERN CROSS
Rigel Kent
(Alpha Centuri)

SOUTH

Times for which our star charts are made:

MARCH		JUNE	
February 1st	2400	May 1st	2400
February 15th	2300	May 15th	2300
March 1st	2200	June 1st	2200
March 15th	2100	June 15th	2100
April 1st	2000	July 1st	2000
April 15th	1900	July 15th	1900

CHARTS

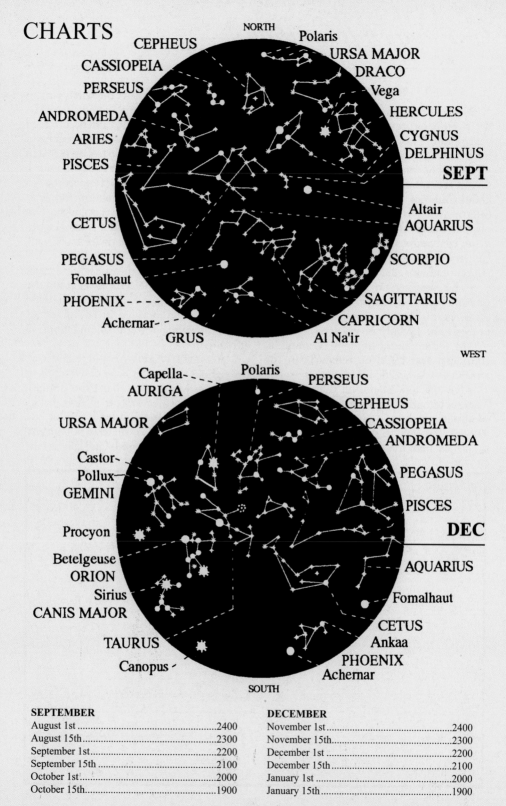

SEPT

NORTH

Polaris
CEPHEUS
CASSIOPEIA
PERSEUS
ANDROMEDA
ARIES
PISCES
URSA MAJOR
DRACO
Vega
HERCULES
CYGNUS
DELPHINUS
CETUS
PEGASUS
Fomalhaut
PHOENIX
Achernar
GRUS
Altair
AQUARIUS
SCORPIO
SAGITTARIUS
CAPRICORN
Al Na'ir

WEST

DEC

Capella
AURIGA
URSA MAJOR
Castor
Pollux
GEMINI
Procyon
Betelgeuse
ORION
Sirius
CANIS MAJOR
TAURUS
Canopus
Polaris
PERSEUS
CEPHEUS
CASSIOPEIA
ANDROMEDA
PEGASUS
PISCES
AQUARIUS
Fomalhaut
CETUS
Ankaa
PHOENIX
Achernar

SOUTH

SEPTEMBER		DECEMBER	
August 1st	2400	November 1st	2400
August 15th	2300	November 15th	2300
September 1st	2200	December 1st	2200
September 15th	2100	December 15th	2100
October 1st	2000	January 1st	2000
October 15th	1900	January 15th	1900

Cruising Information

Weather

The weather is generally pleasant, with temperatures of 78-85° Fahrenheit year-round. The Venezuelan coast varies from desert regions with very little rain to mountainous rainforests that plunge into the sea. In general, rain falls on the mountains and the interior, with conditions becoming drier near low lying coastal areas. Smaller offshore islands are truly desert islands. The many boatyards around Puerto la Cruz and Cumaná are good places to get work done, as the weather is relatively dry.

The rainy season is usually from late June through November. In the really dry areas, there is almost no rainfall, even in the rainy season. Bonaire is very dry.

In some coastal areas in Venezuela, thunderstorms build up regularly in the afternoon and subside before dusk.

The offshore islands all the way from Testigos through to Bonaire lie in the trade wind belt, and there is usually a good breeze. The weather close to the coast of Venezuela is different from the islands. Along the coast from Carenero to Cumaná the winds vary in direction, with light breezes coming from the south through west to north. It often blows hard from the east along this coast from about noon to dusk. From Puerto Cabello to Carenero and from Cumaná to the eastern end of Trinidad, an easterly wind prevails, but it often blows hard during the day and then calms down at night. Many yachts heading east power overnight. This rule is not cast in stone, and it is less likely to be calm at night when the trades are blowing hard.

A very strong northeasterly wind often blows through Coche and Cubagua and the eastern half of the Golfo de Cariaco. In these areas, the wind picks up in late morning, howls through the afternoon, and drops off at night.

A westerly setting current flows throughout the area. It flows consistently as far west as Margarita, though the strength is variable. Farther west, it is more fickle. Sometimes it flows at a brisk one or two knots; at other times, there is no current, or it can even be reversed. One can usually

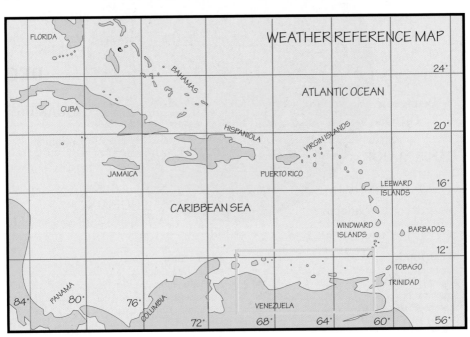

26

	Tobago (Scarborough)	Trinidad (Boca de Monos)	Trinidad (Pointe-a-Pierre)	Punta Pargo	Carúpano	Testigos	Margarita (Polamar)	Coche	Cumaná	Mochima	Puerto La Cruz	I. de Piritu	Blanquilla	Isla Tortuga (Playa Caldera)	Carenero	Los Roques (Sebastopol)	Caraballeda	Bonaire	Puerto Cabello	Chichiriviche
Grenada (Prickly B.)	83	78	103	80	119	86	139	155	190	192	208	220	170	214	274	288	311	390	381	388
Tobago (Scarborough)		63	88	83	153	141	184	192	231	234	249	272	234	265	321	350	363	456	434	443
Tobago Boca de Monos			25	23	95	94	130	135	175	177	189	212	188	211	261	300	304	405	434	388
Trinidad (Pointe-a-Pierre)				47	118	115	154	151	197	200	214	229	213	236	289	324	330	424	401	412
Punta Pargo					72	74	107	113	150	153	167	182	166	189	242	277	283	375	353	365
Carúpano						43	39	44	80	82	100	122	106	118	172	207	215	314	287	295
Testigos							49	68	97	100	114	135	92	128	188	207	225	316	295	308
Margarita (Polamar)								19	47	49	67	88	78	86	137	175	180	277	252	265
Coche									37	40	54	70	78	76	129	167	174	272	240	253
Cumaná										10	32	55	85	68	113	161	158	266	229	241
Mochima											23	43	88	62	105	156	150	260	223	232
Puerto La Cruz												20	96	57	91	148	136	250	209	217
I. de Piritu													102	52	70	138	118	233	186	198
Blanquilla														64	118	116	150	220	216	220
Isla Tortuga (Playa Caldera)															62	94	101	200	168	179
Carenero																83	55	169	124	138
Los Roques (Sebastopol)																	71	109	112	111
Caraballeda																		127	71	86
Bonaire																			102	74
Puerto Cabello																				30

MILEAGE CHART

This table is approximate and is offered as a guide to planning. Distances sailed vary greatly due to wind and current.

keep out of the current by staying within a mile or two of the mainland.

This whole region is considered to be south of the hurricane belt, which is why many people visit during the summer. However, one or two have hit during the last few hundred years. Less severe tropical storms, though rare, are not unknown. It is sensible to listen to the weather, not only because of hurricanes, but also because easterly waves and other disturbances can come through with a lot of rain and wind. Throughout the region, you can probably get the weather in English on Transworld Radio from Bonaire on 800 kHz AM band. They have news on the hour daily and marine forecasts at 20 minutes past the hour. They are not detailed but should give you news of major weather systems. (See also our section on SSB and Ham radio.) Should a storm threaten, go to a secure harbor. In Venezuela, there are endless excellent harbors tucked into mangrove lagoons.

While this area is too far south to be subject to northers, the swells from these systems do affect the area, sometimes creating uncomfortable seas and rolly anchorages in harbors that are exposed to the north.

You can visit Venezuela any time of the year, but the trip back eastwards is tougher in the winter, when the trades are blowing hard. Also, many outer island anchorages, such as Los Roques, are more pleasant in the gentler summer winds.

VHF, HAM, and SSB Radio

Around Margarita and Puerto la Cruz there is often an informal VHF net with information on such things as weather and security. This can be very helpful in Venezuela where such news is not always easy to come by. We give more information under the ports concerned.

Those who have SSB and Ham radios have many weather sources. As the owner of the cheapest shortwave receiver that will pick up SSB, the only weather station I have been able to get is the Caribbean Weather Net on 8104 USB at 0830 local time. Tune in 15 minutes earlier and you can listen to the Caribbean Safety Net first. Other stations you can try (all local time) include: Caribbean emergency/weather net on 7162 kHz LSB at 0630; Caribbean emergency/ weather net on 3815 kHz LSB at 1835; NMN offshore forecast 4426, 6501 & 8764 USB at 0530 & 2330; Southbound II, 12359 USB at 1600; and Cocktail and Weather Net 7086 LSB at 1630 (not normally Sundays). For information on weather fax check website: http://205.156.54.206/om/marine/ radiofax.htm

Navigation

Venezuela is not as well charted as the Eastern Caribbean. For many areas, coastal detail is sparse. Proceed cautiously and keep a good lookout whenever you are close to shore. In this guide, we provide sketch charts

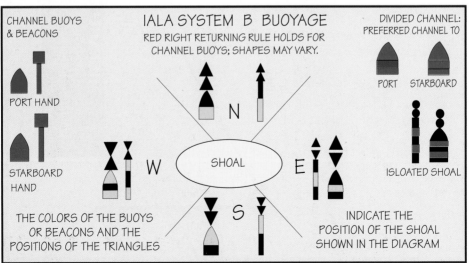

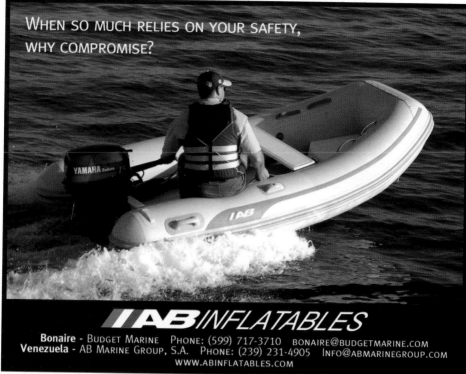

of many areas where the navigational charts are inadequate. As far as we know, these are the only charts available for quite a few anchorages.

The plus side to this is that you have to be part explorer, and this adds to your sense of adventure, discovery, and satisfaction.

Lights

Lights throughout this region are unreliable and should be treated with caution. In more remote stations, they are solar-powered and fully automated. Unfortunately, they are not all checked as often as necessary to keep them in full working order. We have seen a light come on promptly at dusk and die within the hour as the aging battery failed to keep its charge. If you work with the idea that any one light has about a 60 percent chance of working, you will not go too far wrong.

Buoys

The whole area comes under the IALA B system (red right returning). But buoys are not always in place, and there are places where a channel is buoyed in red on both sides. Treat buoys with caution.

Fishing boats

Night sailing along the north coast of Venezuela requires great caution. Fishing trawlers sometimes do not carry lights.

Stay well clear of fishing boats whenever you can. Large nets of tough plastic are set, which could ensnare your yacht. In Venezuela, collisions between trawlers and yachts are not unknown. In one case, the autopilot on the fishing boat was not working, so the crew jammed a chair under the wheel while they went to eat. The chair fell out and the trawler swung hard around and rammed a yacht.

Do not approach Porlamar or Pampatar at night. Many fishing boats set nets in this area.

Oil rigs

New oil rigs are likely to come into being over the next few years if the price of oil stays high. Give all rigs at least a mile's clearance.

Customs and Immigration

Customs and immigration in Bonaire is simple and easy. Venezuela has a huge bureaucracy and it often seems like the left hand doesn't know what the right is doing. There have been many good changes recently, and I am sure there will be more in the years to come.

When you get to Venezuela, official clearance charges are about 50$US, though some port captains and other officials may charge more. We advise using one of our recommended clearing agents (listed under the relevant anchorages) where possible.

Immigration will check each person in for a maximum of two or three months. You can extend month by month up to six months for a reasonable fee. (These charges keep changing as does the value of the Bolívar, so we are not putting them in.) After this, you have to leave the country and when you leave you pay a departure tax (again it is not worth putting in how much, as that changes, too). Once you have left the country, you can return again as soon as you like for another two months.

While you do not need a visa for visits of up to two months, if you plan to stay longer, a multiple entry visa in your passport will make getting extensions much easier. (Get this in Grenada, Trinidad, or one of the other islands.)

Make sure you have all the necessary documents with you. Remember, these requirements change from time to time. For inward clearance, you need: clearance from the last port (and three photocopies), ship's documentation (the original then three photocopies), a letter of authorization (if you are not the owner), and passports (you will need the originals and three copies each of the main page). You also need 700Bs in stamps for both customs and immigration. You also may need 33,000Bs in stamps for permanence requests and 33,600Bs to go into a special bank account.

On departure, you need the customs papers you cleared in with, all passports plus two copies of each, and two copies of the permanence certificate (you get this when you enter). You also need another 700Bs in stamps for both customs and immigration.

From port to port you will need: ship's papers, customs entry from entry port, all passports plus one copy of each, your permanence request (plus 33,000Bs in stamps), another 700Bs in stamps and 33,600Bs, often payable into a special bank account.

You should also carry with some kind of bill of sale or documentation for your dinghy and outboard. If you do not have one visit an inventive desk-top publisher and work out something official-looking.

Time restrictions

Bonaire has a six-month time restriction on yachts, after which they become liable for duty. However, it is possible to make special arrangements if you want to leave your boat in a marina there for longer periods. Check current details with the marina managers.

In one of the best recent changes Venezuela has made, you can now keep your boat in Venezuela for up to 18 months. This makes it practical to leave your yacht in long-term storage afloat or ashore.

Customs and your cruise plan

In Venezuela, customs procedures are complicated, sometimes expensive, and extremely cumbersome. Not only do you have to deal with more officials than anywhere else, but also you are supposed to clear in and out of every major port you visit. This is mitigated in two ways. In several major ports, there are agents who will do it all for you, which makes it wonderfully easy. You just give the agent your ship's papers and a crew list and they do the rest. Make sure you use an agent recommended by us or other reliable people, because there have been a few unscrupulous agents. The cost of the transactions and honest agent's fees combined may be as little as $30 or as much as $70, depending on the port. Don't let it put you off. You will save that much and more on your first purchase of diesel, gasoline, or engine oil.

There are some loopholes that can save you trouble if you plan your cruise. Each major port has a port captain, and he controls an area of the coast around his port. The main ports yachts are likely to visit are Güiria, Margarita (Porlamar), Cumaná, Puerto La Cruz, La Guaira, Carúpano, and Puerto Cabello. Luckily, you can get a clearance from one end of Venezuela to the other and visit all ports in between. For example, if you clear into Porlamar and then clear out of Porlamar for Puerto Cabello, you can go anywhere between the two. This gives you freedom to cruise all Venezuela's offshore islands and most of the coastline. The only time you will have to clear into an intermediate port is if you visit a marina or main town for more than a night en route. A similar rule applies if you clear out of the country. You are allowed 24 hours at any number of stops in between. The 24 hours can be flexible if no one checks you. Thus, you can clear out from Puerto la Cruz to Grenada and spend a couple of weeks getting there. Regulations change, so ask a good agent to update you when you arrive. A few people have been to Bonaire without clearing out from Venezuela. So far, the Bonaire authorities have not been checking clearances from the last port, though this could change anytime.

Protecting the environment

Anchoring

Probably the worst damage yachts do to the environment is to destroy coral when anchoring. Always anchor in sand or mud. If you have to anchor in an area with a lot of coral, dive on your anchor to make sure it is not doing any harm. If necessary, use two anchors to stop your rode from chewing up the bottom as the boat swings around.

Garbage

Take your garbage to a proper facility. If you are away from civilization, dump all your food scraps in deep water (over 600 feet). Choose a location where the wind and current will carry them away from reefs. All plastic bags, wax-lined cardboard, and tinfoil must be stowed and placed in a proper disposal place. The same goes for aerosol sprays, old paint cans, and anything containing potentially harmful chemicals. Plastic bags are particularly bad. Leatherback turtles eat jellyfish and often mistake plastic bags for their prey, with deadly results. If you have a smelly plastic bag from meat or fish, wash it well in sea water before stowing it.

Store paper and cardboard and empty cans till you get back to a dump. If for some reason you cannot do this, hole your cans, shred your paper and cardboard, and dump them in water over 600 feet deep, well away from reefs.

Planning & Cruising

GPS WAYPOINTS

These waypoints may be downloaded from www.doyleguides.com, along with links to help you put them on your GPS. They are for planning purposes only.

We used a Garmin-50 GPS on WGS-84 map datum in our research. Many of the sketch charts in this guide were drawn by plotting a series of GPS readings.

ID	Latitude	Longitude	Comment
PENISULAR DE PARIA SOUTH SIDE (Area 1)			
VA101	N10°40.0000'	W061°53.5000'	I Ensenada Carriaquita
VA102	N10°39.0000'	W061°56.0000'	I Puerto Macuro
VA103	N10°38.5000'	W061°59.0000'	I Ensenada Yacua
VA104	N10°38.0000'	W062°01.0000'	I Ensenada Guinmita
VA105	N10°38.0000'	W062°03.0000'	I Ensenada Uquirito
VA106	N10°37.7000'	W062°04.0000'	I Ensenada Patao
VA107	N10°33.9000'	W062°17.3000'	I Guiria
PENISULAR DE PARIA NORTH/TESTIGOS (Area 2)			
VA201	N10°43.6000'	W062°00.3000'	I Cabo San Francisco
VA202	N10°43.0000'	W062°03.4000'	I Punta Pargo
VA203	N10°42.5000'	W062°08.7000'	I Ensenada Mejillones
VA204	N10°43.0000'	W063°01.4000'	I Ensenada Medina
VA205	N10°43.7000'	W063°10.2000'	I Puerto Santos
VA206	N10°40.9000'	W063°15.0000'	I Carúpano
VA2B6	N10°41.3000'	W063°14.1000'	Punta Hernan Vasquez
VA207	N10°41.5000'	W063°27.9000'	I Isla Garrapatas
VA208	N10°39.5000'	W063°31.2000'	I Isla Esmeralda
VA212	N11°22.0000'	W063°06.0000'	I Testigo Grande
VA213	N11°25.0000'	W063°02.0000'	I Testigos, I. Noreste
MARGARITA/COCHE/CUBAGUA/PENISULA DE ARAYA (Area 3)			
VA301	N10°59.0000'	W063°47.0000'	I Margarita, Pampatar
VA302	N10°56.5000'	W063°49.0000'	I Margarita, Porlamar
VA303	N11°04.7000'	W063°58.8000'	I Margarita, Juangriego
VA304	N10°57.0000'	W064°10.0000'	I Margarita, Boca del Río
VA305	N11°01.0000'	W064°24.0000'	I Margarita, West Coast
VA306	N10°50.0600'	W064°00.8800	I Coche, buoy off northwest shoal
VA3B6	N10°47.0000'	W064°01.0000	I Coche, Punta El Boton
VA307	N10°45.6000'	W063°57.7000'	I Coche, El Saco
VA308	N10°50.7000'	W064°09.5000'	I Cubagua, off northeast point
VA309	N10°41.3000'	W063°51.2000'	I Isla Caribe
VA310	N10°41.3000'	W063°52.5000'	I Isla Lobos
VA311	N10°40.0000'	W064°19.5000'	I Penin. Araya, extremity of NW shoal
GOLFO DE CARIACO (Area 4)			
VA401	N10°27.8000'	W064°11.9000'	I Cumaná

(Area 4 continued)

VA402	N10°28.9000'	W064°11.2000'	I Cumaná, Marina Cumanagoto
VA403	N10°28.5000'	W064°08.6000'	I Cumaná, Navimca
VA404	N10°26.5000'	W064°02.4000'	I Carenero
VA405	N10°27.0000'	W063°58.4000'	I Sena Honda
VA406	N10°27.2000'	W063°56.4000'	I Sena Larga
VA407	N10°27.3000'	W063°54.8000'	I Marigüitar
VA408	N10°26.8000'	W063°51.3000'	I Punta Tarabacoita anchorage
VA409	N10°26.7000'	W063°49.2000'	I Punta Cachamaure
VA410	N10°27.6000'	W063°45.5000'	I Pericantal
VA411	N10°27.9000'	W063°44.7000'	I Punta Gorda
VA4B1	N10°28.1000'	W063°44.2000'	I Punta oricaro
VA412	N10°28.1000'	W063°42.7000'	I Punta Cotua
VA413	N10°28.7000'	W063°40.0000'	I Muelle de Cariaco
VA4B3	N10°32.0000'	W063°48.0000'	I Medregal Village
VA4B4	N10°33.1000'	W063°53.3000'	I Medregal Village
VA414	N10°34.3000'	W063°56.5000'	I Los Manantiales
VA415	N10°34.5000'	W063°57.3000'	I La Marita/Sena Larga
VA416	N10°34.6000'	W063°58.1000'	I Toldo
VA417	N10°34.5000'	W063°58.6000'	I Sena Venado
VA418	N10°34.5000'	W063°59.6000'	I Los Platitos
VA419	N10°34.6000'	W064°00.0000'	I Cangrejo
VA4B9	N10°34.5000'	W063°59.8000'	I Cangrejo Yacht Club
VA420	N10°34.5000'	W064°03.0000'	I Laguna Grande
VA421	N10°34.0000'	W064°04.6000'	I Laguna Chica
VA422	N10°33.8000'	W064°07.6000'	I Puerto Real

MOCHIMA NATIONAL PARK AND PUERTO LA CRUZ (Area 5)

VA501	N10°23.8000'	W064°20.7000'	I Puerto Mochima
VA502	N10°23.0000'	W064°23.8000'	I Ensenada Tigrillo, N of Pta. Tigrillo
VA503	N10°20.5000'	W064°28.0000'	I Ensenada Tigrillo, NW of Punta Gorda
VA504	N10°18.0000'	W064°27.0000'	I Golfo de Santa Fe
VA505	N10°15.5000'	W064°28.0000'	I Islas Arapos, eastern end
VA506	N10°17.0000'	W064°39.0000'	I Chimana Grande
VA507	N10°13.7000'	W064°38.3000'	I Puerto La Cruz (PLC)
VA508	N10°13.0000'	W064°40.0000'	I PLC, off El Morro development
VA509	N10°12.0000'	W064°42.4000'	I PLC, off El Morro Marina
VA5B1	N10°15.5000'	W064°32.0000'	I Bahia Comona
VA5B2	N10°17.0000'	W064°36.3000'	I Chimana Secunda
VA5B3	N10°18.0000'	W064°45.8000'	I Isla Borracha

ISLAS DE PITITU TO CHICHIRIVICHE (Area 6)

VA601	N10°09.7000'	W064°58.6000'	I Islas de Píritu NE
VA6B1	N10°08.4000'	W064°54.7000'	I Islas de Píritu SW
VA602	N10°32.0000'	W066°05.5000'	I Bahía de Buche
VA603	N10°31.6000'	W066°05.9000'	I Carenero
VA604	N10°35.3000'	W066°04.0000'	I Puerto Frances
VA605	N10°37.3000'	W066°44.9000'	I Puerto Azul

0.7 nm

(Area 6 continued)
VA606	N10°37.4000'	W066°50.9000'	I Marina de Caraballeda
VA607	N10°36.5000'	W066°57.6000'	I La Guaira
VA608	N10°37.0000'	W067°01.1000'	I Puerto Calera
VA609	N10°32.8000'	W067°20.6000'	I Bahía Puerto Cruz
VA610	N10°30.1000'	W067°44.3000'	I Ensa Cata
VA611	N10°29.5000'	W067°48.5000'	I Ciénega de Ocumare
VA612	N10°28.9500'	W067°57.1000'	I Isla Larga
VA613	N10°28.9000'	W068°01.0000'	I Puerto Cabello
VA614	N10°48.5000'	W068°16.0000'	I Morrocoy Nat. Park, Boca Paiclas
VA615	N10°50.7000'	W068°13.0000'	I Morrocoy Nat. Park, Boca Grande
VA616	N10°56.0000'	W068°14.5000'	I Chichiriviche

VENEZUELA'S OFFSHORE ISLANDS (Area 7)
VA701	N11°51.0000'	W064°36.0000'	I Blanquilla, center, PA
VA7B1	N11°50.1000'	W064°39.1000'	I Blanquilla, Playa Yaque, PA
VA7B2	N11°48.8000'	W064°36.6000'	I Blanquilla, south coast, PA
VA702	N10°57.9000'	W065°13.8000'	I Tortuga, Playa Caldera
VA703	N10°59.1000'	W065°20.0000'	I Tortuga, Los Palanquinos
VA704	N10°59.1000'	W065°23.4000'	I Tortuga, Cayo Herradura
VA705	N10°57.7000'	W065°24.8000'	I Tortuga, Las Tortuguillas
VA706	N11°46.6100'	W066°34.8500'	I Los Roques, Sebastopol Channel
VA707	N11°54.1600'	W066°35.1100'	I Los Roques, Boca del Medio
VA708	N11°58.0000'	W066°37.8000'	I Los Roques, northeast channel
VA709	N11°55.0000'	W066°44.5000'	I Los Roques, Noronsquis
VA710	N11°54.5000'	W066°45.0000'	I Los Roques, northeast of Crasqui
VA711	N11°53.5000'	W066°48.4000'	I Los Roques, Sarqui
VA712	N11°53.0000'	W066°50.5000'	I Los Roques, Carenero
VA713	N11°47.5600'	W066°54.1600'	I Los Roques, Dos Mosquises
VA714	N11°49.0000'	W066°57.5000'	I Los Roques, West Cay
VA715	N11°57.6000'	W067°28.0000'	I Aves de Barlovento, Isla Oeste
VA716	N11°56.0000'	W067°27.0000'	I Aves de Barlovento, Isla Sur
VA717	N12°05.0000'	W067°42.0000'	I Aves de Sotavento, northwest of reef
VA718	N11°59.6000'	W067°41.0000'	I Aves de Sotavento, Isla Larga
VA719	N11°59.0000'	W067°42.0000'	I Aves de Sotavento, Sapproach
VA720	N12°02.5000'	W067°41.2000'	I Aves de Sotavento, Curracai

BONAIRE (Area 8)
BON01	N12°00.5000'	W068°15.0000'	I Southern tip
BONA2	N12°09.0000'	W068°16.8000'	I Kralendijk
BONA3	N12°09.0000'	W068°23.0000'	I Kralendijk

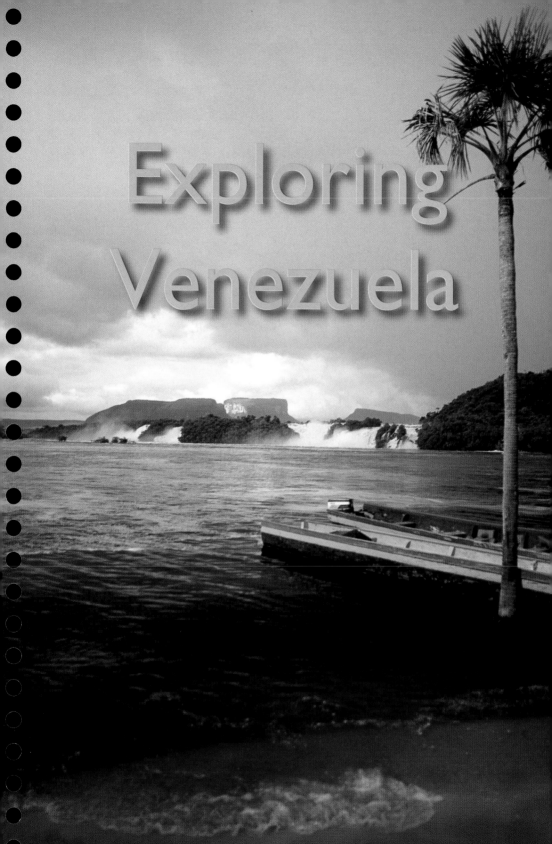

Exploring
Venezuela

*V*enzuela's offshore islands and national marine parks are open and easy for those on yachts, who are the envy of shore-based tourists. But for cruisers, Venezuela also offers a real chance to get off the boat and do some serious exploring. Venezuela is large and offers an outstanding variety not only of scenery, but also of ways of life. When I think of some of the available destinations, it is this experience of different life-styles, combined with mind-boggling scenery, that makes touring Venezuela so appealing. Few places in the world can offer you in reasonably close proximity; year-round snow, desert, tropical forest, perfect beaches and table mountains. Throw in Angel Falls, the world's highest waterfall, and it is a pretty unbeatable combination.

Tours have a lot of advantages. You put yourself in the hands of professionals who really know the area and have it all worked out. It is probably the only way to explore some areas. Renting a car in a particular area and exploring on your own can be a great deal of fun. Even the most impecunious can travel by hopping on a bus or por puesto and heading inland. You need to carry your passport while traveling in Venezuela, as there are

occasional police checks. Below we look in more detail at a few of the highlights.

The Canaima National Park

Within Venezuela is one of the world's most dramatic landscapes ~ The Tepuis (table mountains), which rise slab-sided from the surrounding Gran Sabana (big savannah). These mountains are mainly in Venezuela, though they extend into Brasil, the Guianas, and Columbia. The Angel Falls plunge off the edge of one of these mountaintops, to make the world's tallest waterfall. The area is inhabited by the Pemon Indians, for whom the mountains are sacred. The whole area is in the Canaima National Park, which is a World Heritage Site. Tepuis have inspired several works of literature including Sir Conan Doyle's *The Lost World*.

The underlying formation is very old ~ going back to before the continents drifted apart. At some point, a lot of sandstone was laid down. Erosion took away the softer parts, leaving these more resistant sandstone mountains. The erosion part of the formation was not unlike that of the Canyons in Utah and Arizona, and within the tepuis you find similarly dramatic sandstone formations.

Because the sides of these mountains are steep and inaccessible, the mountaintops formed distinctive ecosystems away from the mainstream of south American vegetation. One-third of the plants are found nowhere else in the world.

The highest of these mountains in Venezuela is Roraima, rising nine thousand feet above the plain. This is not a day-tourist destination ~ but if you have some days and with a suitable guide, you can make it to the top; a totally extraordinary experience. You might get to see the pebble toad, which, rather than hopping from danger, rolls like a ball. Easier, and still very dramatic, is a quick visit to the Angel Falls.

Angel Falls

The most popular trip is to fly to Canaima to see the Angel Falls, the highest in the world. The best view of the falls is from an airplane. A single day trip can include this and a canoe trip to a waterfall where you can swim. You can also spend several days in the interior, traveling to the base of the falls in a canoe. Keep in mind that it tends to be warm during the day but cool at night, so warm clothes are essential. You can also just spend one night there and see some of the interior, as described in the following report from Jeff Fisher, who made the trip from Margarita. (It can be more easily done from Puerto La Cruz or Cumaná.)

"We boarded a brand new single engine Cessna that had a capacity for 12 passengers. The plane was full.

We headed south, overflying Isla Coche, then passing a thin strip of the Venezuelan mainland that encompasses the Golfo de Cariaco. We progressed into a mountainous area that is ideal for the cultivation of coffee and cocoa, and this section was lush and green. After a few mountain ranges, the ground became flat and dirt roads could be seen forming large squares, for here is where pine trees are grown for paper and furniture. The Orinoco was next, a brown, slow-moving, wide river, on whose shore is Ciudad Bolívar, where we set down to refuel. This first leg took about an hour.

We continued south and soon found ourselves looking down on some dark brown rock formations ~ iron ore, jutting out from a flat, arid-looking land. This was interlaced with thin lines of bright green vegetation, created by hundreds of small rivers and streams. These soon gave way to small lakes, which became bigger and more numerous as we continued. Dried-up trees could be seen jutting from all parts of the lakes. These wetlands were created during the recent construction of the second most powerful hydroelectric dam in the world, on the Caroni River. The dam, which took 20 years to build and has been in service for 10, produces enough electricity for domestic use and a surplus, which is sold to both Colombia and Brazil.

Hiking in the Canaima National Park

After these flat wetlands, we saw denser vegetation and curling narrow rivers that have bright white sand beaches at the arc of every turn. Majestic, flat-topped mountains rise thousands of feet, almost straight up. Each mountaintop is isolated from the others and has its own unique environment.

Angel Falls, the highest in the world, cascades down the side of one of these Tepuis. It is called Auyantepui and has a surface area of 740 square kilometers, and the waterfall is the outlet for this rain catchment area. The pilot maneuvered the plane between two adjacent Tepuis, close to the top so we could see the falls. Being the dry season, the falls were not as large as in the rainy season, but still incredibly spectacular. The river poured off the top, a massive waterfall at first, but as it fell unhindered, it became like mist or fog, undefined. At the bottom of this long descent, you could see the river continuing. Other tepuis could be seen spilling water off the top, in long misty threads. We circled around, descending to the other side of this plateau, and landed at Kavac, which is at the bottom of the tepui and on the edge of a great savanna, a flat, grassy area dotted with forests. Our overnight camp was a dozen thatch-roofed adobe huts.

We donned walking shoes, bathing suits, hats, and cameras and set off, following the Kavac river upstream. Moriche palms grow along the banks. Indians have traditionally used the leaves of these palms for thatching their huts. The rocks in the river are various shades of red and pink, a result of decaying vegetation and the presence of tannic acid

from the iron ore upstream. We cooled off in a series of pools and small cascades. Eventually we reached a place of many palms, where the sounds of rustling palm leaves and rushing water mixed.

We stripped down to our bathing suits and gave our cameras to the Indian guide who had come prepared with a couple of large plastic bags. We ventured up an amazing passage through a gorge carved out by centuries of this running water. It is only about 10 feet wide, but over 100 feet straight up on each side,

The overhanging vegetation at the top obscures the sky. The water is deep and running, and we swam and pulled ourselves along a rope for about a hundred feet. We clambered over some rocks and roped our way through the water along the next stretch. Water drops like rain are continually falling off these sheer vertical walls, and the sound of thundering water bounces off of them. A gap appeared in front of us from a break in the overhead vegetation and we saw the sky and a giant waterfall that cascades 100 feet into a deep swim hole. Our Indian guide showed off his climbing and diving skills by scaling the rocks and diving in.

We made our way back to the camp along the same route, to a late lunch, after which those of us who were staying the night were showed to our huts. Mine had two parrots in it, one in the rafters and one chewing on my complimentary bar of soap.

After a brief rest, we went off on another exploratory walk, across the open llano to look at a small, typical Indian village and its farm plot. These farm plots are carved out of the

Angel Falls

forest and the trees are burned. They are cultivated for only five years before the soil is exhausted. They were growing yucca ~ a root used as their staple diet, and wild pineapple, wheat, dates, cotton, and corn. Evening found us walking back to the camp, where I heard parrots squawking in the date palms and watched a falling star drop over a tepui.

The following day we rose to a light rain, which soon cleared. We set off on a steep climb that afforded spectacular views of the camp, the llanos behind, and tepuis in the distance. Our plan was to hike up and around to view the gorge waterfall from above. We continued upstream, swimming through another, smaller gorge and then hiking until we got to a beautiful waterfall straight down and uninterrupted. Shafts of light found their way through the overgrowth to illuminate the falling water. The sound was deafening."

Orinoco Delta

Deep in the Orinoco Delta, many indigenous people live amid thousands of miles of waterway. Among these are a group called the Warao, which means "people from the canoe." The Warao Indians live in huts on stilts, which usually have a thatched roof but no walls. They sleep in hammocks and cook on a fire pit made of clay; rivers are their highways, and canoes their cars. Children here learn to paddle before they can walk. They are excellent basket weavers. You can now stay a few nights with the Warao and experience a completely different lifestyle. Along miles of waterway, you can see the plants and animals of the region, including monkeys, parrots, and little crocodiles called babas. In the following report, our adventurer Heather McIntosh (courtesy Jakera Tours) tells us how she found it:

Angel Falls

40

"I was ready for this inland adventure with all I needed in a small backpack ~ the usual tropical ware like sunblock, appropriate clothing, and a raincoat. Sturdy shoes were not needed, as the camp provides rubber boots for the jungle walks. You would expect to use a lot of insect repellent, but I didn't see even one mosquito. The tour van picked me up at 0730 along with two vacationing couples from Norway and France. The ride to the delta takes 4-5 hours on mostly comfortable paved highways. We traveled through hills, river valleys, small and big towns, and open cattle land. Once we entered the savannah lands, I could tell the river was close by the dense tree line on the horizon. Arriving at the river, we were greeted by guides from the Orinoco Delta Lodge. They took our bags and helped everyone board the "lancha" ~ a fast, 15-foot fiberglass open skiff, powered by a Yamaha outboard. The sun is hot, but once we start zooming over the calm water, the air is refreshingly cool. Only 15 minutes along and we stop to watch a family of howler monkeys, swinging about in the trees. Their red fur glows gold in the afternoon sun. The villages of the Warao Indians blend into the jungle, along with lots of fruit trees filling the spaces around the huts. Little children wave as we pass. Our guide pulls into the shady, hyacinth-filled shoreline and serves cold water and soda as we take a breather. Everyone is smiling and relaxed from the magic of this tranquil beauty. Another fast 45 minutes takes us to the lodge, 50 meters of wood and thatch with a high ceiling and all screen walls. Inside it's like a mini-jungle, with live bananas and palms all around the big wooden tables and chairs. A mesh of flowers and jungle line the wooden walkway to the cabins.

The staff welcomes us and quickly serves us cold drinks and a delicious lunch, fortifying us for the afternoon river trip. We paddle a dugout canoe downriver to a Warao home. Their lives appear rich with everything they need or want growing or living right there: calabash, soursop, palms, annatto, mango, fish, lime, avocado, plus a few chickens and a pig. We sample some fresh cassava bread and coconut water. They allow photos to be taken and are obviously used to this. Paddling back to camp is even easier, with the strong push of the current, and we have time to relax, have a beer, swim, and play with the otters before we take a lancha to watch the sunset. A short ride up river takes us to "una buena vista," and we just drift about, drinking Cuba libres as the day passes colorfully into night.

The cabins are clean, quaint, and comfortable, each with a bathroom and a light. I fall asleep easily, only half hearing the howler monkeys crying in the night. I

awake early to watch the sun rise over the trees onto the misty river, burning off the cooler nighttime air.

Before breakfast it is nice to meander about the camp seeing the toucans, puma, otters, and other busy morning critters. We spend most the day traveling the river and its tributaries in the lancha, where we see the incredible scarlet ibis, monkeys, and freshwater dolphins. As you see more and more of the river, its diversity in plants is striking. We have a lunch and siesta at a thatched open shelter, surrounded by giant mangroves. Our guide and a Warao take us on a jungle walk, where they teach us which vines have water in them, which bark to use to treat diarrhea, which trees are best for making canoes, how to make a smoking pipe for tobacco, and how to eat the heart of palm. On the way back to camp we stop at a village, where we can buy baskets of all sorts, necklaces, carvings, and hammocks. Everyone is as friendly and curious about us, as we are about them.

Our guide buys a couple of huge, freshly caught catfish to take back to camp for din-

ner. We found another group at the camp, and this night's socializing was more of a party atmosphere, with music and drinking. But all one has to do is walk to the edge of the camp for a glimpse at the stars and to hear all the jungle sounds. At the camp are a caged puma and a crocodile, and they are wide awake. The puma hears all the noises and paces and runs around his cage. The crocodile's eyes glow from the grass he lies in.

I woke in the morning sad to think I was leaving that afternoon. At breakfast I found out everyone else felt the same way. We relished our last hours. I went out in a dugout canoe, trying hard not to tip over and to paddle where I wanted to go. I passed a family who all came to the water's edge to say "buen dia." Playful otters joined me, but I discouraged them, knowing their play would end up with me in the water. The current pushed me along with clusters of hyacinths back to camp. I could easily have spent all day just paddling and floating along carelessly. Our last adventure was fishing for piranhas. Way back in narrow passes of the river, we threw our lines out. Only the guide and driver caught fish. The piranha eats the bait very fast, and one must be even faster to pull the pole out. Luckily, none of us was counting on this as lunch. Big, bright blue butterflies fluttered about the river, and as we drove back to camp, we came across monkeys. They leaped from tree to tree; a little baby trailed the rest, barely making the cross-

ing. Back at the camp, I visited my friend the puma, who is having his siesta under his little thatch hut. He opens his eyes briefly when I say goodbye. I find the anteater to have my photo taken with him. He loves to be held and licks my arm with this long, thin, soft tongue. We all feel sad as we climb into the lancha. Our last trip on the river goes too fast. Again we see howler monkeys and scarlet ibis along the way. When we land, lots of tourists are waiting for the lancha. Our van is waiting, and we set off across the savannah towards Puerto la Cruz. The ride is silent except for oohing and aahing at the red-orange sunset as we speed over the hills. All I can think about is the Orinoco Delta and when I can return."

Guácharo Caves

While visiting Cumaná, it is worth making time to visit the guácharo cave near Caripe. It is eight miles long, one of the world's largest and most magnificent caves. (Once you've done this one, you'll never need to do another.) It is inhabited by some 18,000 guácharo birds, strange creatures that live in the dark and echo-locate like bats. They only come out at night, to feed on fruits. They are sensitive to light, so no bright lights or cameras are allowed. You follow a guide who holds a dim oil lamp. The strident cry of what sounds like all 18,000 guácharo birds calling at once adds to the atmosphere. There are wonderful stalagmites and stalactites. The cave floor is muddy, and it is best to bring boots. If you forget, you will discover, like many before you, why Caripe has so many shoe shops. The tour takes you a mile back inside the cave and lasts about two hours. There is a nominal entry fee.

Caripe is set amid beautiful mountain countryside, and it is well worth staying there overnight; hiking and horse riding are good ways to see it. The bus takes four hours from Cumaná, and you should choose one that runs along the Golfo de Cariaco for the best scenery. Taxis can make it in two and half or three hours and are not overpriced. If you are cruising Golfo de Cariaco, then the trip to Caripe is much shorter from Muelle de Cariaco.

The Andes

For a real change in climate, visit the Andes. It is hard to imagine, so close to the tropics, year-round snow, but you can find it. The highest mountain in Venezuela is just outside Merida and some 15,634 feet high; it is snow-capped year-round. A cable car takes you up all the way in four stages. The central town here is Merida, which is about 5,000 feet above sea level. You can get to Merida by bus, plane, or rent-a-car. If you fly, beware of afternoon departure and landing times, as Merida is often fogged in.

Perhaps the most dramatic trip in this area is to an Indian village called Los Nevados. It is stuck way in the hell of nowhere amongst totally spectacular mountain scenery. There are two impossible way to get to it. The easiest is to take the cable car to the third stop, and then take a spectacular five-hour walk or donkey ride along a precipitous path. The alternative is the road from the bottom, whose surface more closely resembles something like a streambed. In places you have to almost graze the paintwork on the cliff side to stop from hurtling to your death over the precipice a few feet away.

People who have done it both ways tell me the car is by far the more terrifying. Los Nevados is as picturesque as a village can be, with whitewashed houses capped by tile roofs all perched in the middle of the mountains. Several houses take guests overnight and feed them. It is like being in the family, and is a great way to experience another culture. You need good sun protection for the long trip to Los Nevados. For those who want to do things the local way, this trip can be done by bus to Merida, early cable car to the third platform, and then a talk with the waiting donkey drivers.

Whether or not you manage to get to Los Nevados, you do want to get to the top of the mountain by cable car, and you will experience firsthand at least minor height fatigue, but the snow and the dramatic mountain scenery makes it all worthwhile for the tropical traveller.

Apart from this, the surrounding scenery driving out of Merida is lovely, once you get used to all the little cautionary memorials to drivers who ended up going over one the various cliffs. If you rent a car in Merida, stay at least one night in Los Frailes, a wonderful hotel built in a monastery dating from 1643. It is set amid bubbling streams and fields of yellow and blue flowers. (You may be able to book a room through an Avensa agent. Otherwise, go online, and a Google search

will give you the current phone number.) Take a sedate horse ride in the magnificent countryside around the hotel and go in the morning, as it often mists over in the afternoon. Drive to El Valle or La Azulita. Try to avoid the busy holiday seasons (Christmas, Easter, and July to September). The days are often warm and the nights cool, so take some warm clothes and a raincoat. While in the Andes, enjoy the wonderful trout (trucha), a local speciality.

Also in this general area are Los Llanos, a wildlife-rich, wet savannah area where you can see such animals as crocodiles, giant otters, jaguars, pumas, river dolphins, anacondas, caimans, capybaras, anteaters, red howler monkeys, and over 250 species of birds including scarlet ibis, jabirus, hoatzins, scarlet macaws, sunbitterns, and numerous birds of prey. There is a biological station, ecolodge, and ranch you can stay in called El Frio Ranch. You can check them out at: www.elfrioeb.com.

If you are touring around and you come to a village where there is no obvious hotel, ask "Hay habitaciones?" You will often find there is a little guest house (posada). If you are planning to get off the beaten track, best do it in the dry season, as some roads wash out in the rains.

A little known fact about Merida is that it has a bull ring. Ask at the local tourism office. There are way more things to do and

places to see than we have mentioned here, but we must at least mention the capital of Venezuela.

Caracas.

Caracas, up in the mountains at 2,400 feet, is far from the sea. But it is the capital of Venezuela, and its cultural center, with the most important museum of modern art in South America. It is full of good private clinics, good restaurants, and entertainment. It is a big and bustling city of about four million people.

Caracas is well known for its medical facilities. Most doctors speak English, and treatments or operations are both good and very inexpensive. When shopping, the most popular buys for the tourists are gold jewels and shoes, crafts that arrived with Italian immigration in the fifties.

Many people do speak some English, you can find phones on most corners, including guys that will let you use their mobile for a fee, and there is the *Daily Journal*, an English-language paper.

Downtown is interesting. You will be in the middle of a very crowed place full active politics at a time when Venezuela is going through a peaceful revolution. Places worth visiting include the house where Simon Bolívar was born (Plaza el Venezolano), and the Plaza Bolívar with some nice Colonial buildings around the National Assembly Palace. For a great nature walk, don't miss Parque del Este en Los Palos Grandes; it is huge park with wild animals, where hundreds of locals take their daily walk. El Avila is an 8,500 foot mountain in front of Caracas. In a couple hours you can hike up to a gorgeous view of the city. If walking is not your thing, take the cable car to the top. In Altamira, everybody knows where the entrance to "Sabanas Nieve" is. Here you find lots of birds, animals and some waterfalls. It is cold by Venezuelan standards, and attractions include a huge hotel, ice skating, an amusement park, and a casino (Alva Magica Call Centre: 212 901 5555. www.avilamagica.com.)

El Hatillo, a little town south in the city, has a huge mall, "El Hatillo Centro Comercial," and a pleasant residential area called La Lagunita. This is the area that old caraqueños describe as the residential area of the "new rich."

Caracas is not totally safe, so to avoid making yourself a target, dress conservatively, do not wear shorts. It is safest to stay in the Este of Caracas; you can find some small, reasonable hotels in the Altamira area. (La Posada Corporativa Octava Transversal de los Palos Grandes is good: 212 286 -662/283-4817. The area of Chacao and Los Palos Grandes is pleasant to visit. Most embassies are here, as well as private clinics and restaurants. From there you can take the metro (www.metrodecaracas.com.ve) to downtown (capitolio) or any other part of the city.

El Avila - Oscar Hernandez photo

Av. Principal and Calle Madrid are packed with good restaurants. (For restaurants, check the website www.miropopic.com.)

For a great view of the city, visit a place called 360 in the top of Altamira Suites (Primera Av. Los palos Grandes), a five-star Hotel in Los Palos Grandes very close to Plaza Altamira.

To get to Caracas from Puerto La Cruz, it is best is to take "Expresos Aereo ejecutivos" or if you are in Cumana, Expresos de Orient.

While in Caracas, use the official taxis, which are white with a yellow plate. Most malls have taxi stands and you can call for one at: 0212 209-3111. If you want a weekend taxi guide contact Jose Luis D LaCoste a Maracucho 0416 612-8084. He is reliable and not expensive, and speaks English (he is married to an American.)

If you need any advice or help, contact Oscar Hernandez, Jr. a sailor himself, who updated this version of the guide. He speaks both English and French.

(oscar.hernandez@yahoo.com or oscar_hernandez_ve@yahoo.com).

For legal or insurance advice, or for a marine survey contact Lujis Gerardo Ochoa Fernandez.

A good contact in Caracas is the big El Capitan chandlery, who deal with everything nautical and fishing. If they don't have it, they can get it, and deal with the paperwork. Do, if you go to Caracas, visit them, and if you don't, you can call them.

Eating out in Venezuela

Restaurants in Venezuela are plentiful, good, and inexpensive. You may like to know

46

about some local specialties:

Arepas are cornmeal griddle cakes, often sliced and filled with butter, cheese, meats, and fish. In Venezuela, arepas are used as bread, and filled arepas make a complete meal.

Pabellón criollo is a staple dish in Venezuela and consists of shredded meat, fried plantain, rice, black beans, white farmer's cheese, and arepas.

Ayacas are mainly served around Christmas and are made of cornmeal, chicken, olives, spices, and raisins, all of which are wrapped together in a banana leaf and steamed.

Paella, the popular Spanish dish of rice with meat and seafood, is equally popular in Venezuela.

Bienmesabe is a coconut cream trifle whose name means "It tastes good to me."

Another popular Venezuelan dessert is flan, a custard with caramel topping.

Places to visit in Caracas.

La Candelaria, Spanish Quarter
Las Mercedes, restaurants and malls
Teleférico de Caracas, to visit El Avila
Plaza Francia, Main sua Altamira
Plaza Venezuela
La MezquitaIbrahim Al-Ibrahim
Ateneode Caracas
Cinemateca Nacional
Teatro Teresa Carreño
Galería de Arte Nacional
Museode Arte Contemporáneo de Caracas SofíaImber
Museo Jacobo Borges
Museo de Bellas Artes
Teatro Municipal
Teatro Nacional
Museode Arte Popular de Petare
Centro de Arte La Estancia
Museo Alejandro Otero
Museo Audiovisual
Museo de la Estampayel Diseño Carlos Cruz Diez
Museo del Transporte Guillermo José Schael
Museo del Teclado
Museum La Estancia (old coffee farm), in Altimera
Museo Sacrode Caracas
Museo de los Niños
Museode Ciencias Naturales
Palacio Municipal
Casa Amarilla
Paseo Los Próceres

Parque del Este - Oscar Hernandez photo

ANCHORAGES IN VENEZUELA

Updated by Oscar Hernández

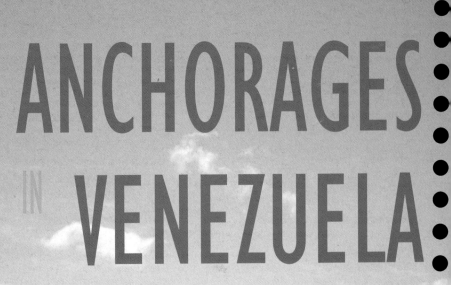

Venezuela at a glance

Regulations

Before you go to Venezuela, you must have valid, up-to-date yacht documentation and a passport. U.S. nationals, Canadians, Australians, New Zealanders, UK nationals, South Africans, and most Western and Scandinavian Europeans do not require a visa for sailing or flying to Venezuela, though if you plan to stay a long time, having a visa helps with extensions. Other nationals should check with an embassy. If you are leaving Venezuela to return overland, check on the visa requirements before you go. You may need a visa to get back in the country overland.

Yachts can stay up to 18 months, which is a reasonable time for leaving your yacht in dry storage.

When you enter Venezuela, immigration normally stamps you in for two or three months (this depends on the officer). After this, you can leave the country and come back in again for another two or three months. The length of stay out of the country does not matter. You can also come in for two or three months and then apply for extensions of up to a month at a time.

You have to clear in and out of major ports visited in Venezuela. (See also cruising information.) You are allowed to stay over in most offshore islands on your way in or out of Venezuela. Ports of Clearance include: Güiria, Puerto Cabello, Carúpano, Cumaná, La Guaira, Porlamar, and Puerto La Cruz.

The taking of conch is illegal throughout Venezuela at this time. It is only legal to buy or catch lobsters from 1st November to the 31st April.

Holiday

Jan. 1st - New Year's Day
Carnival - Monday, Tuesday and Wednesday the Monday to Wednesday 40 days before Easter (Carnival Monday is February 19, 2007; February 4, 2008; February 23, 2009, February 15, 2010.)
Easter - Easter Wednesday to Sunday (Easter is April 8, 2007; March 23, 2008; April 12, 2009; April 4, 2010)
April 19th - Declaration of Independence
May 1st - Labor Day
June 24th - Battle of Carabobo
July 5th - Independence Day
July 24th - Birth of Simón Bolívar
October 12th - Resistance Day
December 17th Death of Simón Bolívar
December 24-25th Christmas
December 31 st. (Unofficial, but it can be hard to get things.)
Midweek holidays are sometimes moved to the following Monday.

For calculating dates of moveable holidays like Easter and carnival check links on www.doyleguides.com

Shopping hours

Most shops open 0800-1200 and 1500-1800, but there are many individual variations. Banks sometimes cannot change money until a new rate arrives, and this can be anywhere from 0900-1100. Some shops are open Saturday mornings,and big supermarkets often open at 0900 and stay open till 1900 or 2000, Monday to Saturday.

Telephones

The easiest way to stay in touch is to get a mobile phone. Otherwise, much of the Venezuelan telephone system is run by Cantv. There are many card phones and the cards are available from Cantv outlets in the larger cities and some hotels and other shops. Make sure you are getting them from an official card agency and that they are wrapped and sealed in the original packing. You will also find many independent communications kiosks, where you can pay for a call.

If you are using a card phone, you

usually dial 00 to get an overseas line and then the country code (1 for USA and most Caribbean islands, 44 for UK, etc.). However, read the directions.

A Venezuelan telephone number begins with an area code (e.g., 0210). You do not dial this if you are in the same code area. If you are dialing from overseas, leave the first zero off the area code. This is followed by the Venezuelan number which is 7 digits.

The country code for dialing into Venezuela is 58. Thus if the Venezuelan number is 0295 264-1646, from the U.S. you would dial 011 58 295 264-1646.

Mobile number area codes are 0412, 0414, or 0416 depending on the company.

Currency

Currency in Venezuela is the Bolívar, currently fixed at $1=2,150Bs. You can still expect U.S. dollars to have excellent buying power when converted to Bs.

Transport

Venezuela has several large airports with international links as well as local flights between cities. Inexpensive round trip tickets are often available between Valencia Airport (nearest seaport is Puerto Cabello) and Miami.

Renting a small plane is often the best way for a small group to go sightseeing.

Regular taxis are not expensive. You can bargain for whole-day trips. It is usually less expensive to hire a taxi for a day than to rent a car. The taxi will be older and have many more miles on it, but it comes with a driver who knows his way around.

Unless you know what the local taxi rates are, you should always ask, "Cuanto Cuesta?" ("How much?") Before you get in the cab. Otherwise you risk being overcharged.

The mainstay of the local transport system is buses for long distance and "por puestos" for short and medium distances. Por puestos are taxis that ply particular routes and pick up passengers along the way. They will often drop you off at your destination even if you are a little off their route. Longer trips (those taking many hours) are usually made by bus. In most towns you find a bus station. Both buses and por puestos are very inexpensive.

*V*enezuela had a thriving Indian community before Columbus arrived. The earliest European settlement was in Venezuela on the island of Cubagua, where the attraction was the rich pearl beds. Indians were conquered and used as slaves, so the Spanish never needed to import African slaves. The Venezuelans broke free of the Spanish in 1811 after a long, hard revolutionary struggle. Simón Bolívar was the major leader in this fight for independence.

Today, Venezuela is a modern country with a Spanish tradition and language. It is a major oil producer and industrialized enough to be self-sufficient in most respects. Anyone who listens to the news will know that Venezuela is not without political problems. The down side of this as far as yachting is concerned is an apparent breakdown of civil order in some areas resulting in crime, sometimes violent. Since these guys often have guns, it would seem to be modern opportunistic piracy, not desperate, poor people. Before visiting Venezuela, go to our website: www.doyleguides.com, and check on the links we give to security which will help you assess which areas present a risk.

Having watched yachting tourism growing in the Eastern Caribbean, you cannot but be impressed by the vigor and entrepreneurial spirit of the locals, who move very quickly to figure out what yachts need and then provide it. Whether it be men coming out in dinghies to sell you fruits, or restaurants ashore touting for your business, the locals are aware of your presence and economic potential.

In Venezuela, on the other hand, there is little awareness that yachts spend considerable sums. I sometimes feel that Venezuela will not come out of its economic doldrums till the locals become more motivated to make a buck. In the meantime, you are not regarded as a source of income, and whatever

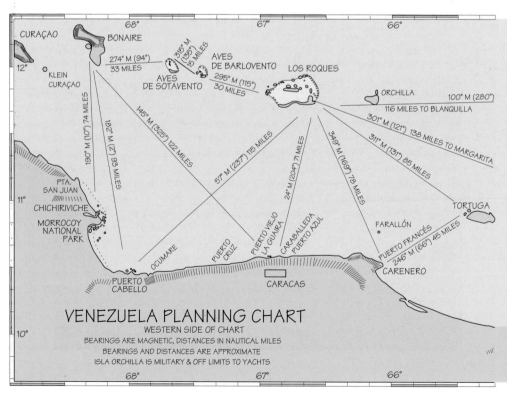

VENEZUELA PLANNING CHART

WESTERN SIDE OF CHART
BEARINGS ARE MAGNETIC, DISTANCES IN NAUTICAL MILES
BEARINGS AND DISTANCES ARE APPROXIMATE
ISLA ORCHILLA IS MILITARY & OFF LIMITS TO YACHTS

relationships you form will be spontaneous rather than commercial. This is refreshing, but it also means that you will not be specially catered to, and while your dollars will buy you much, they don't mean much. Most Venezuelans are very warm, generous, and hospitable, and you will have a great time. A few of the richer Venezuelans are not particularly tolerant. They have welcomed cruising yachts before and found them wanting. Some private yacht clubs regard a cruising yacht much as the U.S. coastguard views an old fishing vessel overloaded with Haitian refugees.

There are one or two private yacht clubs where foreign flag vessels are allowed,

and we have found the people in these very welcoming. However, there are some members who would prefer not to be bothered and they are looking for reasons to exclude foreign yachts. Try not to help their cause. Although you may pay fees in a yacht club, it is a private club and not a commercial marina. You cannot make demands, and complaints will just make you unpopular.

While Venezuela has excellent medical services, many small fishing villages are so far away from large towns that the locals have a hard time getting to a doctor. So if you have medical skills and stock up on extra first aid gear, you probably can make a contribution in some outlying areas.

Organization of this book

Venezuela is larger and more complex than the Eastern Caribbean, with far more potential cruising areas and routes to take. One of the criticisms we received in the first edition pertained to the organization of the our guide. For example, Margarita and Cumaná,

physically close, were at opposite ends of the book. We addressed this in the last edition by dividing the area of Venezuela we cover into seven separate sections (plus Bonaire as another section). You can quickly locate these in the book by looking at the color bars

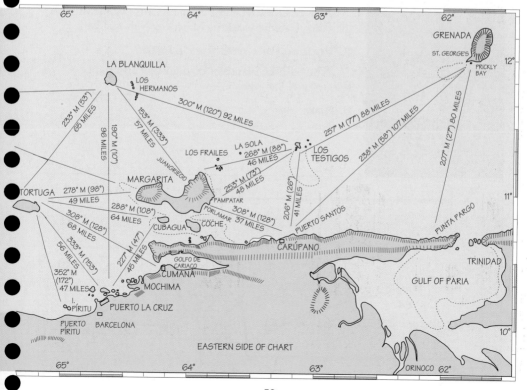

Opposite:
Ensenada Uquirito

which bleed off the right side of the pages. People have liked this organization so we have kept it in this edition.

The map below is self-explanatory, and we hope this system works well for everyone. The areas covered by each section are as follows:

1. Gulf of Paria to Guiria

The southern side of the Gulf of Paria to Güiria. An easy cruise from Trinidad.

2. Eastern Venezuela

The northern side of the Gulf of Paria to Morro de Chacopata and the offshore islands of Los Testigos.

3. Margarita

The islands of Margarita, Coche, and Cubagua to the northern side of Peninsula de Araya.

4. Cumana & Cariaco

Cumaná and the Golfo de Cariaco to the western side of the Peninsula de Araya.

5. Puerto la Cruz & Mochima

From Mochima through and including Puerto la Cruz. This includes all the Mochima National Park.

6. Islas Piritu to Chichiriviche

The coastline west of Puerto La Cruz to Chichiriviche including Carenero and the Morrocoy National Park.

7. Venezuela's offshore islands

The offshore islands of Blanquilla, Tortuga, Los Roques, and Las Aves.

8. Bonaire

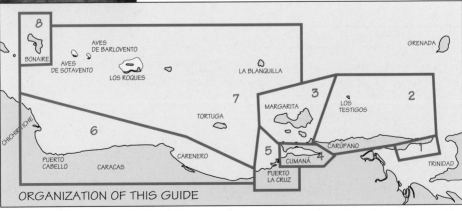

ORGANIZATION OF THIS GUIDE

Gulf of Paria to Güiria

AREA 1

Gulf of Paria to Güiria

The Gulf of Paria side of the Península of Paria has about 25 miles of cruising with half a dozen interesting, beautiful and mainly deserted anchorages en route to Güiria (the nearest port of clearance). This starts within 10 miles of Chacachacare, yet to date it is infrequently visited. It is an obvious small cruise for those who want a break from Trinidad. You have to clear in Güiria, but Venezuelans are usually quite generous about allowing you a few stops on the way in and also out, so you can cruise to Güiria, clear in and out, and then cruise back out. The gulf water is never clear, though for most of the time it seems clean.

Very few yachts visit this area at the moment. I have not heard much about security problems; it might be worth asking on the Trinidad net before visiting. I notice Onsar have it as a security risk, but I have nothing to back this up.

Güiria is also the port of clearance for those who want to explore the Macareo River. We do not cover the Macareo River in this guide, but anyone who wants to go there should visit Boaters Enterprise in CrewsInn in Chaguaramas, Trinidad. There you can get a photocopied cruising guide of sorts and latest notes and tips from cruisers who have been there.

Navigation

The current along the southern side of the Gulf of Paria is mainly to the east, though this changes with the state of the tide, and currents are generally strong, up to one to two knots. This makes progress easy ~ you either have the wind or the current with you. But the resultant wind against sea can make the water very rough, especially in the area around Islas Patos and Macuro. There is no problem in light wind (15-20 knots), but

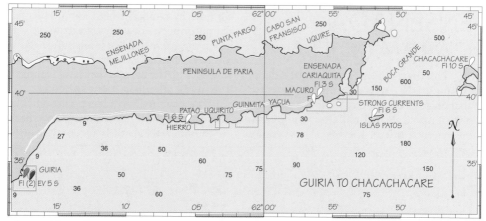

Map labels: 45' | 15' | 10' | 05' | 62°00' | 55' | 50' | 45'

250 | 250 | 250 | CABO SAN FRANSISCO | 250 | 500
ENSENADA MEJILLONES | PUNTA PARGO | UQUIRE
PENINSULA DE PARIA | ENSENADA CARIAQUITA | BOCA GRANDE | CHACACHACARE Fl 10 S
MACURO Fl 3 S | 50
40' | 150 | 600 | 40'
PATAO UQUIRITO GUINMITA YACUA | 30 | STRONG CURRENTS Fl 6 S
Fl 6 S HIERRO | 30 | ISLAS PATOS
9 | 78 | N
27 | 180
36 | 50 | 120
35' | 9 | 60 | 90 | 150 | 35'
GUIRIA | 75 | 75
Fl (2) EV 5 S | 50 | 75 | GUIRIA TO CHACACHACARE
9 | 36 | 60 | 75
15' | 10' | 05' | 62°00' | 55' | 50'

when it blows hard (20 –25 knots), the seas can seem like a washing machine. If you time your passage till the current flows to the west, the seas calm down. Locals tell us that this happens on the rising tide. We met east-going current at all times. If the going gets too rough when you are trying to sail back, you can take a long tack south into calmer seas where the currents are not as strong.

Half a dozen attractive anchorages that are well protected from the east lie along the 12 miles of coast between Ensenada Cariaquita and Ensenada Patao. They are all open to the south and in the unusual event of a strong southerly would be untenable. They can also all roll a little for a couple of hours around high tide. This is worst in Macuro and gets better as you sail west. For the rest of the time, they are generally calm. We noticed bugs could be a problem around dusk and dawn, especially after rain, but were otherwise not bad. The bays are thickly silted, and the sticky mud makes for excellent holding.

A road now runs from Güiria to Macuro, but it is rough and seldom used. It was only finished in 2000, and now as before, nearly everything comes and goes by sea. Thick rainforest rises up from close to the coast into the hills that form the central ridge of the peninsula. These mountains range from 800 to 3,200 feet.

Agriculture has been practiced for generations, ever since early French settlements before Bolívar's revolution. The main crop was coffee. Today a little agriculture still goes on, but it seems to be on a rather small scale. Gypsum was quarried from the rocks in many places along the coast, and in deserted bays you can often see the remains of old docks and machinery. The largest quarry was at Macuro and closed in 1999. We saw one quarry that still seemed to be active behind Ensenada Patao. Fishing is still the major industry and you see many fishing boats up and down the coast as well as anchored in the bays.

ENSENADA CARRIAQUITA

This bay is almost two miles deep, making it the largest and most protected anchorage along this coast. No road reaches here; it is wild and natural. One fishing camp lies on each side of the bay. These camps are used by families from Güiria. Hills fall sharply on each side with some dramatic valleys and giant mangrove trees in the head of the bay. Ensenada Carriaquita has a more closed, "into the heart of darkness" feeling to it than the other bays along the coast.

The bay shoals to 12 feet quite quickly. Thereafter it shoals more slowly as you head in. You can carry about 10 feet to the north-

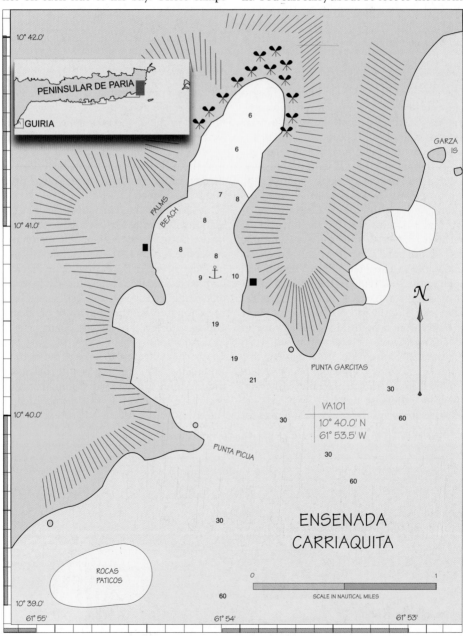

ern end of the palm-lined beach that is on the western shore. There is 6 feet almost to the head of the bay. The inner part is the most protected, but also the more buggy. The bay does tend to have a mangrovy, muddy smell some of the time. It is home to many birds, especially herons and sea birds. We heard howler monkeys early in the morning.

Ensenada Carriaquita

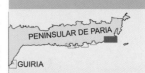

PUERTO MACURO

Puerto Macuro is a delightful small town of around 3,000 people. We were astounded by how beautifully painted it was (December 2000). Everything, even the ruins, were in artistically designed Caribbean colors. This was so different from other Venezuelan towns, there had to be a reason. Apparently, a few months before we came, President Chavez had paid a visit. In advance of his arrival, 300 national guardsmen had

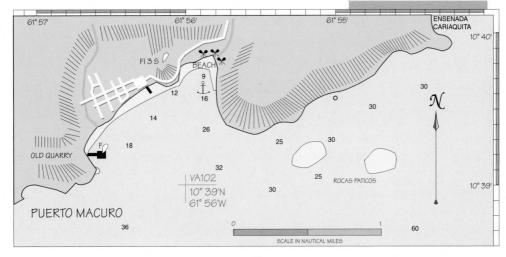

been sent in to paint the town. They did an excellent job, aided by the menfolk of Macuro.

The gypsum quarry had recently closed down, and while fishing was a major activity, locals were also looking towards tourism for the future. Already quite a few Venezuelans come from Güiria to spend the weekend. There are several small guesthouses where they can stay, and several restaurants that only seem to open on the weekends or by special request.

Navigation

Puerto Macuro is at the end of the road from Güiria. A disused gypsum quarry and loading dock lie at the western end of the bay. The dock is well lit at night with fixed white lights. The village is in the middle of the bay, and a new light structure lies to the east of the village up a hill. By our observations, it flashes white every 3 seconds. The best anchorage is right up to the east part of the bay in about 12 feet of water. It can get very rolly for a few hours around high tide, and if you were staying awhile, a stern anchor

would make life a lot calmer.

If you are approaching from the east, you have two dangerous shoals to avoid. It is most sensible to go outside them both. Rocas Paticos lie about half a mile offshore just before the point. In rough weather, you can often make out one or both shoals by the breaking water.

Ashore

Macuro has several broad streets, and the one-story houses look large and comfortable ~ often opening out onto interior courtyards. The main landing dock is often in use, so it is probably best to beach your dinghy. The town square is close to the dock, with well-used public seats. The library opens onto the square. Close to the dock are the large ruins of the old customs bonded warehouse. The stone walls still stand, and just enough roof remains to make it a favorite place for storing and building fishing boats. There are banks of card phones in the town, so calling should not be a problem if you can buy a card. There is nowhere to change money and no one will take U.S. dollars,

so it may be smart to visit Macuro on your return trip from Güiria when you have some Bolívares.

You will find several family-style restaurants, which seem to be officially open only when tourists are in town. However, if you were to track down the owner, they would probably open for you. A couple of small stores sell basics, including bread.

It is possible to hike from here over the central mountain ridge to the Atlantic coast. Two main trails take you over. One leaves town heading east past the light structure. It starts as an old agricultural road and later turns into a trail. It reaches the small village of Don Pedro at the eastern part of the Atlantic coast. Another road heads out from the other end of town and takes you over to Uquire. Either road will take you through magnificent and wild tropical rainforest. We walked a little on the road to Don Pedro but did not make either trip. Even on our short hike, we were surrounded by brilliant blue morph butterflies and heard lots of different birds. I suspect the local who told us the hike took three hours was being optimistic. Venezuelan's do this as an organized hike from the village with a guide and are met by a fishing boat on the other side and return by sea, so they only have to hike one way. You could probably arrange this, or join one of their hikes. For the less organized, a hike anywhere along these paths is great even if you don't go far.

Macuro's main street
the waterfront path
(opposite)
Boatbuilder (below)

61

Ensenada Yacua

ENSENADA YACUA

Two miles west of Puerto Macuro, you come to a delightfully large, open bay, surrounded by a magnificent, jagged mountain ridge. There is evidence of an old gypsum loading area. In the middle of the bay is a fine old estate house that was apparently very active about 15 years ago. An old barge lies as a wreck ashore, and a more troublesome wreck lies in the middle of the bay with just a mast sticking up. Approach with caution. The most protected anchorage is up in the eastern part of the bay; you can carry 12 feet quite close to shore. A rather fine beach with palms in places lies on the northern edge of this bay, perfect for a little exploration.

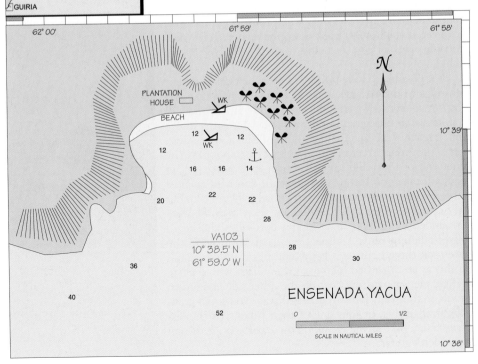

ENSENADA YACUA

VA103
10° 38.5' N
61° 59.0' W

SCALE IN NAUTICAL MILES

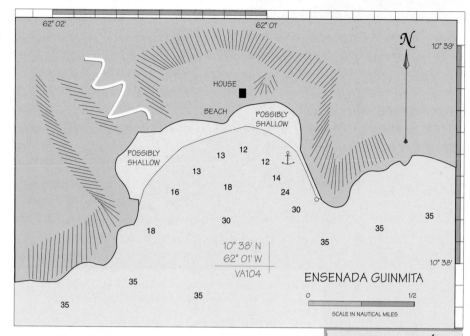

ENSENADA GUINMITA

10° 39'

HOUSE

BEACH

POSSIBLY SHALLOW

POSSIBLY SHALLOW

POSSIBLY SHALLOW

13   12

13   12

18   14

16   18   24

30

30   35

18   35   35

10° 38' N
62° 01' W
VA104

35

35

35

35

ENSENADA GUINMITA

10° 38'

0   1/2

SCALE IN NAUTICAL MILES

ENSENADA GUINMITA

Ensenada Guinmita is another open bay with plenty of protection from the east and lovely hill lines to admire from the anchorage. A rough road leads down into the bay from the western part, and there is a small house halfway along the beach. The beach is well clad with vegetation, including a few palms. The anchorage to the eastern part of the bay is the best protected; feel your way in till you are comfortable.

PENINSULAR DE PARIA

GUIRIA

PENINSULAR DE PARIA

GUIRIA

ENSENADA UQUIRITO

Although Ensenada Uquirito is a little smaller than some of the other bays, it is still pretty big with good protection in the eastern part. The rock and roll at high tide is not as bad here as further east. The dramatic mountains make a great view from the cockpit. Towards the north, the water shoals quite rapidly to less than 6 feet, so approach reasonably slowly with an eye on the depth. There is plenty of well-protected anchoring room in the eastern part of the bay in 12 feet of water. A ruined dock lies in the middle of the bay with some old machinery, including a rusted-out vintage truck close by ~ reminders of the gypsum industry. A rough road winds down in the western part of the bay. A fam-

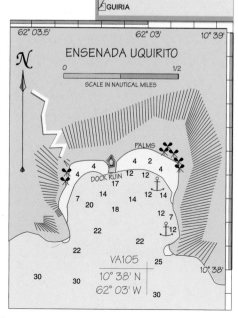

ENSENADA UQUIRITO

62° 03.5'   62° 03'   10° 39'

0   1/2

SCALE IN NAUTICAL MILES

PALMS

4   4   2

4   4

DOCK RUIN   12   12   4

17

7   14   12   14

20   14   12   14

18   12   7

22   12

22   7

22   22

22   25

30   30

VA105   25

10° 38' N
62° 03' W

30

10° 38'

ily lives behind the beach; the house is only visible from some places, but the boats are often moored off the beach.

ENSENADA PATAO

Ensenada Patao is well protected, as the land has a little more of a hook to it than in the previous bays. There is plenty of room to anchor in the protected northeast corner in about 12 feet of water. Behind the beach vegetation is a large salt pond, which would be interesting to explore. There are some cut cliffs and evidence of continuing quarrying in the hills behind the western half of the bay.

PENINSULAR DE PARIA

GUIRIA

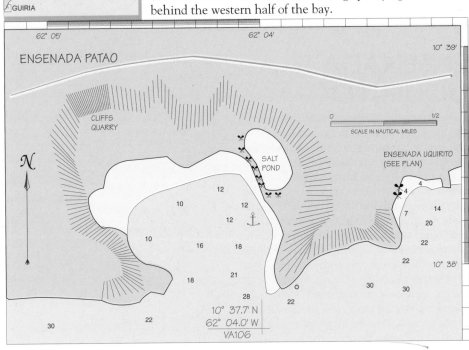

ENSENADA PATAO

CLIFFS
QUARRY

SALT
POND

SCALE IN NAUTICAL MILES

ENSENADA UQUIRITO
(SEE PLAN)

10° 37.7' N
62° 04.0' W
VA106

GUIRIA

Güiria is the port of clearance and a sizeable Venezuelan country town. It is a boom or bust town depending on the state of the oil industry, which uses the harbor as a base for their supply boats. When the oil boys are in town, there are plenty of ex-pats, and the bars, restaurants, and discos get busy. Last time I visited, it was very quiet. Since then it has livened up some with rise in oil prices, but is far from a bang-up boom. Compared to the larger cities, it is often relatively safe to walk around town even late at night, but ask first.

Like many Venezuelan towns, Güiria has reached a kind of balance where the rate of deterioration and decay is offset by an equal measure of building and renewal. The buildings are mainly one story, and from the outside, they appear deceptively small. Take a glance through an open doorway and you will see the houses are often large, with inside patios and gardens. Despite this, many locals prefer the more social street pavement as a hangout, and plastic chairs are put out by the roadside; families gather to chat, neighbors visit, children play. Luckily there are few enough cars racing around to make this rather charming habit relatively safe.

Area I Gulf of Paria to Güiria

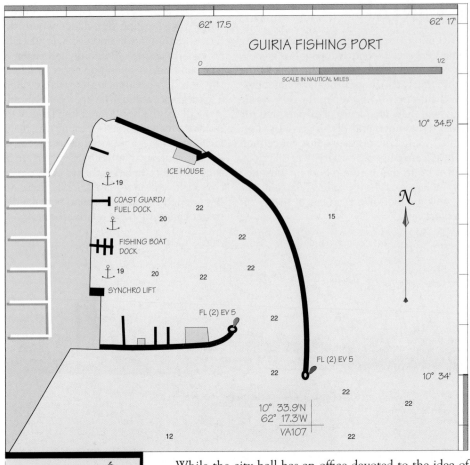

GUIRIA FISHING PORT

62° 17.5

62° 17'

0   1/2

SCALE IN NAUTICAL MILES

10° 34.5'

ICE HOUSE

⚓ 19

COAST GUARD/
FUEL DOCK   22

⚓   20   15

FISHING BOAT
DOCK   22

⚓ 19   20   22

SYNCHRO LIFT   22

FL (2) EV 5   22

22

FL (2) EV 5

22   10° 34'

22

10° 33.9'N
62° 17.3'W
VA107   22

12   22

N

opposite:

Aerial Guiria **photo
courtesy Premica**

PENINSULAR DE PARIA

GUIRIA

While the city hall has an office devoted to the idea of tourism, as yet it is just an idea; the main trip they promote is a boat ride to Macuro. You will be taken for a gringo, but not a tourist ~ these are as yet unknown here. As a result, you will find your money goes a long way, but you are unlikely to find internet cafes, and even changing money can be hard. The shops are geared to the practical, and the best stores are hardware shops of various sizes selling everything from tools to furniture.

The locals are quite proud of their big beach that is a few kilometers to the north of town. Pictures make it look quite tropical and wild, but after the Grenadines, the gulf water will leave you unexcited, but not cold.

Navigation

The large harbor is protected by a long sea wall, with plenty of room to anchor within. Red and green lights mark the entrance and flash twice every five seconds. When we were there the green one would stop working a few hours before dawn. Güiria is acceptably safe if you anchor near the coast guard. We noticed that all the fishermen removed their outboard props

before they went ashore, as this seemed to be the number one item that was stolen. The biggest risk would be to lose stuff from your dinghy while you went ashore.

You need to anchor out of the main channel. If you anchor either side of the coast guard dock, the presence of the coast guard will probably add to your feeling of safety. You can tie stern to the sloping wall if you want, to keep your boat from swinging around, but you will not be able to get in close enough to walk ashore. We anchored between the fishing boat dock and the synchro-lift dock. If you want more privacy, I can see no reason not to anchor southeast of the icehouse dock, off the main wall.

There is a little dinghy dock in the northern part of the harbor, but this is completely open to the public. We used a stern anchor on our dinghy and went bow to the wall close by the coast guard dock. With a long locking line you can lock to a tree or around a rock.

Regulations

Güiria is the major port of clearance in this area. The coast guard makes spot safety checks. They look for life jackets, fire extinguishers, first aid kit, navigation lights, a horn, a chart of the area, and a working main engine. They also check your boat papers. There was no charge, and we found them friendly and pleasant. If you have been through one of these checks before and still have your inspection paper, you can show this instead.

Most vessels call in advance for an agent to clear them when they arrive. Most agents listen to the VHF. You can, like us, bumble ashore and walk into one of the agencies and ask them to clear you in. Agent Albernie and Agent Petrosini are very close to the dinghy dock by the beach (see our town plan). The agent known as the Windward agent, because they used to be the agent for this line and still have a sign to this effect, are farther in town. The agents usually charge about $100 U.S. for inward and outward clearance for a foreign port. They charge somewhat less if you are already cleared into Venezuela and just want a port clearance. The fees cover all government clearance charges. Changing U.S. dollars may not be easy, so ask your agent if he can help. They will need your passports and boat papers and the clearance from your last port. Someone in each agency is reputed to speak some English. We went without Venezuelan visas in our passports and had absolutely no problem. The officials did come on board to do the paperwork, with the agent.

Guiria Street

Services

While Güiria has several banks, these only seem to change U.S. dollars occasionally. You probably can get them to give you some Bolívares on your credit card. Probably by now they have ATMs. Your entry agent may well be able to help you change some money; otherwise try the bookshop on Calle Bolívar between Juncal and Tringhera. They like U.S. dollars and will change some when they have enough cash.

The customs dock is also the fuel dock. Diesel is at the end of the dock, while gasoline is just partway down. If you plan to go in with your boat, time it for around high tide, or you will have problems stopping your deck going under the dock. You make arrangements with the small station at the head of the dock. The ice plant is on the outer harbor wall. The ice is finely chipped and comes out of a large pipe.

The port has a huge sychro-lift capable of taking major ships. It is run by Premica. The American manager, Jerry Johnson, is well worth meeting and can give you good general advice even if you don't need hauling. They have excellent engineers, machine shops, and welders and are most used to working on steel ships. They are not geared to hauling small yachts, and while they can do it, the lift is so large it would not be economical. They do compete when it comes to vessels the size of tugs, and they have had a few larger yachts visit and be satisfied with the work.

A weekly ferry service to Chaguaramas, Trinidad, is usually in operation. Try for information at: 0294 982-0169.

Ashore

The best bet for fresh produce is the market. It is one and a half blocks off our map between Calle Trehinga and Pagallo. They open about 0700, and by 1100 you will be looking at leftovers. For cans and basics, Las Palmas on Plaza Bolívar is the best general grocery. This is not a supermarket, but one of those old-fashioned stores where you lean over a wooden counter, stare at the produce in the back, and ask an attendant to bring you what you want. For a delicatessen, bakery and patisserie, visit the very fancy Chaceca bakery on the corner of Sucre and Juncal. This surprising place is all dark glass from the outside and full of tiles and marble on the inside. They have lots of delights inside, including fresh strawberries. Seats are laid out for lunch, and you can eat a sandwich or chicken lunch here.

Start your evening at Sam's Pub, if he is still around. This is the local hangout for ex-pats and a good bar as well. Sam is an American from Dallas; he has worked in the oil trade all over the world and ended up here during a boom time. This quickly turned to bust, but has started to look back up again. Sam is a great source of local information and will be able to answer most of your questions and tell you about any new restaurants. Sam had a restaurant part to his bar and plans to reopen this in a few months when the oil boys return.

If after a few beers all you want is a cheap meal, then wander half a block to Restaurant Plaza. This family style restaurant at the back of a bar is in a large room with plants down one wall. It is owned and run

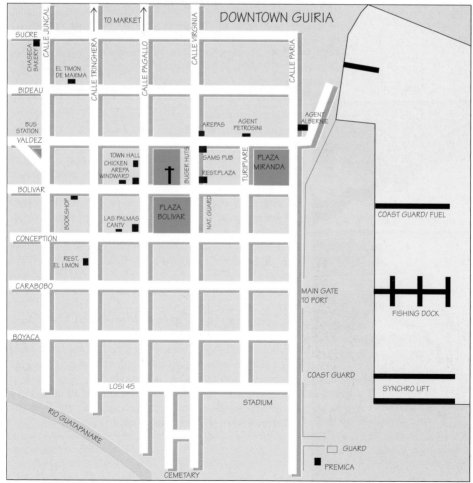

Guiria fishing boats

by Clirita and Nanoco. If you don't want to watch the television while you eat, sit at the far end. Food here is family style with good-sized portions at very reasonable prices. Other choices for a cheap meal include the row of hamburger stalls with seats on the pavement right opposite the Plaza, Look out for a small trailer run by Eleazar and his wife; they offer Trini rotis and local food, in a clean and breezy spot. The Chicken Arepa on Plaza Bolívar, also makes an excellent lunch spot.

Güiria also boasts a couple of really quite good restaurants. El Fondo El Limon is open all day every day except Sunday. The restaurant is under a long roof at the back of a patio that has a "Limon" tree (in this case a lime). They do good fish and shrimps and a great local dessert.

The fanciest is El Timón de Maxima on Calle Bideau. This family run restaurant has been beautifully designed and built with lots of fancy brick and stone and would look smart even in Puerto la Cruz. The owners are very welcoming, and their food is first rate.

Güiria also has several discos; one of them is right above Sam's pub. If you are into nightlife, ask Sam; he will steer you in the right direction.

Eastern Venezuela

AREA 2: THE NORTHERN SHORE OF PENINSULA DE PARIA AND LOS TESTIGOS

South part of Testigo Grande; the big beaches face east

Eastern Venezuela

This area includes the northern shore of Península de Paria and the islands of Los Testigos. For most of us these are both the gateway into Venezuela and part of the slog back to the Eastern Caribbean.

The northern coast of the Península de Paria is wild and rugged country, with tall mountains covered in rainforest rising straight up from the sea. The further east you go, the more rugged it gets. Out towards the eastern end there are few roads and the communities depend on boats to reach other villages. Hiking ashore is wild with monkeys, snakes, and many birds.

The northern coast of the Península de Paria area has seen more than its share of

armed robberies in the last few years, considering the small number of yachts that cruise here. I would avoid it until there is news of improved security. Los Testigos seems fine, but I would not advertise exactly when I was leaving or which direction I was headed.

Los Testigos lie offshore, about 40 miles north of Puerto Santos. This lovely group of islands has long been a favorite with visiting yachts. It is a natural gateway for those coming to Venezuela from Grenada, and it is a pleasant sail from Trinidad. It is also not a bad place to kick off from if you are heading southeast for Trinidad or northeast into the Eastern Caribbean.

We start with Los Testigos and then follow the coast of the Península de Paria from east to west.

LOS TESTIGOS

Los Testigos (The Witnesses) are a delightful group of islands with about 160 inhabitants who live by fishing. They are here year round and have a school and church, but for shopping or for an outing on a public holiday, they zoom over to Carúpano in their pirogues.

Natives of Los Testigos can apply to build a house anywhere in the island group. Most choose to live on Isla Iguana or on Playa Tamarindo. However some have built elsewhere and a few houses are now dotted in other areas.

Since there is no ferry and no airport, yachtspeople are among the very few outsiders to visit. So far, things have gone quite well between the locals and the yachting fraternity, and we should all do our best to make sure it stays that way. Under no circumstance should you take garbage ashore or get in the way of any fishing boats. Be sensitive if you are using a camera. Most of the people are friendly and more than reasonably patient with those like me who speak "poquito Español." Those who speak Spanish will obviously find it easier to communicate. One or two yachtspeople with medical skills have offered a helping hand and given yachting a good name.

You will find gorgeous beaches, huge sand dunes, lots of fish, interesting snorkeling, magnificent views, and a vast colony of frigatebirds. Los Testigos make a convenient first landfall from Grenada and are a wonderful introduction to cruising in Venezuela. We have not heard of any serious security problems here.

Passage from Grenada to Los Testigos

It is an easy sail to Los Testigos, with wind and current on your side. The distance from Prickly Bay to the nearest Testigo is 80 miles, but it is another five into the anchorage. The current often reduces the distance sailed by 15 or 20 miles. This was

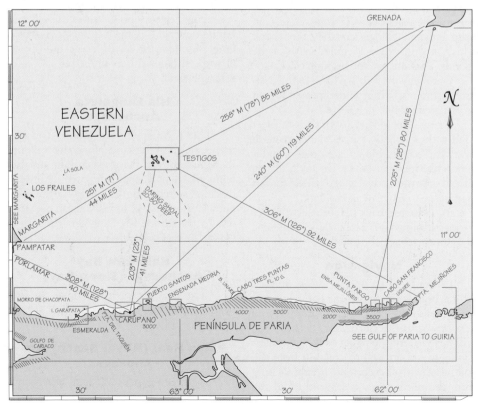

Eastern Venezuela

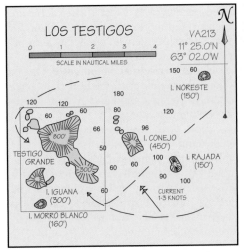

little islets around Testigo Pequeño, then power or tack close to shore to stay out of the current. Narrow passages between islands are best avoided, as the currents create overfalls.

Every few months the wind will switch to the southwest and blow quite hard for a few hours. Should this happen, head for the Isla Iguana anchorage (see below).

Two other lights have been reported in Los Testigos; a flashing green light on Testigo Grande at 11°22.452N, 63°07.750W and a flashing red light on Isla Iguana at 11°21.874N, 63°07.744 W. These are probably helpful to local fishermen, but we would strongly urge that you only navigate in this area during daylight hours.

There are several anchorages, all of which roll from time to time. You can often improve the situation by using a stern anchor to keep you head-to the swells.

a bit too much for one single-hander who underestimated the current and was wrecked while still asleep.

The course is about 245° true (258° mag). Most yachts sail overnight, leaving Grenada just after dark. For yachts that go 6-7 knots, a magnetic course of 245-250° usually gets you in sight of the islands the next morning. If visibility is bad, it is better to err to the south of Los Testigos. Here, your echo sounder should pick up the 25-foot bank which extends some 15 miles south of the islands. This will get you back on track.

Generally the winds will be in the easterly quadrant and they sometimes get lighter as you go south.

Testigo Grande has a light some 807 feet high with a 10-mile range. It used to flash every six seconds, but a recent report said it is now fixed and hard to see. In any case, you should time your arrival after daylight, for this is no place to navigate in the dark.

You can beat back to Grenada from Los Testigos, though it is a tough slog. The same goes for the trip to Trinidad.

Navigation

Currents set to the northwest and are strong, usually one to two and half knots, but up to four knots have been reported. Avoid getting set to the northwest, because you will have to struggle to get back. Engineless yachts would do well to come in from the southeast with the current. If approaching from the north, pass to seaward of all the

Anchorage off Isla Iguana

You can anchor off the village at Isla Iguana. This is fine for checking with the coast guard or for a brief visit to the village, but it does roll. It is much calmer if you tuck up close under the lee of Isla Cabra (Goat Island), though this is often full of local fishing boats.

Isla Langoleta Anchorage

This is a popular anchorage. You are within reach of the sand dunes, the walk up the mountain, and Playa Tamarindo, and the main village on Isla Iguana is within dinghy reach. A stern anchor can help cut the roll. For visiting the sand dunes, you can take the dinghy pass inside Isla Langoleta through a cut in the reef quite close to shore.

Balandra Bay Anchorage (Sloop Bay)

The best spot is right down in the southeast corner, and it is calmest if you take a line ashore.

Playa Real (Royal Beach) Anchorage

A picture-perfect soft sand beach and

inviting water colors make this anchorage the most beautiful in Los Testigos. Anchor close to the gap between Testigo Pequeño and Testigo Grande. Here, waves crash on the windward shore just a few feet away. The holding is good, and there is plenty of room, but it does roll a bit. The calmest anchorage is a quarter of a mile southwards, tucked into a small bay off Testigo Grande,

with a line ashore. However, this can be out of the breeze. There is more room and it is still reasonably calm in the same area but anchored a little farther out.

There is also room for one boat to anchor in the charming little bay between Isla Calentador and Testigo Pequeño. Note that although there is a deep-water passage between Isla Testigo Pequeño and Isla

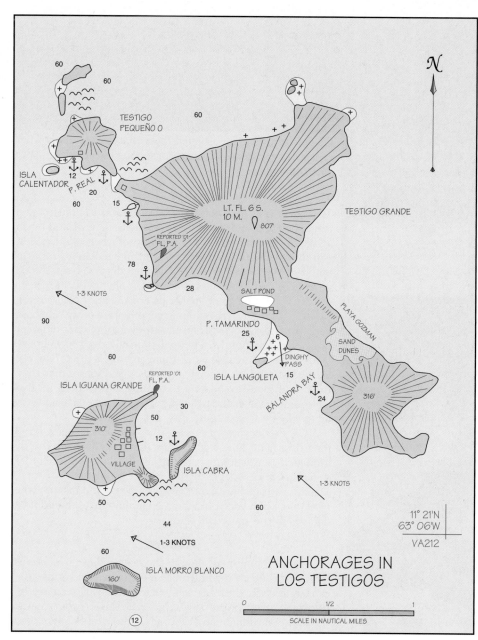

ANCHORAGES IN
LOS TESTIGOS

11° 21'N
63° 06'W
VA212

Eastern Venezuela

Los Testigos showing Isla Langoleta anchorage to Isla Iguana

Calentador, there are isolated rocks that stick well out from either shore. Explore by dinghy or snorkel before bringing the yacht through.

Regulations

There is a small coast guard outpost on Isla Iguana in a round building under the Venezuelan flag. They stand by on VHF: 16 "Guardacosta." You can anchor where you like, but you should then visit the coast guard immediately. You can outboard over from most anchorages, but those who row should go in their yachts, as the current in the channel is strong.

It is up to the coast guard officer to decide how long you can stay before carrying on to a proper port of entry. This can vary with the coast guard officer, as they are rotated to different posts every few months. They will probably give you 48 hours. If you are enjoying it so much that you want an extra day, you can go back and ask. If you really want to stay longer than that, the best thing is to sail over to Carúpano and check in. It is a pleasant reach each way. You can then come back and stay up to your visa expiry date.

Los Testigos are a protected area. You are welcome to troll for fish, or hand-line off your yacht, but spear fishing is strictly forbidden. Scuba diving is also against the law, as it is felt that some yachts were depleting the lobster population.

All garbage must be retained on board and taken to the next port when you go. Under no circumstances should it be dumped in the sea or left ashore.

Ashore

There is one small shop in the main village, which is so basic that you may not find much more than a cold drink. You can buy fish from the fishermen year round and lobster in season (November 1st to April 31st). One or two locals prefer to swap the lobster for liquor, and they may approach you.

Those stout of heart and shoe should make the hike up to the lighthouse (allow two to three hours round trip). The path begins at the northwest end of Playa Tamarindo on the northwest shore of the salt pond. It is rough and involves scrambling in places. You may occasionally lose your way and have to backtrack to the last mark. The cliff-hanging view from the top is dramatic enough to make the climb worthwhile, especially if you remember to take your camera. The path is marked in three ways; blue-painted rocks, notched trees, and little heaps of stones. If you get lost, go back to the last mark and keep looking until you find the next one. There are many cactuses, balsam plants, and Spanish moss on the trail. You may see big iguanas.

There are wonderful sand dunes at Playa Gozman. They top the hill, and you can see them from Balandra Bay. The swimming and body surfing looks exciting, and there are acres of sand to play in. The sand gets the hottest hot, so take shoes. There is a tiny beach for the dinghy in Balandra Bay, and the trail is quite clear.

Snorkeling is pretty good all around. The water is sometimes greenish, owing to effluent from the Orinoco, but the abundance of fish makes up for it. Isla Rajada is said to be best for snorkeling.

When it is time to leave Los Testigos, you have an easy day sail to Margarita (44 miles) or Carúpano (39 miles)

NORTHERN SHORE OF THE PENINSULA DE PARIA

For those heading east to Trinidad, following the coast along Península de Paria was considered the easy way to go. However, since security has become an issue, it is advisable to sail or motorsail directly to the Windwards from Margarita or Los Testigos. If you sail north into the latitude of the Windwards, you will get some lessening of the west-setting current. Maybe security

will improve and you can use the following information.

The rugged north coast of the Península de Paria has a few anchorages, which offer fair to good protection provided there are no northerly swells.

The prevailing wind in this area is northeasterly to southeasterly all the way from Pta. Mejillónes to Morro de Chacopata. The winds often calm down after nightfall and stay light till mid-morning. There is not usually much current within a mile or two of land. Farther out, the prevailing current is west-setting. Winds are typically calmer in the summer and stronger in the winter. There are exceptions to this rule: you occasionally fight a knot of current close to the coast in strong winds.

Many of those heading back east motor by night, when the wind is calm, and anchor during the day, when the wind is blowing.

Those heading east can break the trip into manageably short runs. If you get up at first light, you can motor until the wind starts blowing hard, then beat or motor sail the rest of the way to the next anchorage.

There is just one long stretch, between Puerto Santos (or Ensenada Medina) and the next reliable harbor, which is Punta Pargo. This is 50-60 miles, depending on where you start, and it is probably best done as an overnight trip.

The westward passage along these shores is no problem, though if winds are light, the sailing will be improved by taking a swing out to Los Testigos to get the wind on the quarter.

Those heading back to Grenada often head out from Punta Pargo or Cabo San Francisco. It can be a pleasant run or a real slog, depending on the wind direction.

Passages between Trinidad, Grenada & the eastern part of Península de Paria

Getting to Cabo San Francisco or Punta Pargo from either Trinidad or Grenada is usually a pleasant sail. The return trip is a little harder. From Cabo San Francisco to Trinidad is only 25 miles and easily accomplished in a day's sail, even though it is to windward.

Eastern Venezuela

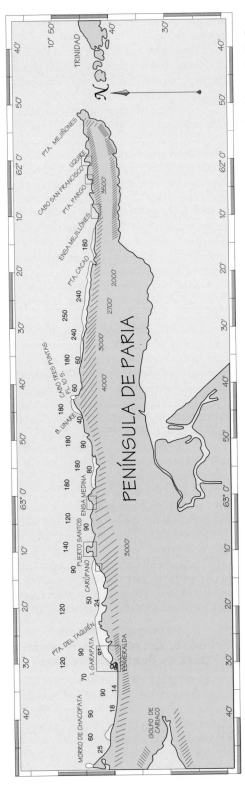

From Punta Pargo to Prickly Bay in Grenada is about 80 miles, and the course is about 13° true or 26° magnetic. Remember to allow for current. The light flashing every 10 seconds on Trinidad's Chacachacare Island shows up very well, as does Grenada's Point Saline (2+1 every 20 seconds) light with its 18-mile range. As you get closer to Grenada, you will see two quick-flashing lights, one on the end of Point Saline and the other on Glovers Island. It is impossible to predict the wind direction from observations along Venezuela's coast. The wind often changes after the first 10 to 20 miles. It can be a wonderful trip with sheets eased in a southeasterly wind, or it can be a real struggle to windward in a northeaster. If you can lay Grenada easily, do not be tempted to ease off too soon, as the current is often strongest just south of Grenada. Plan to arrive in daylight so you can avoid the Porpoises Rocks. If you have to come in at night, then entering in St. George's is easier.

UQUIRE TO ENSENADA MEJILLONES

Some people prefer this part of Venezuela over all others. Certainly, you could not wish for wilder terrain farther away from civilization. Tall mountains of rainforest rise abruptly from the sea. Fast mountain rivers create pools and waterfalls. Ashore, you are in the wild. There are monkeys, parrots, and jungle cats. But before you rush up in shorts and flip-flops, remember there are also poisonous snakes and giant centipedes along with lesser biting bugs. At least one vampire bat has taken a meal from a yachtsman in Cabo San Francisco.

While this area can be as calm as a lake, all too often there are huge, sloppy swells along the coast which make the anchorages rolly, though they are normally tenable. Since you never know when a swell may arrive, it makes sense to anchor a few hundred feet offshore rather than go stern-to the rocks.

It is about 70 miles from Cabo San

Francisco down to Puerto Santos. With the wind and current behind you, it is certainly doable as a daysail.

Heading east, you are more likely to be motor sailing at night, when the wind is lighter. It is not too bad, though you can get an uncomfortable swell. There are quite a few villages with lights as far as Cabo Tres Puntas, after which it is black. The Cabo Tres Puntas light sometimes works.

For those without a GPS, the problem at daylight is to know where you are. Ensenada Mejillónes makes a good landmark. Five distinctive-looking rocks lie in line out to sea from the eastern end of this bay. Península de Paria is at its narrowest point here, and in the middle of the bay, the mountains are a little lower than on most of the rest of the coast.

UQUIRE

Pta. de Mejillónes is the eastern point of Península de Paria. About eight miles west is Uquire (Providencia on some charts), the first sizeable settlement you come to. It is easy to recognize, as there is a distinctive island that looks like three huge boulders leaning into each other on the eastern headland.

There is also a beach and sizeable village that boasts lamp posts. The water is very deep in the bay, making anchoring tricky, but some yachts like to visit Uquire because you can sometimes get cold beers and fuel.

CABO SAN FRANCISCO

Cabo San Francisco is the next bay west of Uquire. It is the most dramatic anchorage along this coast. Towering, jungly mountains drop straight into the sea. Red splashes from bright tropical flowers peek through the green. Clouds hang off the land, rising like steam. There are two small fishing shacks, one on a stony beach and the other hidden up a hill. Fishermen sometimes use this bay as a base. There is a large anchoring shelf in the southeast corner of the bay with depths of 15 to 34 feet. Anchoring bow and stern with your bow to the swells is advised. Cabo San Francisco and Punta Pargo, the next bays west, are two of the best protected bays along this coast.

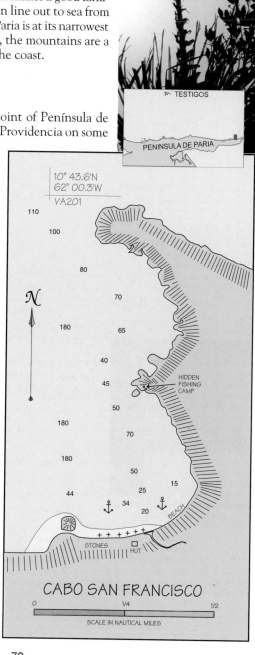

CABO SAN FRANCISCO

SCALE IN NAUTICAL MILES

Eastern Venezuela

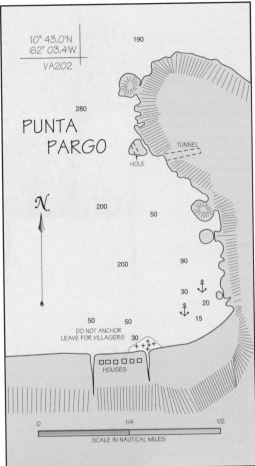

10° 43.0'N
62° 03.4'W
VA202

190

280

PUNTA
PARGO

TUNNEL
HOLE

N

200

50

200

90

30

20

15

50

50

DO NOT ANCHOR
LEAVE FOR VILLAGERS   30

HOUSES

0   1/4   1/2

SCALE IN NAUTICAL MILES

Ashore, there are just a few small trails to fishing lookouts, but the adventurous can explore up the river.

PUNTA PARGO

Punta Pargo is the next bay after Cabo San Francisco. It is more open than San Francisco with a delightful, palm-backed beach and a fair-sized village. Anchor right in the east of the bay under the headland. I would advise bow and stern anchoring away from the rocky shore with your stern a couple of hundred feet out, in case a swell comes up.

If you are arriving from the west, Punta Pargo is five miles from Ensenada Mejillónes. Once you have passed Ensenada Mejillónes, you can follow the coast a few hundred yards offshore. About two miles farther on, you will notice a large rock with a hole right through it. Punta Pargo is inside the next major headland you see from this rock.

It is a good idea to introduce yourself to the villagers in whose territory you are anchoring. They are generally helpful and friendly and will direct you to the best hikes. Follow the river for some great natural swimming pools.

Snorkeling and dinghy exploration are outstanding all along the eastern shore. Just inside the rock with a hole through it is a long tunnel that goes way back into the cliff. There are several other intriguing holes and little beaches tucked in the rocks.

TESTIGOS

PENINSULA DE PARIA

SJE '93

Approaching Punta Pargo from the west

80

ENSENADA DE MEJILLONES

You can find a passable anchorage tucked right up in the eastern corner of Ensenada de Mejillónes, where you get some protection both from the headland and the off-lying islands. There is a large anchoring shelf with 19-40 feet on it. Bow and stern anchoring is advisable, with your bow into the swells.

Ashore there are a few houses and lots of wild terrain to explore.

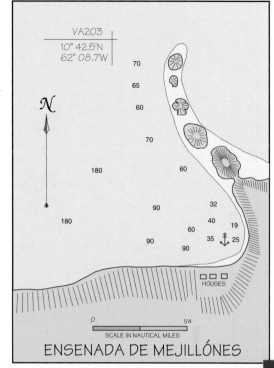

ENSENADA DE MEJILLÓNES

Eastern Venezuela

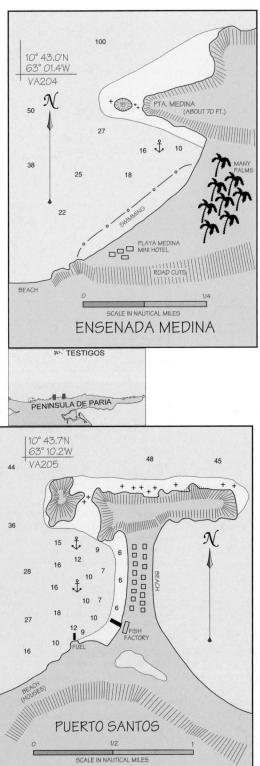

10° 43.0'N
63° 01.4'W
VA204

N

100

50

27

+ 15 +
PTA. MEDINA
(ABOUT 70 FT.)

16 ⚓ 10

38

25 18

MANY PALMS

22

SWIMMING

PLAYA MEDINA
MINI HOTEL

ROAD CUTS

BEACH

0   1/4

SCALE IN NAUTICAL MILES

ENSENADA MEDINA

TESTIGOS

PENINSULA DE PARIA

10° 43.7'N
63° 10.2'W
VA205

44

48   45

36

15 ⚓ 9 6

12

16

28

7

10 6

N

16 ⚓

10 7

BEACH

27

18

10 6

12 9

FISH
FACTORY

10

FUEL

16

BEACH
(HOUSES)

PUERTO SANTOS

0   1/2   1

SCALE IN NAUTICAL MILES

ENSENADA MEDINA

There are no really well protected anchorages between Punta Pargo and Puerto Santos. This is no problem when you are heading west, however when you are struggling east, Ensenada Medina is well worth considering, as it is 9 miles east of Puerto Santos, giving you a shorter hop to Punta Pargo.

Ensenada Medina has a gorgeous beach, and you can take interesting walks. However, it is not all that well protected and is frequently too rolly for comfortable overnighting. If you are lucky enough to get it in a calm mood, you could spend a day or two here.

The best anchorage is tucked right up in the northern part of the bay in the lee of Punta Medina and its small off-lying island. You can use bow and stern anchors to cut the swell.

There is a small hotel facility on the south end of the beach. A snack bar opens on weekends and holidays and whenever there are enough people around. We had one report that they were no longer serving yachtspeople, but check it out for yourself. If you do get here in a period of calms, talk to the management about their inland hotel in a wild ranching area. You could visit it and return in a day.

PUERTO SANTOS

Puerto Santos is the best-protected harbor between Punta Pargo and Esmeralda. The bay is picturesque, though the water frequently has brown scum across the surface, possibly effluent from the fishing industry. A little diesel fuel and engine oil are usually added to this. All in all, not the best place to give granny her first swimming lesson. The cleanest and most pleasant anchorage is tucked up close to the island, in the northern part of the bay.

Services

Water and fuel are available at the fuel dock. There is a good 12 feet of water at the head of the dock and about nine feet of water a third of the way down. It is easy to get water and fuel in jerry jugs here. Bringing the yacht in presents a problem, because the dock is one mass of fishing boats most of the time. An incoming swell does not help. Water comes out of a one-inch water pipe, and for alongside filling, you need your own hose and connection. Check it out by dinghy first, then come in and join the fray. Block ice is available from the fish factory.

Ashore

There are a few bars and small shops where you will find essentials. Otherwise, Carúpano is easily reached by por puesto. There is a pleasant walk over on the windward beach.

CARÚPANO

Navigation

Carúpano is the main town along this coast, and it is a port of clearance. It is about three miles west of Puerto Santos, though you will not see it till you pass Punta Hernán Vásquez, a headland about a mile to its east.

Lights around Carúpano are unreliable.

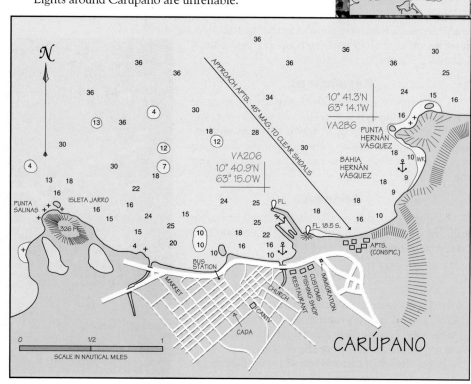

Playa Medina

Carúpano Harbor is small and somewhat exposed to the swells. You can tuck in between the harbor walls or anchor in the bigger bay inside them both. When you have finished in town, there is a pleasant anchorage that is just as protected as Carúpano inside Punta Hernán Vásquez. Puerto Santos is a much better anchorage, fuel and water are more easily available, and it is only a few miles farther up the coast. Some people prefer to leave their boats in Puerto Santos and take a por puesto to Carúpano.

Regulations

Carúpano is a port of clearance for entering or leaving the country. If you need to clear in or out, you should anchor your yacht in town. Customs and immigration are quite close to the head of the dock; the port captain is farther west along the waterfront near the bus station.

Services

Water is available on the inner side of the harbor wall, but diesel has to be trucked in. Telephone calls can be made from Cantv.

Ashore

Carúpano is attractive and green with public squares and parks. There is a pleasant walk along the waterfront. CADA is good enough for a major provisioning, and near the local market there are several wholesale stores. Most are willing to deliver to the docks.

Just to the left of customs you will find a fisherman's

shop with some marine hardware and a pleasant little seafood restaurant ($D).

We are told that Carúpano has a spectacular carnival, though small compared to Trinidad's. It attracts people from all over Venezuela.

Carupano to Punta Esmeralda

It is 15 miles from Carúpano to Esmeralda, and the coastline is indented and interesting with numerous rocks. It is also poorly charted, and the water is often too murky to be readable. In completely calm conditions when the water is clear, this is a great area for those who want to explore uncharted waters off the beaten track. For anyone else, it is best to give this coast a wide berth.

If you look at our sketch chart of Carúpano, you will notice that there are several frightening shoals dotted up to a mile out to sea west of the town. To avoid these stay over a mile offshore.

Further west along the coast in the direction of Punta Esmeralda, give a good clearance to Punta del Taquién and all its attendant rocks and sail outside Islas Garrapatas.

If you are approaching Carúpano from the west, head more for Puerto Santos than Carúpano until the conspicuous new apartment blocks to the east of the town bear 45° magnetic. You can then head toward these buildings.

From the west, Carúpano is hidden away. The first thing you see is a huge block of apartment buildings that lies just to the east of the harbor wall. Shortly afterwards more apartment buildings come into sight. These are a couple of miles to the west of Carúpano.

PUNTA ESMERALDA

For those sailing westwards from Carúpano, Margarita is only 42 miles, which makes an easy day sail. However, if you are struggling east against the wind, Punta Esmeralda is a convenient stop along the way. It is only about 28 miles from Margarita, or 22 miles from Isla Caribe, just the other side of Morro de Chacopata.

The island is high (325 feet), as is the headland off which it lies. Farther south are three smaller islands. Unlit oyster rafts are often anchored in this area. Their positions vary, so keep a good watch. The bottom

Eastern Venezuela

85

Punta Esmerelda

shelves gradually from 12 feet into the shallows. The water is generally murky, and the bottom sticky mud. Occasionally, enough swell enters the bay to create a bit of a roll. Despite the cloudy water, the anchorage is scenic and for those who wish to explore ashore, there is a poor but picturesque fishing village. Tie your dinghy to the stone wall to the north of the village. Elsewhere thick, gooey, black silt lies close to shore.

Punta Esmeralda is the last anchorage before Morro de Chacopata. We deal with that part of the coast in our next section.

In the next section, we visit the islands of Margarita, Coche, and Cubagua, then return to the coastline of the Península of Araya from Moro de Chacopata round to the Golfo de Cariaco. In this part we also deal with the small islands; Isla Lobos and Isla Caribe. So if you want to continue with this coast, head to the end of the next chapter (Page 113).

Margarita to Araya

Porlamar - Oscar Hernandez photo

Margarita

In this section we start with the island of Margarita, then cover the islands of Coche and Cubagua, before finishing with the smaller islands of Caribe and Lobos, and the coastline of the Península de Araya from Morro de Chacopata past Araya to the entrance to the Golfo de Cariaco.

Margarita is the biggest and most important of Venezuela's offshore islands. It has a carefree holiday atmosphere and is the most popular holiday destination for Venezuelans. A major attraction is that it is duty free, and watches, electronics, and jewelry are cheaper here than on the mainland. Venezuelans are limited by how much they can take back each time they visit, but they are not limited by the number of visits they make. It also attracts many international visitors (often from Europe) who are more interested in the warm, dry climate, the lovely beaches, and the interesting mangrove channels.

Gambling has come to the island in a big way, and you can find casinos in most 5-star hotels. El Yaque beach by the airport is world-famous for kit-boarding.

Enjoy some of the island's attractions while you are here. One of these is the capital, La Asunción, which is back in the mountains. La Asunción was founded in 1565, and its pretty white washed buildings with red-tiled roofs are a refreshing change from all the modern high-rises in Porlamar.

Do not miss the Playa La Restinga and Laguna Grande. We put this under our Bahía Mangle anchorage, but you could also make the trip by taxi.

There is an informal marine net that operates on VHF: 72 at 0800, with weather and an exchange of views, ideas, and cultural events. This is run by yachtspeople and is dependent on how many are in the harbor, so there may not be a net when the yachts are scarce.

Margarita has some security problems, but not as many as the mainland. Yachts still anchor here, and most go unmolested, though you need to take a lot of care to secure your dinghy. You still need to be aware

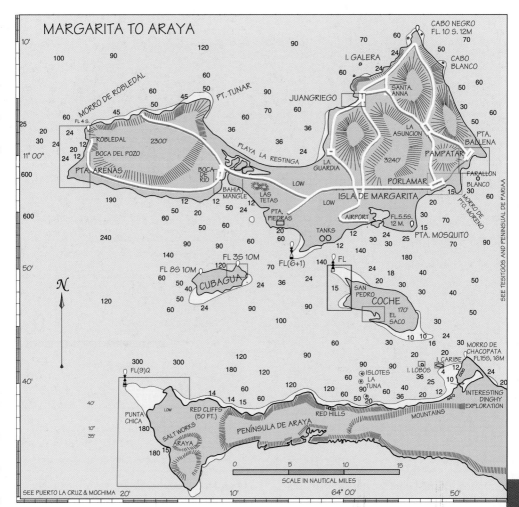

MARGARITA TO ARAYA

of what is going on around you when you go ashore, and you should get local recommendations about which areas are safe to visit at night.

Regulations

You anchor and clear customs in Porlamar. We strongly recommend you use agents to help you. (See *Regulations* under Porlamar.)

Navigation

If you are approaching Porlamar from the east, Los Frailes, a group of rocks about 8 miles northwest of Margarita, show up clearly, as do the mountains on the northern part of Margarita. As you get nearer, Pta. Ballena will appear as a distinct headland just to the south of the mountains. The land to the south is lower, and one can see huge blocks of multistory buildings before the land itself. Farallón Blanco makes another feature; it is a small, but distinctive white Island (Isla Blanca on some charts). From a distance, Morro de Puerto Moreno looks like an island. Marina Margarita Yachting is one and half miles west and a little north of Farallón Blanco.

It is about 48 miles from Testigos to Pampatar. The course is 239° true, 251° magnetic. Most people steer 240-245 to allow for the west-northwest current. Porlamar is about four miles beyond Pampatar. You can change course and head for Morro de Puerto Moreno when you see it.

Do not approach Porlamar at night as

Margarita to Araya

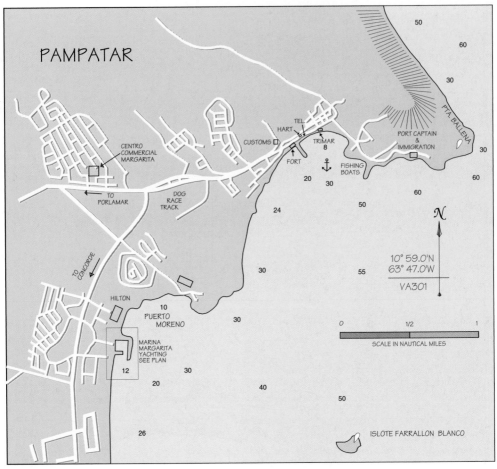

many fishing boats set nets in this area.

PAMPATAR

Yachts are no longer allowed to anchor in Pampatar, so visit by land.

Pampatar is a quiet, picturesque fishing town with several beaches. Historically, it was important because of its deep-water harbor. At the head of the big new dock you will see Castillo San Carlos de Borromeo, a castle with ornate turrets. This was built in 1662, after the Dutch sacked the town and destroyed the original fort. The fort enabled the Spanish to fight off many hostile attacks, but they were driven out by Simón Bolívar in 1817 during the struggle for independence. The Spanish tried to blow up the fort with 1400 pounds of gunpowder, but the fuse didn't work. It has been renovated and is open to the public. From the top, you get a commanding view of the bay.

PORLAMAR

Porlamar is the largest and busiest town in Margarita. It is very modern, with smart shops and fashionable restaurants. The eastern part of town is full of impressive, tall buildings that are either hotels or apartments.

Navigation

There are no problems entering. Anchor off the docks beside the Concorde Hotel. You may need a second anchor to hold your bow into the swells when the wind comes south of east. The closer to the docks you can get, the less rolly it is. However, beware of the big shoal patch in

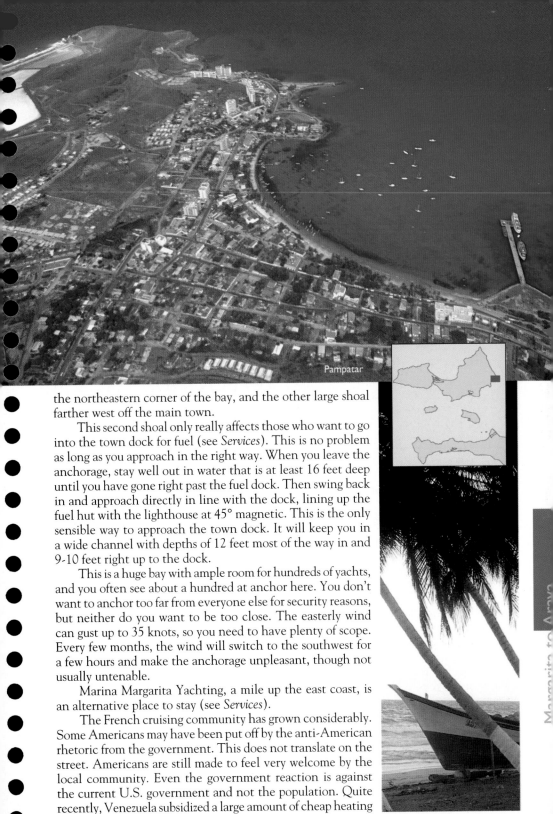

Pampatar

the northeastern corner of the bay, and the other large shoal farther west off the main town.

This second shoal only really affects those who want to go into the town dock for fuel (see *Services*). This is no problem as long as you approach in the right way. When you leave the anchorage, stay well out in water that is at least 16 feet deep until you have gone right past the fuel dock. Then swing back in and approach directly in line with the dock, lining up the fuel hut with the lighthouse at 45° magnetic. This is the only sensible way to approach the town dock. It will keep you in a wide channel with depths of 12 feet most of the way in and 9-10 feet right up to the dock.

This is a huge bay with ample room for hundreds of yachts, and you often see about a hundred at anchor here. You don't want to anchor too far from everyone else for security reasons, but neither do you want to be too close. The easterly wind can gust up to 35 knots, so you need to have plenty of scope. Every few months, the wind will switch to the southwest for a few hours and make the anchorage unpleasant, though not usually untenable.

Marina Margarita Yachting, a mile up the east coast, is an alternative place to stay (see *Services*).

The French cruising community has grown considerably. Some Americans may have been put off by the anti-American rhetoric from the government. This does not translate on the street. Americans are still made to feel very welcome by the local community. Even the government reaction is against the current U.S. government and not the population. Quite recently, Venezuela subsidized a large amount of cheap heating

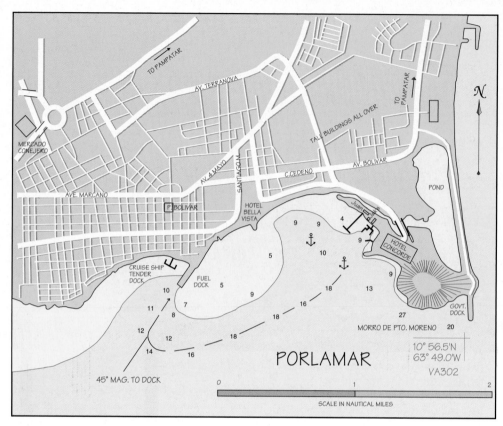

fuel for thousands of Americans in need.

Regulations

For clearing in, get Juan Baro and his mother, Liliana, (at Juan Marina), to do it for you, they can do it faster, and after all the driving around that is necessary, probably cheaper than if you do it yourself. You find them in the Juan Marina offices.

However, if you want to do the clearance yourself, you will need to check with Customs, Immigration, Port Captain, and National Guard. You may have to arrange for the doctor and customs officer to visit your yacht. The charges are variable. If you do it yourself, you should ask for and keep a receipt for any money paid out. Most offices have been combined into a single office, but unless you want to do it as a challenge and practice in dealing with local bureaucrats, we highly recommend you let Juan handle it. He clears hundreds of yachts in and knows the requirements.

Unfortunately, clearing in is only good for Margarita. When you want to move on, you have to clear out. When you do this, you can get a clearance to some distant port. This covers you for anything in between, except stays in other major towns like Puerto La Cruz, where they will insist you do it all again.

Communications

Two cruisers from Malta have installed harbor-wide wifi. They charge about $58US per month, $18US per week, or $4US per day. Check www.wifimargarita.com. You can also ask Juan about this service and how to hook up.

Juan Marina (0295 263-1332, Juanbaro@hotmail.com) has two Cantv telephones available, and they can receive faxes for cruisers. Apart from this and his clearance service, Juan Baro also looks after and cleans dinghies while you go ashore, carries supplies to your dinghy, and sells French bread daily. He is also a classical music fan, and may be able to share some with you.

(See also *Services*.)

Cantv communications centers can be found in most malls as well as on downtown sidewalks, areas where you are unlikely to have any problems. But it makes sense to buy a mobile phone: you can get them from $30, including the sim card. GSM makes the most sense, especially for overseas calls. You can get a local number post-paid by credit card or use the pre-paid cards. Digicel is currently the best deal.

If you need to get anything sent from the U.S. quickly, there are Federal Express, DHL and UPS offices, as well as Domesa, a local international courier service, in town.

General Yacht Services

Dieselman makes the rounds in the bay supplying fuel and water to boats directly from his tender. This is the best way to get it. But if for some reason this is not available, water, diesel, gasoline, and engine oil are also available at the main town dock in Porlamar. It is easy to get there, but you must go in the right way (see *Navigation*). Be sure to pick a time when you don't have to compete with the local fishermen for services. (Varying regulations may also make this impossible from time to time.)

Nodona Tours is a small store that has basic foodstuffs and ice. They are located next to Margarita Divers, in the long

Juan Baro

93

building that runs along the waterfront.

Just north are some more shallow draft docks, used primarily for local charter powerboats. The next dock north is a long one over the shallows, for dinghies only, at the head of which is a building shared by the coast guard auxiliary and Juan Baro of Juan Marina (VHF: 72). Juan is an ex-sailor with 12 years of varied experience who understands yachting needs. Juan speaks English, French, Italian, and Portugese. His dinghy dock has 24-hour security and he can help with clearance both national and international, phone, fax, and mail service, laundry, car rental and tour arrangements. If you need something made or repaired, talk to him. Juan offers a free bus to Sambil, a big mall out of town, on Mondays, Wednesdays, and Fridays, leaving at 0930 returning at 1300. This is a pleasant mall where you can easily spend some time. On Tuesdays, Thursdays, and Saturdays (same times), he goes to Rattan, a huge Depot Shop where you can find almost anything. It is great for tools and repair supplies, carpentry, and more. Times and destinations may change from time to time, so check with Juan.

If you look from the anchorage toward the fishing fleet to the east of town, you will see a sandy path going up a hill. La Impecable laundry is to be found up this hill. Like most laundries in Venezuela, you need only bring the dirty clothes; they supply the soap and will wash, dry, and fold for you. A couple of blocks into town is a more modern laundromat called Ediko's that offers both do-it-yourself or drop-off service; it is air-conditioned and has internet machines.

Marina Margarita Yachting (sometimes called the Hilton Marina) is a large, very well protected, man-made harbor with a depth of 12 feet. The marina is open and works, but at about half-capacity, without much ongoing push towards completion. Only the north docks have water and electricity. Still, there is usually plenty of room for most yachts, including catamarans, and they have 24-hour security. The coast guard has a base on the west side. The commodore is Pedro Ordaz (0295 261-0486 / 6857. VHF: Ch.10 "Marina.") As it is next to the Hilton, you will find taxis, restaurants and casinos a short walk away.

I have not been in this marina, but a satellite image shows there may be some obstructions close to the outer wall as you enter (looks like the outer wall crumbled). Use your eyes and go carefully. A GPS approach to 10°58.4N 63°49.0W should get you close enough to eyeball your way in. Go in by day.

Chandlery

The big Vasmesca chandlery store is a couple hundred yards down the road into town on the main road behind Juan Marina (Raul Leonie Avenue). Richard is the best contact; he speaks perfect English and is very helpful. They can handle imports from the U.S. and give support for electronics repairs and other maintenance. If you are staying here a long time, you can ask about a mailbox. They also have a branch in Puerto La Cruz.

In town, Offshore Marine (VHF: 11) is on Calle Marcano and geared to yachts with a wide range of general chandlery, including guides, water makers, electronics, fishing gear, coolers, and ropes, and they are the agents for Mercury outboards.

Another shop is two blocks past Plaza Bolívar on the corner of Igualdad and Martinez and is called La Casa Del Pescador. They are the agents for OMC Johnson supplying parts and fishing gear. Nautica Pampatar in Avenida Juan Bautista Arismendi in front of Rectimar is another convenient nautical store.

Technical Yacht Services

For bimimis, awnings, and sail repair, contact Simón Sails Service (VHF 72). Israel and Juan, originally from Orient Canvas, are good for general upholstery and sails. Contact them on VHF: 72 or visit at Marina Carmelo N.13, beside Playa Concorde.

Rectificadora y Torneria de Precision, run by Douglas Matto, can do metal fabrication and repair. Talk to Vemasca about electronics.

Provisioning

Banco Mercantil in Sambil or on 4 de Mayo Av. is best for exchanging dollars at

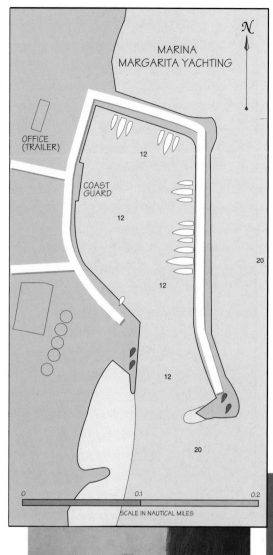

Margarita to Araya

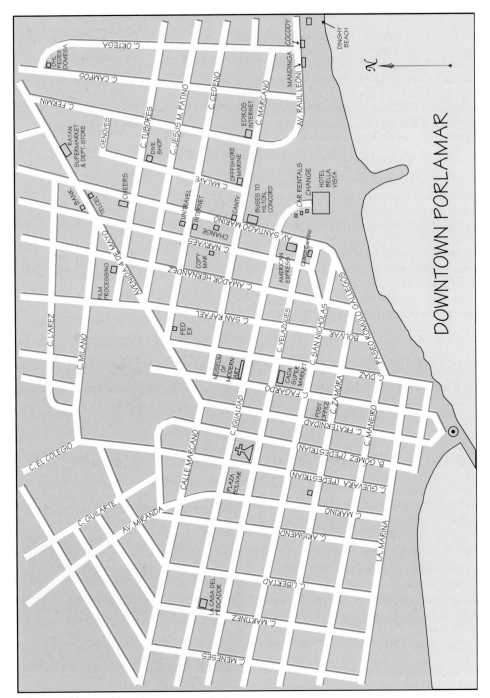

DOWNTOWN PORLAMAR

the official rate. But most banks have cash machines that take Cirrus, Mastercard and Visa, and this is the safest and simplest way to handle your cash, taking only as much as you need. In front of the Margarita Hilton is a change place (cambio) called Cuzco."

Centro Commercial Margarita, in Av. Bolivar, two miles from Juan Marina, heading east and north, has one of the best supermarkets and is the most popular with

Marina Margarita Yachting - Oscar Hernandez photo

cruisers. (See our Pampatar chart).

Otherwise, if you want to go into Porlamar, provisioning is a breeze at the two large supermarkets. The newest and fanciest is Ratan on Ave 4 de Mayo. This is both a large food shop and a complete department store with everything from household goods to bicycles. The goods are stacked so that unopened cases lie above items on display, and there are discounts for buying by the case. You will be able to find someone who speaks English, and you can find a cab on the street outside. Cada on Calle Velasquez is another big supermarket.

There are also several large malls in the vicinity that have inside multiple stores for complete shopping needs. The newest and biggest is called Sambil where there are also 5 movie theaters showing the latest in U.S. films, in English with Spanish subtitles.

The most interesting place to shop for food, handicrafts, and clothing is the Mercardo Conejero (Rabbit Market), which has recently been renovated and is much cleaner than before. It is best to go early in the morning, when everything is in full swing. The market is a riot of color and movement as everyone wanders from stall to stall looking for bargains. Most things are half the price you would spend at the malls. A couple blocks south of Mercado Conejero (take a taxi, do not walk) are some huge new hyper-stores. Traki seems to be very popular. Nearly everything you find in these shops is imported to Venezuela.

Fun Shopping

The boutique shopper will have a ball, because Porlamar is one vast shopping mall. A good place to start looking for bargains is along Blvd. Guevara and Calle Gomez, both pedestrian streets lined with shops. Santiago Mariño and Avenida 4 de Mayo are the really fancy streets with the highest quality shops. Clothing and leather can be good buys. There are huge variations in both prices and quality.

Taking on fuel and water - Oscar Hernandez photo

Hotel Bella Vista is a useful landmark and meeting place as it is near the main shopping area. Some car rental agencies are placed outside, and a whole range of shops and services, including a travel agency, are inside. In the cool of their air-conditioning you can find comfortable armchairs in which to sit. They have restaurants and an oyster bar out by the pool where dozens of succulent oysters can be had for just a few dollars. There is a variety of entertainment at night. In the same area, you will find a big Centro de Conexiones Cantv, and many fancy stores with prestigious brands.

Transport

Buses into town stop regularly in front of the Concorde hotel.

Unitravel does complete tours and excursions to the interior as well as to other islands, either by bus, ferry, or plane, along with international flights. They speak English, Italian, and French. Flight connections between Margarita, the mainland, and the rest of the world are very good.

In front of the Margarita Hilton, there are several car rentals: Ramcar, Los Amigos, Budget, and Excellency. The last one is the least expensive.

If you are interested in hiking, contact Kelbert Bortone. He organizes tracking, bird watching, and fauna and flora tours in most of the mountains in Margarita, the highest of which is over 3,000 feet.

The hikes include spectacular views. You can call him at: 0141 093-6323, or email: Kelbertk7@hotmail.com. Kelbert also builds houses and sells real estate.

West of Hotel Bellavista Marina El Faro is a dock from which daily ferries and charters leave to Carupano and Coche.

Ashore

Robert Strong, a cruiser from the U.S., created a service to facilitate medical support for cruisers and visitors willing to take advantage of good doctors and inexpensive prices in Venezuela compared with the USA. The idea started while he as dealing with a medical emergency in Margarita. Check him out at: surgicalservicesinternational.com

Try also the excellent Medymed group in Caracas (0412 231-9469), a large, top-quality facility, covering many specialties. They speak English.

For dental work, check Dra. Juaquina Guerra de Martins (Tel: 0295-267-2715, 267-2294, Cel: 0414-395-5248) CC Rattan, Piso 3 Of. 5.

While wandering around town, check out the Museum of Contemporary Art (closed Mondays) on Calle Igualdad. The downstairs contains the work of Francisco Narvaez, who was born in Margarita and before his death became one of Venezuela's most sought-after artists. His work often fetches higher prices than the most famous European artists. Upstairs the museum shows exhibitions of other modern artists.

While in Margarita, consider visiting El Reino de Musipan (www.musipan.net/index.php). It is a giant theme park about Venezuelans throughout their history. It is a lot of fun, and you will have the opportunity to see the real idiosyncrasy of the country. It is on the Playa El Yaque (the big windsurfing beach) close to the airport.

Restaurants

There are hundreds of restaurants in Margarita, which open, close, and change with astonishing rapidity. We mention a few that are currently good value. Most of these restaurants open daily at midday and stay open through the evening. Jak's is a quaint restaurant on the beach right by the dinghy dock at the Concorde serving Thai, local, and international foods, open everyday except Sundays 0900 to 2100. It is a favorite and convenient place for visiting yachtspeople to get together. El Pescador de la Marina is next door facing the day-charter boat dock and serves great seafood. If you are dying for Italian food, try Restaurant La Italiana, a smart and reasonably priced restaurant on Avenida 4 de Mayo. Just down the road, Dagenaro Pizzeria cooks pizzas in two big, wood-fired ovens. Cheers is a pleasant place for lunch or dinner. Heavy-duty air-conditioning and ice-cold beer make a welcome break from the heat of the city. They serve good steaks and seafood, as well as rice and pasta dishes, but save some room for something off the dessert trolley. Cocody (open evenings only) is on the waterfront. You can even pull your dinghy up on the beach outside. They have an open air-deck over the sand with an attractive white fence around it with access to the beach, which is nicely landscaped and well lit. They serve French, Venezuelan, and international food.

For a more varied and formal meal, with authentic local entertainment and music, visit the Mandinga restaurant just down the beach.

In front of the Margarita Hilton are some small restaurants. Mogamy is a good place for lunch and not too expensive.

Water Sports

Why not try diving in Venezuela? There are two dive sites within easy reach of Porlamar and others that are a longer boat ride away. One of the close ones is Farallón Blanco, a small island between Porlamar and Pampatar. You dive to about 40 feet. This is the site of a curious underwater religious statue put down by the first divers to dive here. (There is a similar one on the island.) In addition, you will see enormous brain corals, large sea fans, and lots of reef fish including barracudas. In the same area there is an underwater patch of rock called Mucura. Here huge boulders are riddled with holes that are home to many reef fish, including really large, brightly colored parrotfish. It is somewhat farther away to go to Los Frailes. The current there is strong, so it is for advanced divers only and is usually done as a drift dive. There are moray eels, really big barracudas, and lots of oysters. (See also Isla Cubagua.)

Walter Vedovello's Margarita Divers at Concorde Marina can take you on any of the above dives. They normally do two-tank dives. They will also fill your tanks and help however they can.

There is another dive shop downtown in Porlamar called Venaquarium. They take groups to Frailes, Cubagua, Testigos, and Blanquilla. In addition, they have a well-stocked shop for buying diving gear.

Margarita to Araya

99

Coast just north of Juangriego - Oscar Hernandez photos

JUANGRIEGO

Juangriego (John the Greek) was named after a Greek pirate who was shipwrecked here. It is a delightful town with a touch of the Riviera. It is peaceful and pleasant, yet there are enough shops to satisfy most needs, a picturesque church, many brightly painted fishing boats, and some cozy waterside restaurants. There are good shops for clothing, watches, and souvenirs. Ask about security, as there have been a few problems, but efforts are being made to change that.

Paul and Yvonne from Holland, recent arrivals who run Hotel Patrick close by on Calle el Fuerte, have recognized some of the problems and are trying to get some things done. They have a VHF radio and offer showers and a laundry at the hotel. They have been working with the local mayor and other officials on the idea of a floating dock, better security, and a customs clearance agent.

Navigation

Juangriego is open to the northwest. You would not want to be here during a northerly swell, when bad seas can flood the town. In the spring and summer it is perfect, and far more comfortable than Porlamar when the winds switch south of east. Anchor anywhere in the bay clear of the fishing boats.

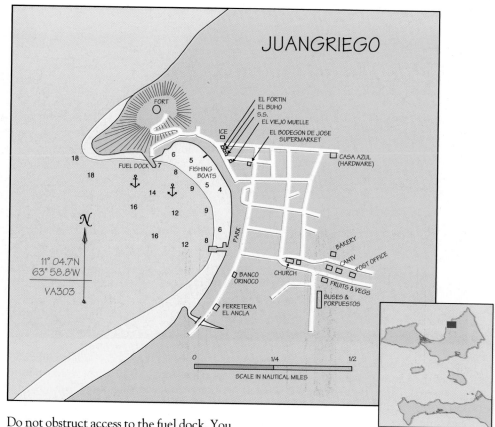

Do not obstruct access to the fuel dock. You can pull your dinghy up the beach, or anchor it and take a line ashore like the local fishing boats do. As you come in with the dinghy, watch out for long lines streaming from the fishing boats.

Communications

Hotel Patrick close by on Calle el Fuerte has a broadband internet connection in the bar free of charge for its clients, and is putting in a wifi system which should be bay-wide.

S&S La Casita de las Crepes on the waterfront is open everyday from 0830 and has an internet facility. Telephone calls can be made from the Cantv office near the post office or from the card phones scattered around.

Services

You may be able to get gas and diesel on the fuel dock. There is seven to eight feet off the dock, but there may be scattered boulders on the bottom left over from building the wall, so approach slowly.

There is an ice factory close to the waterfront, or you can get it from the ice truck that supplies the fishing boats on the fuel dock.

Ashore

There are several small supermarkets; the closest is El Bogedón de Jose, open everyday from 0900 to 2100. Although there are no chandleries, there are two good hardware stores in town.

Several agreeable little restaurants are clustered up in the northeast corner of the bay. El Viejo Muelle ($D), El Fortin ($D), and El Buho ($D) all serve good seafood and are beautifully positioned on the waterfront to sit and watch life go by. Nestled in between these on the waterfront is S&S La Casita de las Crepes ($C-D) open everyday from 0830 serving American food as well as local fare. They have an internet facility as well. For good Chinese food, check Tao Wan

Margarita to Araya

Juangriego from the air

restaurant on Calle Bolívar (the main street, where the Cantv Communications Center is situated). Banco de Venezuela is situated in the Malecon. Pizzeria La Mamma serves excellent pizza.

Hotel Patrick is close by on Calle el Fuerte. They have a restaurant (Coya Cabana) and bar, where you can play pool, darts, chess, cards, or just sit in the TV corner and watch a DVD. They have a nightly happy hour and occasional live music.

El Fortin (Small Fort) de la Galera is a short walk up the hill, where you are rewarded by good views all around. This little fort played an important part in the Venezuelan struggle for independence. In 1815, while Bolívar was in exile in Haiti, his cohort, Juan Bautista Arismendi, mounted an attack on the Spanish garrison here and killed all the soldiers. This provided a stronghold for the return of Bolívar, who landed here in 1816 with 4,000 rifles and a small force supplied by Haitian President Tion. He gathered up a small army and headed for Carúpano. The war of independence continued, and in 1817, the Spanish general Pablo Morillo recaptured the fort and slaughtered hundreds of patriots. If you look down you can see a lagoon. It is said this ran red with blood after the slaughter, and it is called Laguna de Los Mártires (Lagoon of the Martyrs).

Two miles east of Juangriego, you will find a historical replica town called Taguantar. It includes mud houses, historical statues, and antiques, and is the creation of Alexis Marin. This is a good place to buy beautiful local handicrafts, visit a rum distillery, and eat typical Venezuela food.

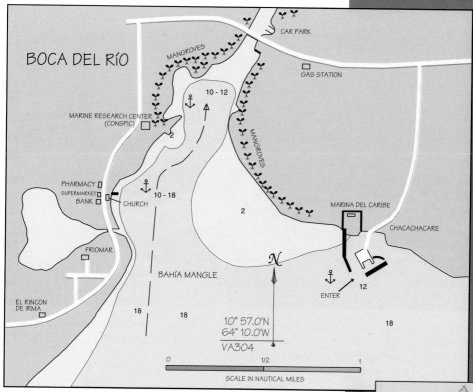

BOCA DEL RÍO

CAR PARK

MANGROVES

GAS STATION

10 - 12

MANGROVES

MARINE RESEARCH CENTER
(CONSPIC)

PHARMACY
SUPERMARKET
BANK
CHURCH

10 - 18

MARINA DEL CARIBE

CHACACHACARE

FRIOMAR

2

BAHÍA MANGLE

N

ENTER

12

EL RINCON
DE IRMA

18

18

18

18

10° 57.0'N
64° 10.0'W
VA304

0   1/2   1

SCALE IN NAUTICAL MILES

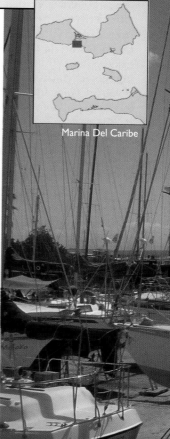

Marina Del Caribe

BOCA DE RIO, PLAYA LA RESTINGA & LAGUNA GRANDE

Your visit to Margarita will be more fun with a visit to the intricate mangrove channels in Laguna Grande and the beach at Playa La Restinga. This can be done by car, but you can also sail right up into Bahía Mangle and anchor in the mouth of the lagoon, or for better security leave the boat by Del Caribe Marina at Chacachacare close by.

Navigation

The entrance to the Boca De Río (Mouth of the River) anchorage is not difficult, but unfortunately the water comes in patches of green and brown that bear no relation to the depth. As you come in Bahía Mangle, favor the Boca del Río side of the bay, but do not hug the shore too closely. You can anchor right off the town. This is sometimes a lovely anchorage, especially in the winter, when the winds are north of east. However, in the summer months, this bay is subject to a nasty chop, so it is better to continue up into the first mangrove bay, which is completely sheltered. There is a shoal that extends about 120 yards to the south of the mangroves on the western

Boca del Río

shore. When you get about 200 yards from the entrance, swing out into the middle of the channel to avoid the shoal (see sketch chart). As the water is murky, I would recommend a slow approach, taking soundings. Alternatively, if you anchor off the village, you will probably be approached by one of the men who do the river trip. They will guide you up into the bay in return for being chosen to take you to Playa La Restinga. If you are going up in the mangroves, take mosquito coils for the night. Chacachacare, on the eastern side of Bahía Mangle, is a busy fishing port sharing the same breakwater with Del Caribe Marina.

Communications/shopping

Valerios Telnet Service, an internet station is in Boca del Río on the main road. At the end of town there is a chandlery, Ferremar, and a bank with a teller machine.

Services

Astilleros & Varadero Del Caribe is run by Philippe Philippart, an ex-pilot and diver who was previously in the oil industry. It is located in Chacachacare next to the fishing harbour. Argentinian Marcelo Bieder is the operations manager. They have a 50-ton Travelift, extra wide to accommodate up to 24-foot beam. In addition, he has a railway

that will haul larger catamarans and trimarans. Divers are available to help with the haul. There is storage for about 100 to 120 boats and a crane for mast work. They can also do all kinds of repair work and major reconstruction, gelcoat-peeling, electrical and mechanical work. There are baths and showers as well as washing machines. The office has phone, fax, and email service. Duromax, on site, has a good supply of parts, paints, and supplies. Diesel, gasoline, propane, and ice can be arranged through the office. A public bus service runs into Porlamar during the day, and a taxi service is available. A vegetable truck makes frequent stops, and there is a seafood restaurant next door.

Cruisers can live aboard while working on their boats, and you can process customs and immigration through the office. Ask in the office about Mr. Cucho, who can supply food to the boats while people are staying on them. They have plans for a restaurant and barbecue facilities.

At the entrance to the boatyard there is a store selling essentials and the bus stop. At the entrance of town, there is an ice factory.

You can anchor on the west side of the western breakwater in about 12 feet. However, there have been some serious security problems in this anchorage, so check on the

Mangrove channel

current status. (A new police station by the bridge may help.) Access to the marina is through the space between the two breakwaters; anchoring inside is limited as the fishing boats are moving around in there. The floating dinghy dock is on the east side of the marina.

Boca de Río has a medical lab and a dental clinic called San Francisco de Asis.

Ashore

The trip through the mangrove lagoon to Playa La Restinga is not expensive and should be done with a local guide, on one of their boats, which might be described as "Lagoondolas." They are small, open boats with a protective canopy and big outboard. The journey through the mangroves takes you along miles of twisted, maze-like channels. There are placid lagoons, narrow tunnels formed by mangrove branches, and pretty canals that have been called such names as "tunnel of kisses" and "canal of lovers." Huge pelicans perch in tiny branches, looking as out of place as a bank manager on a seesaw.

Your destination is Playa la Restinga. This is an almost deserted, ten-mile-long beach. The only buildings are right by the landing and consist of a bunch of rough-and-ready restaurants open to the sea breeze. Stay for lunch, as the seafood is good and prices reasonable. Langostinas are the specialty.

Playa la Restinga is exposed to the wind, and as far as the eye can see, waves break in white lines along the shore. You can enjoy body surfing and playing in the waves. The beach has thousands of shells with a few unusual ones tucked among the clams. An hour or two is not too long to walk here, and you should keep this in mind when arranging the return time with your boatman. When you go back, it is by a short and quick route.

Laguna Grande is also known for its scarlet ibis. This bird is best seen at dusk, and you would have to arrange a special trip.

If you bring a bag, you can collect your supper from the sea. Thousands of guacucos (clam-like shellfish) get washed up along the shore. You can take the live ones as they get washed in or dig for them in the shallows.

Fishing boats in chacachacare

Margarita to Araya

Robledal, west coast of Margarita

You need 20-30 per person. Rinse them countless times, or leave them in saltwater overnight, to get rid of the sand. To make a delicious soup for 3-4, pour a one-pound can of tomatoes, the same can full of water, and the clams in a pot. Add half a can of white wine. Add salt, pepper, and a little thyme and garlic. Bring to the boil and simmer for 20 minutes (reject any clams that stay closed). If the clams are still sandy, just forget them and enjoy the liquid part of the soup.

If the soup isn't as filling as you hoped, you may wish to eat out. El Rincón de Irma ($D) is set in a pleasant garden and open every day. There is also Friomar. While here, check out the Sea Museum.

The best cold coconut drinks in Margarita, "cocadas" can be found at the crossroads between Boca del Río and Macanao.

WEST COAST OF MARGARITA

The west coast of Margarita has an attractive coastline backed by red mountains. You can find good anchorages here, though in the winter it should be treated with caution, as it is susceptible to northerly swells. It is a convenient stopping place while circumnavigating Margarita and a stopping place en route to Isla Tortuga or Blanquilla. Punta Arenas (Sand Point) is very low with a lovely, secluded beach. Along the west coast, there are two fishing villages separated by another beach. This area is visited only occasionally by yachts. So far, we have not heard of many security problems.

Give a good clearance to the southern part of the west coast, as it is shoal. Keep in at least 14 feet of water. You can anchor anywhere else along the coast; just south of Boca de Pozo (Pool Mouth) is especially attractive. If you want to visit the village of Boca de Pozo, anchor outside the fishing fleet in about 12 feet of water. You can carry on down to Robledal (Oak Tree) and anchor off the dock in nine feet of water. There is a six-foot shoal about quarter of a mile southeast of Robledal dock. It is soft mud. Your chart might show a light at Morro de Robledal. This has been replaced by one that flashes every five seconds and is situated on the hills above the point. The light is unreliable.

Ashore

You can find small shops and bins for your garbage in either village. Robledal is a little more picturesque, with whitewashed houses set amid flowers. Here you will find a good general store, two bars, two pharmacies, and a modern, small hotel called L'Oasis. L'Oasis is owned by Vermonter Reed Fendler, who is occasionally in residence and has a European and North American clientele. They have a good little restaurant serving Venezuelan and South American food, which is open for breakfast, lunch, and dinner.

Boca de Pozo has a pharmacy, bread shop, and a place to buy ice, all set round the square, which is clearly marked by the huge aerial.

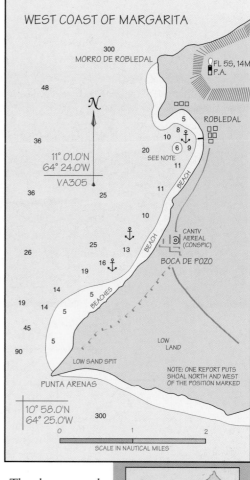

WEST COAST OF MARGARITA

MORRO DE ROBLEDAL 300

FL 5S, 14M P.A.

ROBLEDAL

48

SEE NOTE

36

11° 01.0'N
64° 24.0'W

VA305

36

26

19

45

90

BEACHES

BEACH

BEACH

CANTV AEREAL (CONSPIC)

BOCA DE POZO

LOW LAND

LOW SAND SPIT

PUNTA ARENAS

10° 58.0'N
64° 25.0'W   300

NOTE: ONE REPORT PUTS SHOAL NORTH AND WEST OF THE POSITION MARKED

0   1   2

SCALE IN NAUTICAL MILES

Fishermen in San Pedro - Ellen Sanpere photo

Isla Coche

```
10° 50.06'N   VA306
64° 00.88'W  (POSITION OF BUOY)

                    NOTE: NO ANCHORING OFF THE
5        4          NORTH ANCHORAGE BEACH
                    IF FISHERMEN WISH TO
              4     USE IT.

    4    3       3

         2    PUNTA PLAYA       6

         4
11   10
         10
12       10    9
    12    12

              12
         13    10        AIR
                         STRIP
N    13       10

    14

10° 47'N
64° 01'W
VA3B6                  SAN PEDRO
18                HOTEL          150-200 FT.
                  +
               ++
PUNTA
EL BOTÓN          13

    20
WEST COAST OF ISLA COCHE
0              1              2

    SCALE IN NAUTICAL MILES
```

170° MAG. TO POINT CLEARS REEF

Isla Coche is an unusual island of dry hills in pastel hues of red, yellow, and brown covered with dry scrub and cactus. It was originally inhabited by Indians, and its name comes from their word for deer. It was colonized by Europeans in the sixteenth century, when the pearls started giving out over in Cubagua and more were discovered in the waters surrounding Coche. It also proved a good source of salt, which they still produce here. It has a population of about 4,500, and the capital, San Pedro, is a sprawling town of fisher folk, which used to be reminiscent of Mexico in the 40s. Now the dirt roads are shiny tarmac, and there are tourists. I hope at least beady-eyed vultures still sit on roofs and stare down.

Hiking in the hills is really pretty, and the vultures take on a new look, soaring gracefully overhead. To the north of town, Punta Playa is a long and lovely sand spit. Coche is affected by a wind funnel that goes from here right though the western part of the Golfo de Cariaco. With lots of wind and the big beach and Punta Playa, it has become a hotspot for wind and kite surfers. It is also a popular day-charter destination from Margarita. A huge new hotel is planned on Punta Playa.

They have shrimp farms here, las camaroneras, that you could visit, and some people like to visit

Western Isla Coche, Punta Playa and San Pedro

the huge mounds of conch shells down by Punta Conejo at El Saco.

There are two main anchoring areas; the western end of the island and at El Saco on the south coast.

WESTERN COCHE PUNTA PLAYA TO PUNTA EL BOTON

Navigation

The high parts of Isla Coche can be seen from afar, but the low-lying land, like Punta Playa, can only be seen when you are close.

If you are coming from Porlamar, it is necessary to avoid the shoal that extends a mile and a half north of Punta Playa. If you round Punta Mosquito about a mile offshore and head due west, you should find it. It is marked by a buoy at 10°50.06' north and 64° 00.88' west. Once you have rounded the buoy with a reasonable margin, you can head toward Punta el Botón. Should the buoy be missing or out of place, then a course of 170° magnetic to Punta el Botón should keep you clear of the reef. Take care around this shoal: from time to time I get messages saying the buoy is out of place, or that the shoal has extended.

The strange, castle-like building in the hills is an abandoned government project, intended as a holiday resort for unruly youths.

Isla Coche Hotel - Ellen Sanpere photo

Margarita to Araya

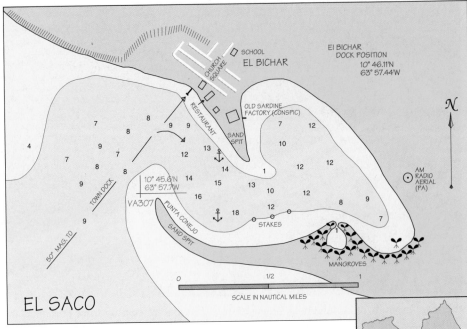

EL SACO

The Punta Playa anchorage is attractive, and in the early morning, it is a pleasure to watch the pelicans and cormorants coming to work. It must be used with consideration for the fishermen who fish all along the beach. Yachts anchored here can be in their way, so move if asked. Daytime anchorage is no problem, as the fishing is nearly always done at night. If the wind is howling out of the northeast (which it often does here), they will probably not be fishing, and you can stay the night. If you see fishing boats with nets moored in this area, move before dark. This is no problem, as it is less than a mile down the beach to the San Pedro ferry dock. There is a good anchorage north of the ferry dock down to El Coche hotel, in nine or ten feet of water and you will be out of their way. This is also a more convenient anchorage for visiting the town. I have heard about occasional security problems here, but a large number of yachts do visit and feel welcome.

Ashore

If you run short on some essentials, there are several small basic stores in town and a couple of well-stocked supermarkets: one on the main street, one in Plaza Bolivar. But why cook on board? You can choose between the local restaurants in town and the half-dozen hotels catering to the windsurfers. The most popular among yachts is the Isla de Coche Speed Hotel, right on the beach with a dock, close by the airport. You can even call them on the VHF, and if their launch is available, they will come and collect you and. Apart from lovely surroundings they have free-flying exotic birds, including parrots and macaws.

You can walk above town to Hotel Atti and Casa Rita, or into San Pedro, to Posada del Kitesurfista. This is a fve-roomed posada (guest house) on the main street. It is owned and run by Alex and Maria, a young Venezuelan couple who are happy to do laundry, deliver cold beer and groceries to the dock and be of general help. But better yet, arrange to eat here. They cook breakfast and dinner in a family style atmosphere and make great Key lime pie. Alex has crewed on yachts and so has an affinity for them (kitesurf.wtfe.com).

EL SACO

El Saco is a beautiful harbor on the south side of Isla Coche. It is open to the

Coche

El Saco

breezes but completely protected from the swells and large enough to house every cruising boat in Venezuela. It makes a great cruising rendezvous for a few days away from it all. The long, thin land spit at the entrance often contains so many pelicans and cormorants that it looks brown.

Navigation

If you are sailing from San Pedro, keep about half a mile to a mile offshore to clear any shallow places along the coast. The white buildings of the disused sardine factory can often be seen when you round Punta El Botón.

While there is plenty of water in El Saco, you do have to cross a wide bar to get in. The depths on the bar vary from about seven to nine feet, with lots of bumps and dips. The deepest water seems to be on an approach of 50° magnetic toward the dock at El Bichar. There is a partially hidden, red-roofed church behind the dock, which helps locate it. Binoculars also help. Approach the town dock until you are close, then head up into the lagoon. Once inside, you have 10 to 18 feet of water in the first part of the lagoon. The prettiest anchorage is on the south side of the harbor close to the southern sandspit,

which is so narrow that you can see the water on both sides. You can also anchor anywhere in the bay.

If you are going into the second lagoon, enter near the stakes, as this has the deepest water. Inside, our soundings showed most of the inner lagoon to be 10-12 feet deep. Proceed gently.

The inner part of this harbor is protected enough to ride out a tropical storm, but might be marginal for a bad hurricane, as the low-lying outer spit might be covered in a storm surge.

Ashore

The village of El Bichar sprawls up the hill. The waterfront, with a church and square and a street behind, is the most picturesque part. There are one or two small stores, a couple of bars, and a pleasant beach front restaurant called El Pescador de la Isla ($D). It is open daily from when the owners wake up to midnight. They keep plenty of cold Polar on ice and serve good, inexpensive fish and chicken plates.

The protected lagoon is ideal for dinghy exploration and windsurfing. Ashore, you can hike into the dry hills, or go look at the big conch pile on the point.

Margarita to Araya

111

Cubagua, Ensenada de Charagato

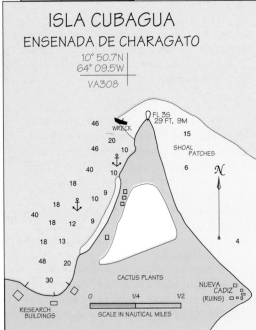

ISLA CUBAGUA
ENSENADA DE CHARAGATO
10° 50.7'N
64° 09.5'W
VA308

FL 3S
29 FT, 9M
46
WRECK
15
20
46   10
SHOAL
PATCHES
40   10
6
18
9   N
18   10
40   18   12   9
18   13
4
48   20
30   CACTUS PLANTS
NUEVA
CADIZ
(RUINS)
0   1/4   1/2
RESEARCH
BUILDINGS
SCALE IN NAUTICAL MILES

Isla Cubagua

Isla Cubagua is a pretty island of sandy beaches and dry hills. The yellow-brown hills change color with the sun, and on a clear day puffy white clouds perch on Margarita's mountains in a surreal way.

Isla Cubagua was the first European settlement in America. It happened because Christopher Columbus saw some natives with pearls along the Península de Paria. Within a year, two adventurers, Christobal De LaGuerra and Pedro Alfonso Niño, discovered the source of the pearls to be the pearl beds off Cubagua. In 1492, fifty fortune hunters arrived and founded Nueva Cádiz on the east side of the island. They took Indians as slaves and forced them to dive for pearls. They worked them so hard, whipping them when they would not dive, that hundreds of Indians died. At the height of the pearling industry, Cubagua pearls provided Spain with a wealth almost equal to that of the gold transported from Inca lands. In one year alone, Cubagua exported 820 pounds of pearls.

In 1520, a force of 300 well-armed Indians attacked the town and forced the Spaniards to leave. But the Spanish came back in force and rebuilt the town stronger than before, fortifying their houses against attack. A fort was also built over on the mainland to secure a water supply.

After a few decades of heavy exploitation, the supply of pearls decreased and new beds were sought in Coche and Cumaná. On Christmas Day in 1541, an earthquake and tidal wave destroyed Nueva Cádiz. Now Cubagua is uninhabited save for a small research station and a few fishing camps.

Navigation

The best anchorage in Cubagua is the Ensenada de Charagato at the northeastern tip. This is a large anchorage, well protected from the prevailing winds, and you can anchor anywhere along the shore.

As you approach, you will see the conspicuous wreck of a car ferry. This caught fire in the late 70s. There were frequent explosions from the gas tanks of the cars on board, and it took a week to burn. Pass outside this wreck and sail up into the bay. The anchoring shelf is widest off the beach, and holding is good in sand between the dense weed patches. Day-charter boats use this anchorage, but there is plenty of room to anchor well away from them.

Regulations

Pearl fishing has been prohibited since 1962.

Ashore

The remains of Nueva Cádiz are a 40-minute walk. Skirt the salt pond and follow the shoreline south until you come to the ruins. Only the bottoms of the walls remain, but you get an idea of the size of the town as it continues down into the sea. The ground glints with reflections from thousands of oyster shell fragments.

Water Sports

The water is often refreshingly chilly here and the visibility is not always good, but snorkeling and diving on the big wreck are excellent, with lots of fish and reef creatures such as basket stars. You also see large starfish. Advanced divers can go inside the ferry hold and see the cars still sitting there. The wreck of a barge is close to the wrecked ferry.

The Península de Araya, Isla Caribe and Isla Lobos

Navigation (See our Area 3 chart on page 85)

When you round Morro de Chacopata heading west, you pass through a five-mile opening between this point and Isla Coche. The

NOTES ON HEADING BACK EAST

Before hading back, check on the current security situation. Make you way back to Testigos and then head off from there, unless security along the Península de Paria has improved. If it has improved, then following the coast along Península de Araya and Paria is the easiest and shortest way to go to Trinidad. For those sailing to the Windwards, this is considered the soft option, though it is probably a bit faster to motor sail directly to the Windwards from Margarita.

The prevailing wind in this area is easterly; somewhat north of east from Cumaná to Chacopata then northeasterly to southeasterly from Chacopata to Punta Pargo. The winds often calm down after nightfall and stay light till mid-morning. There is not usually much current within a mile or two of land. Farther out, the prevailing current is west-setting. Winds are typically calmer in the summer and stronger in the winter.

There are exceptions to this rule, and those that attract the demons of adverse winds and seas can occasionally fight a knot of current close to the coast and the winds blowing hard all night.

From Araya to Chacopata there is a degree of protection from ocean swells because of Margarita, Coche, and Cubagua. The trip from Chacopata to Punta Pargo is in open ocean. This part of the coast can be placid, or it can be stirred up and rough.

Those heading east can break the trip into manageably short runs. If you get up at first light, you can motor until the wind starts blowing hard, then beat or motor sail the rest of the way to the next anchorage.

There is just one long stretch between Puerto Santos (or Ensenada Medina) and the next reliable harbor, which is Punta Pargo. This is 60-70 miles depending on where you start, and it is probably best done as an overnight trip.

water here is relatively shallow between 16 and 30 feet deep. You have to pass to the north of Isla Caribe; shoal water extends all the way out from Morros de Chacopata to Isla Caribe. You can pass on either side of Isla Lobos.

Just off the north coast of the Península de Araya, about 10 miles west of Morros de Chacopata, lie three rocks called Islotes La Tuna. These are too small to give any shelter and you need to treat them with caution as submerged rocks extend for several hundred yards around them. There is plenty of room and water to pass midway between the two northern ones.

An extensive shoal lies northwest of Punta Chica on the westernmost point of the Península de Araya (see sketch chart page 117). It extends a couple of miles out, and you have to go way round it before it is safe to head back down towards Araya or Cumaná. You have to be similarly careful

in the other direction when you are leaving Araya to head east. A buoy that marks the extent of the shoal is sometimes there, sometimes missing. On our sketch chart of Araya we have given GPS coordinates that might be helpful. Otherwise, just give a good wide berth. The water is deep outside it, so if you have an echo sounder with an alarm and set it on 40 feet, it should give you enough warning.

You can find anchorages at Isla Lobos and Isla Caribe down towards Morros de Chacopata, and there are about four good places to anchor off the western end of Araya. There is not much else in the way of anchorages here.

ISLA CARIBE

Isla Caribe makes a pleasant overnight stop. It has a fair beach with a couple of fishermen's huts. Approach the island from

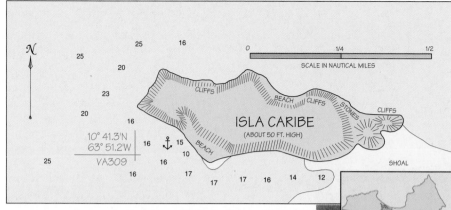

the west or northwest and anchor off the beach in about 16 feet of water.

Do not attempt to pass round the south side of Isla Caribe, between it and the mainland. A long, shallow bank extends from the mainland to the eastern end of Isla Caribe. This is marked as mainly 9-10 feet on the charts, but many places seem much shallower; a good place to avoid.

ISLA LOBOS

Isla Lobos are two small, hilly islands that are joined by a rocky shallow. This breaks up the sea and gives good protection. The islands have some ruins on them, but today the main inhabitants are hundreds of cormorants who line up in ranks on the flat parts of the shore like a small, dark, avian army. There is even a thimble-sized beach; in all a great spot for a night or two.

Approach from the west and anchor between the two is-

Isla Caribe

Margarita to Araya

Isla Lobos

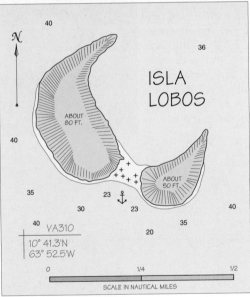

lands. To get the best protection from the seas, edge up as close as you dare to the rocks.

WEST COAST OF PENINSULA DE ARAYA

The west coast of the Península de Araya is an appealing area of light sand beaches, soft red-brown cliffs, and dry, scrubby plants. It is well known for its salt production from the naturally occurring salt flats. At peak production, the salt factory can produce 120,000 tons of salt a year.

In the old days, when salt was the only means of preserving many foods, Araya was an especially important possession. The Spanish, who owned it, became increasingly frustrated because the Dutch kept sneaking in on them and stealing boatloads of salt. In response, they built the largest fort in Venezuela, the Castillo de Santiago de Araya. It was started in 1618 and completed in 1665. It held a complement of 300 men and 45 cannons. This effectively stopped the pilfering and everything went well until 1726, when a hurricane passed by and winds and waves not only damaged the fort, but also rendered the salt ponds useless and the fort unnecessary. The Spanish didn't fancy leaving it there for someone else, so they blew a large part of it up. The salt lagoon later reformed and is still productive.

Navigation

If approaching from the east, give Punta Arenas a wide berth, as a shoal extends southeastwards about two-thirds of a mile.

There are four good places to anchor along this coast. All of them offer wide areas in which to anchor, and they are fine for a one-night stop. For longer stays, they suffer the disadvantage of being on a very busy seaway of ferries and fishing boats. Always leave a good light on at night and be prepared to rock with the wash of passing craft.

Keep in mind this is an area where lots of thefts and worse have been reported. If you are going to anchor along this coast, Punta Arenas has a better reputation than the other anchorages. You could also make a day visit, which would be safer. There are plans for a big new boatyard somewhere in Araya.

The southernmost anchorage is just west of Punta Arenas, where there is an attractive, inhabited beach. This is also considered the safest spot. About two miles up the coast there is another long and mainly deserted beach with a perfect anchoring shelf. Perhaps the most interesting spot is between Punta Barrigón and the old fort. There is a long stretch of beach here with little cliffs, and you can choose your spot. This also positions you to explore the old fort Santiago de los Caballeros ruins. The other anchorage is off the town itself, which is perfect for those who like to check out the local bars. You can also anchor much further north.

The fort is 400 years old and was built by the Spaniards to protect the area from Dutch invaders and salt thieves. Nearby is Choro-Choro (part of the town called Araya on our chart), the main town of the península. You will find locals making handicrafts and see some old faces of people who worked for years in the salt mines under harsh conditions. There was a film called Araya in 1959 directed by Margot Benacerraf, which won a first price in the Cannes Film Festival. Some of the locals appeared in that film and they had their first chance to see it some 30 years after it was done.

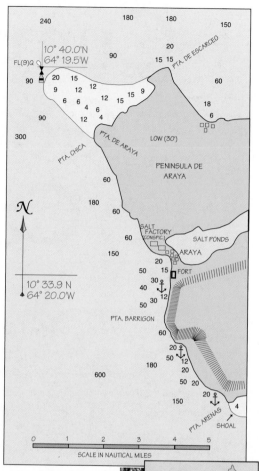

Margarita to Araya

Cumaná &
Golfo de
Cariaco

AREA 4

Oscar Hernadez photo

Cumaná

This section covers Cumaná and the Golfo de Cariaco. This is a delightful cruising area, well protected with lots of anchorages, and away from Cumaná, a generally good reputation for security.

Cumaná has the honor of being the first city founded by the Spaniards in the American continent, in 1521. It is a handsome town set on a river about three-quarters of a mile inland. There are pleasant plazas, colorful streets, and a walkway along the river. Cumaná is the capital of the state of Sucre and its main commercial center. The waterfront area is called Puerto Sucre. It is less alluring than the town but compensates with some good haul-out facilities and a first-class marina.

Cumaná is a conveniently placed gateway to the Golfo de Cariaco, and it is only about 10 miles from Mochima National Park.

Cumaná was an important Indian town before Europeans arrived and derives its name from the Cumanagoto tribe, who lived there. The Cumanagotos were great seafarers and known as the owners of the sea throughout the islands.

Franciscan missionaries were here in 1506, but the town didn't become a European stronghold until pearls and gold were found. The town was officially claimed by the Spanish in 1521, and Indians were taken from Cumaná to dive in the pearl beds at Cubagua.

Gold and pearls passing through Cumaná made it an attractive target for pirates, who would pass by for a little looting and mayhem. This led to building of the fort called Castillo de San Antonio de la Eminencia. Construction started in 1660 and was completed nine years later, just in time to repulse Henry Morgan, who was passing by on his way from sacking Maracaibo.

Cumaná is in an active earthquake zone,

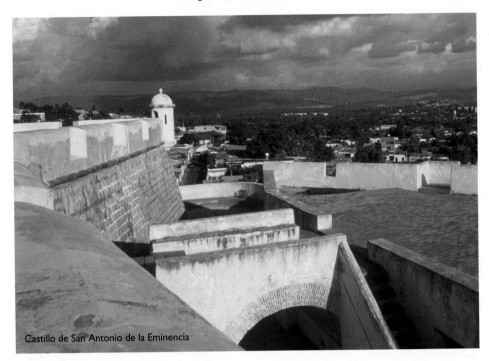

Castillo de San Antonio de la Eminencia

and the fort was destroyed repeatedly by successive tremors, once in 1684 and again in 1853. It was rebuilt by 1906, only to be destroyed by a disastrous earthquake in 1929, which was accompanied by a tidal wave 20 feet high. The fort is now repaired as a tourist attraction. At some point there were tunnels leading from the fort into town, but these were blocked by the earthquakes.

Regulations

Cumaná is a port of entry and if you are already cleared in to Venezuela, you will have to check in again here if you are going to stay long. Marina Cumanagoto or Navimca will do all the paperwork for you.

Navigation

The approaches to Cumaná from the north and west are clear. If you have to, you can anchor on either side of the big ship dock (see sketch chart, above). The southern side is bigger and has a much wider anchoring shelf; the northern side is a little more central. Both anchorages get rolly during the afternoon, when the winds reach their peak strength, and can be a security risk at night. For the most part the only place people an-

chor is behind the wall down in Navimca.

There is also the possibility of dinghying up the river into town. There is usually enough water to get all the way up to the river walkway in town. It is an adventurous way to go, though probably slower than walking. The river route does go through some exceptionally seedy and probably dangerous areas. I would ask locally about the wisdom of this route before attempting it.

Most people opt to go into the marina; advance booking is possible, but if you have to wait a few days, you can spend time on the northern shore in one of the pretty bays such as Laguna Grande. You can stay in touch with the marina on the VHF. The anchorage right outside the marina is uncomfortable. The entrance to the marina is down a narrow channel that is currently well marked by buoys (red right returning). Optimally, it has a minimum depth of 8.5 feet at low tide, and you can come in with nine feet of draft or more at high tide. But the channel does from time to time silt up due to the currents; the marina is pretty good about keeping it dredged, so if you draw more than six feet or so, call the marina to find out the present state of the

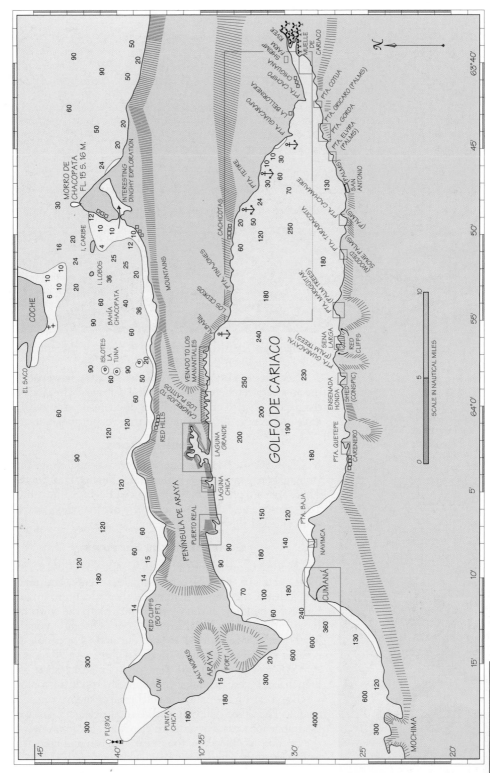

GOLFO DE CARIACO

Cumana with the marina in the foreground. The Peninsula de Araya can be seen on the far side.

channel. The berths immediately in front of the entrance bounce a bit when the wind is strong.

Security is a little improved since now the navy patrols the area between here and Coche and Cubagua. They look at the papers of small craft, which has discouraged criminals. It is not perfect: in 2005, there were three major incidents.

Communications

You can use Marina Cumanagoto as a mail drop: (c/o Cumanagoto Marina, Av. Perimetral, Cumaná, Edo. Sucre). There are card phones in the marina with a U.S. direct line. You can send and receive faxes at the marina office, as well as do email at the marina office.

General Yacht Services

Marina Cumanagoto (Tel. 0293 400-0347/ 0414 795-0999, VHF: 16, 22, 23) is pleasant and secure, and many people leave their boats here while they adventure inland. Since the building of the Marina Plaza Mall, the town has come to the marina. This has proved one of the most popular places for the wealthy locals to hang out, and yachtspeople are popular here. They are now starting a hotel with 90 rooms.

Manager Eduardo Jaime Vera speaks English, Italian, and French and is very helpful; if your Spanish is poor, ask for him when you call on the radio. He will be happy to give you good advice. The office will help with customs clearance as well as arrange for taxis. For customs clearance, ask for Alexis in the operations office. He, too, speaks English and French as well as Spanish. There is water and electricity (110/220 volt, 60 cycles) on the dock, and the marina has a fuel dock with

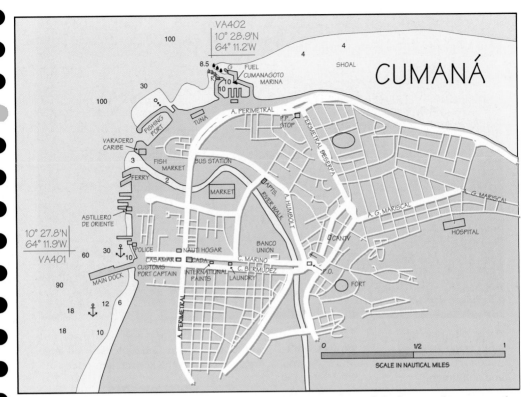

diesel and gasoline. Ashore there are showers, and toilets. The marina accepts many major credit cards.

Miguel makes his living by getting parts and arranging repairs. He speaks no English but manages with sign language. He usually comes down in the morning to find out what there is to do and returns in the afternoon. Miguel is the son of Old Bolívar, who did the same job before him.

The Marina Plaza Mall right at the marina has nearly everything you want: restaurants, fast food, laundry, telephone service, bookstore, cybercafé, supermarket and shopping in general. The mall is busy right into the evening, but most shops are closed on Sundays.

Chandlery

Two chandleries in town will take care of your boat needs. Casa Mar offers a good price on all the Venezuelan inflatables. They also stock Yamaha outboards, Sigma and international paints, and a good supply of nautical hardware. Nearby is the main branch of the Nauti Hogar chandlery (VHF:

18). Here you will find a complete range of boat gear including Yamaha and Evinrude outboards and spares, Jabsco pumps and parts, fishing gear, Yamaha gen sets, and some electronics.

Technical Yacht Services

You can get any kind of work done in Cumaná. There are several good hauling facilities.

The busiest used to be Varadero Caribe (0293 43- 0804, VHF: 13), run by Michael Plaut and his family, who speak perfect English. I understand that for the time being they are no longer hauling yachts, but are working for the oil industry. Things change, so it is good to know of this yard, which was very reasonably priced, and you nearly always knew exactly what a job was going to cost before it was started. They use a couple of massive marine railway systems with ways of easily shunting boats to the side. It is a commercial yard, and they are used to working on fishing boats of wood and steel. They are capable of doing excellent yacht work, too, including excellent Imron or

Cumaná and Golfo de Cariaco

123

Marina, with Marina Plaza mall behind
- Oscar Hernadez photo

Awlgrip topside spray finish. They also have a full machine shop, which allows them to undertake large repairs in stainless, bronze, and aluminum.

Next door, Astilleros de Oriente has a 70-ton Travelift and can haul boats up to a nine-foot draft and 24.5-foot beam. They are more expensive than Varadero Caribe, but they can usually haul immediately and do still work with yachts. They also have a dry dock. Ask for Elias Tobias (0293 43- 4119).

If you want to get off your boat while the work is done, there are several inexpensive hotels nearby where you can be a lot more comfortable.

Provisioning & shopping

You will find almost everything you need while you are in the marina, in the Marina Plaza Mall.

The main roads in town are the two that run from CADA to the river. The area between the river and Cantv has lots of appealing, small shops. Avenue Mariscal also has many shops.

You can get cash on your credit card from cash machines at most banks. There is a big CADA for supermarket shopping, if you want something other than the supermarket at the marina.

You can buy fish at the fish market near

Varadero Caribe, and the tuna plant just west of the marina sometimes sells off large boxes of frozen tuna at excellent prices.

Restaurants

Two good restaurants may be found in the marina. El Navegante ($C-D) is the fancy one, air-conditioned with original nautical decor (notice how they have done the air-conditioning ducts) and a picture-window view of the marina. The Coffee Shop ($D) is open to the breeze and is open for breakfast, lunch and dinner, serving snack-type food as well as a varied menu of traditional and seafood dishes. Both will prepare take-out meals. For a good Italian meal, Gozas on the ground floor of the Maina Plaza Mall would be hard to beat.

Camino Real in Calle Miranda is a good place for Mexican food. It opens at 1730. El Timonel in front of Playa San Luis is a good Spanish restaurant serving excellent seafood. For a real local flavor, take a taxi to La Negra on Avenida Perimetral, Sector Caigure. This is a wonderful place, very local, with an ocean view, that serves Venezuelan food from this area, and they treat overseas visitors very well.

Ashore

The big central bus station for out-of

Oscar Hernadez photo

town buses is marked on our sketch chart.

While visiting Cumaná it is worth making time to visit the guácharo cave near Caripe. (See our section on sightseeing). If you go by bus, make sure you take one that follows the waterfront of the Golfo de Cariaco.

In downtown Cumaná, the colonial quarter (Centro Historico) near Plaza Miranda is nice to visit. Iglesia Santa Ines on Calle Sucre is worth a look, as is adjoining Castillo Santa Maria de la Cabeza, which was built in 1669 under Governor Sargent Sancho Fernández de Angulo y Sandoval, Governor and Captain General de la Province de Nueva Andalucía (imagine having to introduce him). It often served as both fort and governor's residence. But make the big Castillo de San Antonio de la Eminencia a priority, as it offers some great views.

Another local attraction is the tobacco factory Bermudez, in front of Plaza Bermudez. You can watch them make Crispin Patiño, a world-famous premium tobacco, all handmade by women.

Olga Bello and Rosa Marothy run a pleasant and inexpensive bed and breakfast called Hostal Bubulinas. It is on Callejón San Ines, toward the river. They have a good inexpensive restaurant and like to help visiting cruisers.

Water Sports

For diving, Hesperia is a diving and aquatic center run by Fernando Garcia. It is in Hotel Cumanagoto. Fernando rents equipment, gives courses, and offers visits to the best places throughout Mochima. (www.scubavenezuela.com.)

THE NAVIMCA HAUL-OUT FACILITY

On the eastern edge of Cumaná is the Navimca haul-out facility (VHF: 16). Giorgio Neri, the president, is a naval architect and R.I.N.A surveyor. This yard for many years built large, seaworthy boats, until Giorgio switched to the yachting industry some years ago. Giorgio speaks English and Italian. Navimca is both very good and inexpensive, and Giorgio and Patricia create a family friendly atmosphere, which cruisers love. They have a 70-ton Travelift and hydraulic crane for masts. Many people take their boats out for dry storage. This is also an excellent yard for big jobs whether you do-it-yourself or get Giorgio to do it for you, as he supervises all yard jobs personally. They can handle Imron and Awlgrip spray painting, osmosis jobs, wood, steel, and glass repairs and fabrication, as well as mechanics, refrigeration, and machining. They have separate areas for storage and working, including a special sandblast area, so your boat does not get covered in someone else's sandblast. For those living on their boats, there are showers, toilets, and a coffee shop/restaurant. Once a year, they take their current customers for big night out.

The approach is not hard. From Cumaná stay well offshore, as shoals extend about half a mile out to sea. If you have an echo sounder with an alarm, set it to 50 feet and follow the shoal around. If you have a GPS, a setting of

10°28.85'N, 64° 08.9'W should get you close enough to see the first channel buoys. The beginning of the marked channel is 10°28.7'N, 64° 08.5'W.

The large basin is slowly being dredged. You are welcome to anchor inside (it is the only protected anchorage in Cumaná) and use their dinghy dock. There is one wall with water and electricity (maximum draft 6') and endless room without facilities for boats drawing less than 6 feet. These depths are increasing as they dredge so call for the latest information. This is a very calm place to leave your yacht while you travel. Eventually the inner basin will be a big marina, but that will take some time. Ask about current security in the anchorage.

GOLFO DE CARIACO

The Golfo de Cariaco is 35 miles long and never more than about eight miles wide. While you can get a nasty chop, it is completely protected from ocean swells, and you are never far from an anchorage. It contains a range of different environments, from dense green hills and palm-fringed beaches in the southeast to desert areas of pretty rocks in the northwest.

It is typically calm at night, and the wind is light and often easterly in the early morning. By mid-morning, the wind starts picking up from between east and northeast, and by mid-afternoon, it is often blowing about 25 knots with short, steep seas. The wind drops again after dark. While this pattern holds throughout the gulf, it is far more intense in the western half. This area seems to be subject to a wind funnel that sweeps down across the islands of Coche and Cubagua, across the Península de Araya, and right over Cumaná only to die in the mountains behind. The winds are also more intense in winter than in summer. At the eastern end of the gulf, the winds start later, blow weaker, and die earlier. As anywhere in Venezuela, a wind of about 20 knots, associated with rain and squalls, will blow from the southwest every few months. It usually only lasts a few hours, but it makes most of the anchorages along the northern coast unpleasant. In normal conditions, the north coast gets some lee from the mountains, and the seas are much less than on the south side of the gulf. In some anchorages the wind manages to come through the valleys.

If you enjoy sailing, the best way to see the gulf is to make

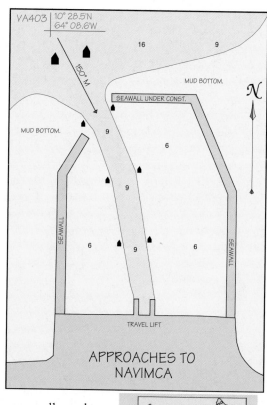

APPROACHES TO NAVIMCA

Typical Golfo scenery, taken close to Punta Cangrejo - Oscar Hernadez photo

large, close reaches from side to side, stopping at anchorages as the mood takes you. This is not hard, because there are many anchorages. In our review of the anchorages in Golfo de Cariaco, we go around in an counter-clockwise direction, starting eastwards down the south coast and returning westwards along the northern shore.

It should be noted that the Golfo de Cariaco is a big area and the charts are not very detailed. There is not much to worry about out in the middle, but close to shore, keep a good lookout. There may be shoals that we did not spot.

CUMANA TO CARENERO

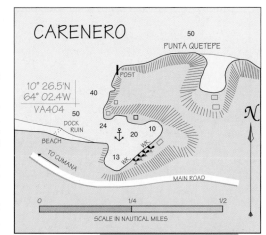

There are extensive shoals off the coast to the east of Cumaná as far as Punta Baja. Toward Punta Baja, they extend nearly a mile offshore. Stay well out or skirt the bank carefully, paying close attention to your echo sounder. Best stay in at least 35 feet of water. Once you have rounded Punta Baja and cleared the bank, you can head directly toward Punta Quetepe.

Carenero is a superb little harbor that cuts its way into the west side of Punta Quetepe. Inside, there is a sizeable anchoring area in 10-20 feet. The bay is pleasant with little beaches, small mangroves, a couple of wrecks, and a few houses belonging to fishing families. The main road runs close by, and you do hear the traffic.

The fishermen do not mind yachts coming in for a night or two, but they would not like boats to start hanging out in the bay. Fish do occasionally come in, and when this happens they close off the whole bay with a net, and yachts would be in the way.

ENSENADA HONDA

As you sail east from Carenero, the water is deep close to shore for two miles, then there are a few shoals less than a quarter of a mile offshore. You will see a headland on which there is a very large shed, a boat-building enterprise that seems to have stalled. About a third of a mile beyond this headland is a tiny but well protected bay called Ensenada Honda (Deep Water Bay). This is a lovely spot with some well-to-do homes and a small beach. The main road is some distance away, so it is peaceful. It lives up to its name: the water is a good 60 feet deep in the middle of the bay. To anchor here, you need to drop an anchor almost on the beach, then put a stern one out to hold you from going ashore.

As you head east from this bay, watch out for oyster floats off the village before Punta Guaracayal. The bay after Punta Guaracayal is shoal, so give the coast a reasonable clearance, but don't stay so far offshore that you miss the next bay, Sena Larga. If you are approaching from the north coast, there are some conspicuous red cliffs on either side of the harbor.

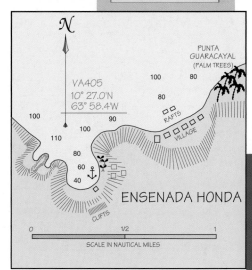

Cumaná and Golfo de Cariaco

129

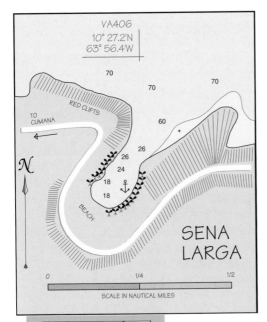

SENA LARGA

Sena Larga (Deeply Indented Bay) cuts well back into the land. The only danger we could see was a rock very close to shore on the eastern headland just outside the bay. Inside, the water is all 18-25 feet deep with plenty of swinging room. No houses, just colorful red rocks, a few mangroves and a public beach at the head. The main road does follow the bay right around. You can follow the coast pretty closely from here down to Punta Marigüitar. If you sail within quarter of a mile of the shore, look out for shoals.

MARIGUITAR

Punta Marigüitar is a prominent headland magnificently decorated with palm trees and beaches. It provides shelter from both the seas and the prevailing wind, which gets broken up by the trees. There are often some boats anchored here associated with the Club Maigualida ashore. There is a mud bank that extends up to 200 yards from Punta Marigüitar, but you can see this in reasonable light. Anchor right up in the head of the bay, off the dock. The water is deep, so you may want to edge close to the shore and use a second anchor. You can tie your dinghy up to their dock.

If you leave the anchorage to head east early in the morning, remember that the mud bank comes out a long way. Do not follow the headland right round into the next bay, as it is shoal, though the fish factory has reclaimed some of the shoal area. Apart from this, you can follow the coast fairly closely to the next anchorage off Punta Tarabacoita.

Ashore

Club Maigualida ($D) is a great place to stop for a meal. It has a pleasant, open-air bar and dining room, the atmosphere is friendly, and the prices are reasonable. They have a mini-zoo in a cage with cristofues, an agouti, a monkey, and a parrot. There is a phone service and a small market.

About three-quarters-of-a-mile dinghy ride round the headland, there is a large and conspicuous building, which is a fish canning plant for sardines and tuna. (Occasionally you get a whiff of the operation from the anchorage.) Just before you get to the factory, there is a dock with a public market at its head, which is active in the mornings. You can also walk back to the village, where you will find a few shops with most necessities. Nearly everyone in the village is employed by the fish factory, and many of them walk around in matching work clothes. They also appear to get around by bicycle, as there are enough here to run a Tour de France.

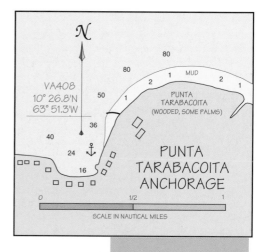

PUNTA TARABACOITA

The anchorage to the west of Punta Tarabacoita gives good shelter from easterly winds. In a northeasterly, you would be better off in Marigüitar to the west or Punta Cachamaure to the east. The headland is wooded with some palms and small beaches between the beach greenery. The most sheltered anchorage is tucked in to the head of the bay as far as you dare go. You can anchor close to the shore in about 20 feet of water. You get a little protection from the shallow mud bank that extends from the shore to the north of the anchorage. A dock comes out to the edge of this bank. Ashore, there are several houses. If you are leaving this anchorage to head east, note that the mud bank continues right round the headland and can be nearly 100 yards wide in places.

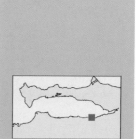

PUNTA CACHAMAURE

Punta Cachamaure is two miles east of Punta Tarabacoita, and the anchorage west of Cachamaure is perfectly delightful and much more protected. The bay is quite wide and very deep. Punta Cachamaure is picture-perfect, with sandy beaches, tall palms and banana plants behind. The hills are bright green and along the shore are several simple fishing huts with thatched roofs. The main road is a bit set back, so it is not too obtrusive. You have to head right over to the eastern shore where you will find bottom close to the beach, about 30-35 deep. You will need two anchors, one deep and one shallow, or one anchor and a line ashore. You can anchor alongside the fleet of open fishing boats or a little farther up off the next beach. Be prepared to cooperate with the fishermen if they need to net.

Ashore, the Holidays Club has a dinghy dock, phone, and water as well as showers and small market. I have no current information about whether they appreciate visiting yachts.

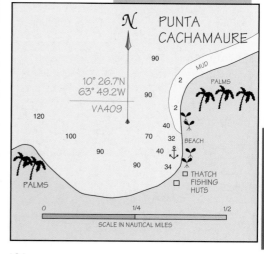

131

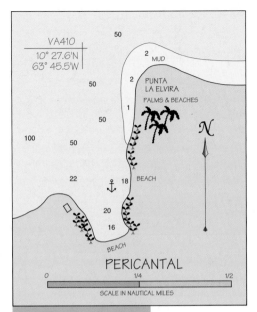

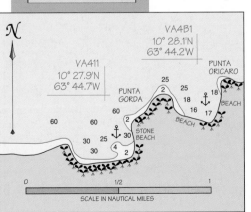

When heading east from this anchorage, give Punta Cachamaure good clearance, as there is a mud bank around the head and down into the bay to its east. The next sheltered anchorage is Pericantal, nearly four miles east in the lee of Punta La Elvira. Along the way, you will pass the town of San Antonio. Watch out for mussel platforms that are sometimes put out here.

PUNTA LA ELVIRA/ PERICANTAL

Pericantal is a super little bay, well protected from the regular trade winds and far enough away from the road that any traffic is well muffled. Punta La Elvira is a magnificent, palm-fringed headland with lots of small beaches. The water in the bay is 16-25 feet deep, perfect for anchoring. There is one house on the western headland. The beach at the head of the bay is used by fishing boats. The prettiest anchorage is off the beach just north of this bay. Fishermen do not usually set nets here, so you can relax and enjoy the peace.

A mud bank extends round Punta La Elvira, so give it a reasonable clearance.

PUNTA GORDA AND PUNTA ORICARO

There are anchorages to the west of both these headlands. They are very peaceful, as the main road has gone back inland. The bay west of Punta Gorda is a quiet, mangrove lined bay. There is a large shoal that takes up the southeast corner of the bay. North of this shoal is a little, red-colored stone beach. You can approach this beach from the northwest and find plenty of anchoring room in 20-30 feet of water. However, you may well prefer to anchor in the bay to the west of Punta Oricaro. (Punta Gorda is surrounded by a mud bank, so do not hug it tightly.) This is a charming bay. The shore all around is wooded, with some lovely beaches. Anchoring depth is an ideal 17-20 feet. The best spot is off the beach, on the eastern side of the headland.

If leaving this anchorage to go east, give Punta Oricaro a couple of hundred yards of clearance.

PUNTA COTUA

The anchorage west of Punta Cotua is really not very well sheltered, but you are getting so far up in the bay that the winds and seas are not quite as bad as they are farther west. In normal winds, you will get some little waves creeping round the corner. It makes a very pleasant lunch spot, and if it is calm enough, you can spend the night. The nicest anchorage is off the beach toward the point. The bottom shelves to a suitable 26-30 feet before you run aground. The best way to anchor would be bow to the beach with a line ashore and a stern anchor to hold you from going aground.

MUELLE DE CARIACO

As you proceed east from Punta Cotua, there are some shoals that extend out several hundred yards and can take the coast-hugger unawares. The problem here is that the water becomes murky and unreadable. Stay closer to the middle of the channel than to the shore. Don't go way over the north side as it is even shallower there. As long as you stay somewhere near the middle, there is plenty of water, and it gets deeper toward the south side as you approach Muelle de Cariaco, the town at the head of the bay. You can feel your way into anchorage anywhere in this large and protected bay, which is about a mile wide. I suggest anchoring about quarter of a mile off town and well back from the mangroves as the best bet for a bug free night. The big building at the entrance to Laguna Cariaco on the north side is a shrimp farm. You can pay a visit and see if you can persuade them to sell you some shrimps.

Ashore

Muelle de Cariaco (The Dock of Cariaco) was an important little trading town where ships were always loading cargo. When a good road was built to Cumaná, ships no longer came, and now it is charming in a sleepy sort of way.

You can leave your dinghy on the dock while it lasts, which will not be too long unless some repairs are done. Close to the dock is a picturesque, tree-lined stretch of road with old houses. The old upper road is well worth exploring for charming views to the east, west, and south.

The main drag in town is from the dock eastwards toward the gas station. You will find several basic stores. One sells ice, and

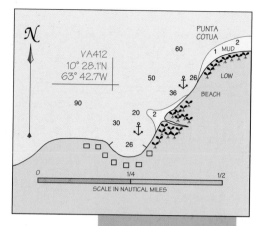

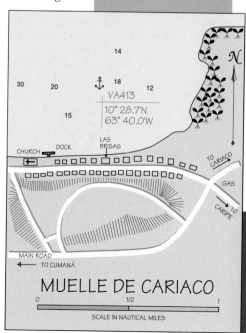

Cumaná and Golfo de Cariaco

133

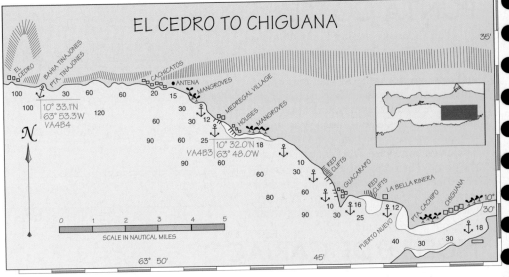

EL CEDRO TO CHIGUANA

you can often find bread.

The hub of travel has left the sea and retreated up the road to the main crossroads by the gas station. The gas station has a small snack bar where you can get a simple meal and be entertained by watching the comings and goings from the different buses and por puestos.

If the travel bug gets you, you can get a por puesto to the village of Cariaco, just a few minutes away, which has more shops, and internet facilities. The local market is excellent, and the locals, who like yachtspeople, will not rip you off. You can also carry on to Carúpano or go back to Cumaná.. Better yet, take a day trip to Caripe to see the guácharo birds (see our sightseeing section for more details). It is only about a 45-minute ride away, and if you start early in the morning you can easily do the round-trip and the caves in a day.

While at the eastern end of the Golfo de Cariaco, you should take a dinghy trip up into Laguna de Cariaco in the head of the bay. This is great for exploring and bird watching. There are plenty of herons, cormorants, pelicans, and parrots. Don't miss exploring up the river on the north side of the Laguna. You can make it all the way till the water is fresh (about one and half miles). If you happen to be here on a moonlit night, come back down the river as darkness falls and you will be surrounded by a host of fish-

eating bats.

If you come and visit on September 1, they have a celebration of the Virgin. In this fishermen take a Virgin Mary statue in a procession that includes visiting places by boat around the bay. If you are around Medregal in February, ask about the Carnival in Cariaco, by all accounts not to be missed.

PUERTO NUEVO

Puerto Nuevo is a large bay between Punta Cachipo and the village of Guacarapo. This is a lovely spot, with some excellent bird watching. If you are coming from the east, take a very wide swing around Punta Cachipo as there is a shoal off the eastern shore. If you are approaching from the west, pass the Bellorinera Restaurant before heading in, as there is a shoal that extends southwest of the restaurant. You can anchor just east of the restaurant in 12 feet of water or feel your way eastwards to a more secluded spot.

Ashore

La Bellorinera Bar and Restaurant ($D) is open daily 0800-2000. It is informal and friendly, owned and run by Atilano and Paulina Bellorin. They specialize in fish, clams, shrimps, and chicken. If you need to go shopping, you can get a por puesto from Guacarapo.

Punta Cachipo

The shoal at the eastern end of the bay is a fabulous bird-watching spot. Best take binoculars and dinghy right out around the Punta Cachipo, go ashore on the eastern side, and make your way back closer on foot. You can see flamingos and many kinds of wading birds feeding together here.

Scarlet ibis also frequent this area and are often seen flying or in the trees between La Bellorinera and Chiguana. Some people have also reported seeing them up in Laguna de Cariaco.

GUACARAPO TO CACHICOTAS

A small road runs behind the coast linking these villages and other houses. The people here live by fishing and cattle ranching.

When the wind starts to blow hard down the gulf, this part of the coast is protected from the worst of both wind and sea. However, small wavelets do turn the corner and follow the coast down, building in size the farther they go. This whole stretch of coast has a wide, rather shallow shelf, making anchoring anywhere very easy. The water is often too shallow within a couple of hundred yards of the shore. In many places, there are fancy docks built out to the edge of the shallows with roofs and sitting areas.

It is a peaceful area with a thin strip of beach that is miles long, which you can have to yourself. Even so, it is not especially exciting. There is one anchorage that is more alluring than the rest. This is a small bay about two miles southeast of Cachicotas (10° 32.42N, 63° 48.39W). What makes this special is the view. The sandy beach of the bay forms the foreground, and the eye gets led back up the green slope to the dramatic mountain range behind.

The bay is quite shallow, but you can feel your way in to the outer edge, and this seems to get you out of the little waves.

Close to this bay at the head of a T-covered dinghy dock is Medregal Village (VHF: 71). This small hotel and restaurant is run by Jean Marc and his Venezuelan wife, Yoleda who welcome yachtspeople. Free services include dinghy dock with good security, hot and cold showers, a swimming pool, direct TV and a game room. They can help with customs clearance, and phone calls, and

Cumaná and Golfo de Cariaco

135

Medregal Village and owner Jean Marc

Oscar Hernadez photos

have a laundry service, mini-market, internet station, and every Saturday organize a bus into town for shopping and sightseeing. Fresh French bread and ice are available and they offer special discounts for cruisers at the bar and restaurant. The mail post service address is Medregal Village, P.O. Box 205, Cumaná, Estado Sucre, Venezuela. Email: Medregal@cantv.net. Medregal Village is a great place to use as a base for visiting this area. They can help you organize trips to Carupano, Cumaná, Caripe Cave, the Chocolate Factory, the Mineral Springs, and Cariaco market. They also provide transport to Carupano Carnival.

If you visit during April and May, anchor as close of the coast as possible, so you will be out of the way of the fishermen.

Services

Medregal has expanded its yacht facilities to include a haulout and boatyard. They can accommodate 88 boats ashore with a maximum draft of 8 feet. The marine hoist can lift 30-tons. The new facilities include a chandlery, carpentry shop, and spray paint and fiberglass repair facilities. It is not too crowded and is a very pleasant place to work in a holiday atmosphere. It is also very dry. They offer a special trench for removing rudders and keels. You are welcome to do your own work or use their services. Federeky Mayer is the boatyard manager.

Los Cachicatos

Los Cachicatos is a small, artisanal fishing village where about half of the houses are vacation homes. There are restaurants, bars, and small markets. If there is any chance of being here in September, come for the Virgin's feast, which is superb.

Once you pass Cachicatos, the small waves are big enough to make some kind of shelter desirable. The next place you can find this is in Bahía Tinajones (10° 33.18N, 63° 53.32W), which is sheltered by the punta of the same name. This is a congenial, small bay with a beach, a green valley, and interesting, rocky ledges. You can find anchorage close to the beach in about 25 feet of water. About a mile beyond Tinajones is the small village of El Cedro.

ALBANIL

Shortly after El Cedro, the coast takes a turn to the northwest to a small bay called Albañil. This shift in direction of the coastline gives fair protection from the seas and almost too much protection from the wind.

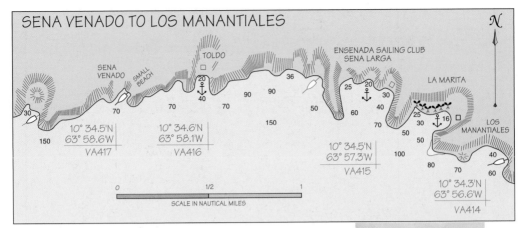

SENA VENADO TO LOS MANANTIALES

N

TOLDO

SENA VENADO

SMALL BEACH

ENSENADA SAILING CLUB
SENA LARGA

LA MARITA

LOS MANANTIALES

10° 34.5'N
63° 58.6'W
VA417

10° 34.6'N
63° 58.1'W
VA416

10° 34.5'N
63° 57.3'W
VA415

10° 34.3'N
63° 56.6'W
VA414

0   1/2   1
SCALE IN NAUTICAL MILES

For the most part, it is very deep close to shore, and you need two anchors. Not an especially exciting area, but it is worth knowing anchoring is possible.

LOS MANANTIALES TO SENA VENADO

This two-and-a-half mile stretch of coast is rugged with many indentations. The coast is mainly steep-to until you tuck into the little bays, where there is usually good anchoring depth. Some bays are so small that the only way to be out of the seas is to anchor bow or stern-to the beach. Always proceed in good light when close to shore, though the only potentially dangerous shoal we found extended southwest off the eastern headland of La Marita. All our old charts showed a rock or shoal 100 yards or so off this headland. We spent some time gingerly powering up and down looking for it, without success. The fishing family who live in La Marita say it does not exist and I think they would know. Proceed with caution.

Los Manantiales
Los Manantiales (Spring Bay) is just west of Albañil. You can find protection by going bow or stern-to the small beach in the eastern corner.

La Marita
La Marita is a fine bay with mangroves and colorful little cliffs round the shore. A beach fronts a lush, verdant valley, which ascends to peaky green mountains behind.

The bay gives outstanding protection, with plenty of room to anchor in 16-25 feet in the eastern part. A single fishing family lives on the beach here. You can also anchor comfortably in the western tongue off the mangroves.

Sena Larga
Sena Larga is also quite delightful, with three little beaches separated by rocky headlands. There are cactus-covered cliffs, open valleys, and small mangroves. The biggest bay with the largest anchoring room is the eastern one, but it is much pret-

Cumaná and Golfo de Cariaco

137

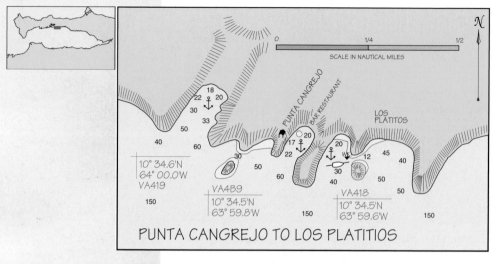

PUNTA CANGREJO TO LOS PLATITIOS

tier to be anchor just off the middle bay in about 22 feet of water. Here you will find the Ensenada Sailing Club, with a dinghy dock, bar, and restaurant.

You can also find a small, protected spot for one boat west of Sena Larga's western headland. You have to anchor stern-to the beach with your bow facing out. There are lots of pelicans for company.

Toldo

Toldo (The Awning) is a small bay with colorful cliffs and a single fishing camp at its head. If no one is fishing here, you can get fair shelter close to the beach in about 30 feet of water.

Sena Venado

Sena Venado (Deer Bay) is half a mile westwards. The only way to get complete protection is to anchor with your stern to the tiny eastern beach and your bow out to sea.

The next bay, about half a mile farther west, is so small that the local fishermen have not even given it a name. It is an attractive, wild little bay with rocky outcroppings sticking through the green vegetation. You have to anchor in the eastern side of the bay to keep out of the swells, going stern-to the beach.

LOS PLATITOS TO CANGREJO

This short stretch of coast is very deeply indented with the added attraction of some small islands. There are three excellent anchorages here, all perfect hideaways. Don't bring the fleet, but they are large enough for a couple of boats.

Los Platitos

Los Platitos (The Small Plates) is a romantic little anchorage in the lee of a small, cactus-covered island where you can see mockingbirds, woodpeckers, and little green parakeets that

Los Platitos

Laguna Grande

flash by like bright emeralds. The protected part of the bay is west of the island. You can pass between the north of the island and the shore in about 12 feet of water, but watch out for shoals on either side. You can anchor in the middle of the bay in about 25 feet of water. Better still, drop hook in the shallows between the island and the shore, drop back, and use a stern anchor to hold you in position. Beware that a wreck has been reported in the middle of this bay ~ it should be visible in good light. The snorkeling is good around parts of the island, with lots of brightly colored worms covering the coral and making a colorful display.

Punta Cangrejo Bay

Punta Cangrejo Bay is just over the headland. You can walk between the two. It is a charming, secluded bay with a fine, thatch-roofed open shelter on the western headland. There is a small shoal patch in the northwestern corner of the bay. It is easy to see, and you have room to anchor to its east. Ashore, there is a bar and restaurant run by Kike Ponce and Elizabeth Garcia.

They have a little guest house with a nice Churuata (Indian House) with a simple restaurant with good seafood. Cruisers are welcome, and quite a few visit.

Between this bay and the next is a distinctive white island. You can pass inside the island with about 30 feet of water under you, but shoals come from both sides, so do it in good light. This next bay is deeply indented and well protected. A large, dry valley heads the bay, and plenty of interesting rocks and cliffs line the shores. The few mangroves that have gotten a toehold are well used by roosting pelicans and cormorants. There is plenty of room to anchor anywhere at the head of the bay in 18-30 feet.

The coast from here to Laguna Grande is rugged and mainly steep-to. There is really nothing by way of a decent anchorage.

LAGUNA GRANDE

This colossal lagoon is breathtakingly

Cumaná and Golfo de Cariaco

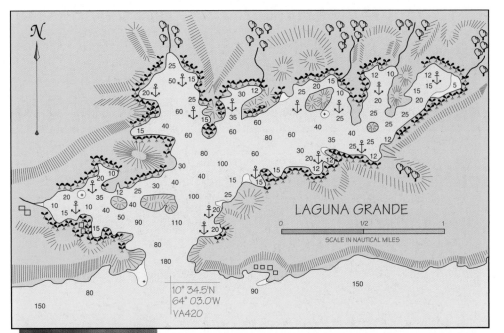

beautiful, with an endless variety of contrasting hills in whites and glowing reds. Small islands have beards of dense green mangroves and wear cactuses like some scraggly Afro. It is a timeless desert landscape, outstandingly colorful and decorative. It must rate high among the Caribbean's hidden treasures and only a few people stop by. A few fishermen's houses lie up in the western corner of the lagoon; otherwise, it is deserted. Nothing happens here, and Laguna Grande will only appeal to those who like desert landscapes.

We noticed a couple of shoals that might give trouble, which we have marked on our chart. However, there may be others, so keep a good lookout. When you enter Laguna Grande, do not cut fine round the western headland, as a shoal extends a long way off. We have put a few anchors on our plan, but you can anchor anywhere that takes your fancy. If you follow the harbor in around the eastern headland, there is a small bay and then a mangrove island. Both these anchorages afford spectacular views. Everywhere in Laguna Grande is ideal for contemplating the view and for dinghy exploration. Those with sailing dinghies can take advantage of the afternoon breeze that sweeps through the hills. The energetic can hike in the hills.

LAGUNA CHICA

When the rarefied atmosphere of Laguna Grande becomes too much, Laguna Chica makes for a cheerful change. It is inhabited by fishermen and boatbuilders. The colors are festive: red hills, bright green trees, white and blue fishing boats. There is always a little activity, with boats coming and going, without

the pace getting hectic. There is a bar/dance hall in the eastern corner of the bay, and it has a shower outside. Late afternoon, when it is cool, is the best time for taking a walk.

We have marked several good places to anchor. The most intriguing is in the little lagoon in the western corner of the bay. Enter carefully in good light, as there are shoals on both

Laguna Grande

LAGUNA CHICA

SCALE IN NAUTICAL MILES
0   1/4   1/2

N

BOAT BUILDER
BAR & SHOWER
BOAT BUILDER
FISHING FLEET

VILLAGE AND CHURCH
GRAVE YARD
NOT SURVEYED

10° 34.0'N
64° 04.6'W
VA421

Cumaná and Golfo de Cariaco

Laguna Chica

sides. There is a perfect place to anchor in the southern corner of the bay, where you can look across the low sand spit to the gulf outside. Turning room is very tight in here, so if a following wind is blowing hard, you may want to drop hook while you are still moving and let the anchor swing the boat round.

Laguna Chica fishing fleet

PUERTO REAL

Puerto Real

You can find good anchorage off Los Cañónes or Puerto Real. Of the two, Puerto Real is far more scenic, and the most appealing anchorage is right up in the eastern corner. This is

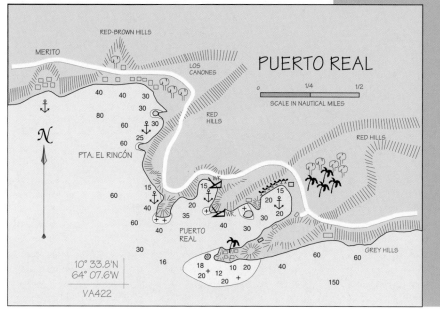

Cumaná and Golfo de Cariaco

a delightful and very protected anchorage. Over the bow, the green valley makes a pleasing contrast with the red hills, and off the stern, the little fishing village built out on the point is picturesque. There is easy access to the beach for walking ashore.

When entering Puerto Real, give good clearance to the eastern headland, as a rocky shoal extends almost half a mile out. The depths over this shoal are mainly 10-16 feet, but there are shallower spots. (See our aerial photo.)

Just northwest is the quaint and clean village of Merito, where two nuns who are in fact sisters, Maria and Beatriz, run a tourism school. They are very welcoming, and as they teach English to their students, they would welcome visitors who speak English. You can also anchor here.

Looking from Merito to Puerto Real

Mochima to Puerto La Cruz

AREA 5

Mochima National Park

ochima is about 12 miles west of Cumaná. The whole area from Mochima right down to Puerto la Cruz is a wonderful national park. The park was created in 1973 with over two million acres, half of which is marine, including 32 islands, the rest coastal areas and peninsulas. The park goes from Mochima down to Puerto la Cruz and includes all the offshore islands. There are dozens of anchorages in secluded bays, by beaches, and among tiny islands. Development is restricted, and wildlife is protected. The common dolphin (*Delphinus delphis*), seabirds, small green parrots, and hawks are all abundant. Fishermen are allowed to use existing camps but cannot build new ones. Areas have been set aside for nesting and feeding for various marine turtle species. There are plenty of fish for the local fishermen including corocoro (white grunt) and pàrgo (snappers). Snorkelers will find a huge variety of anemones.

The Guardacosta and National Guard have been doing their best to keep a handle on crime, but there are incidents, so inquire in Puerto la Cruz about the current situation, and cruise cautiously. In some cases, it may be safer to use many of these anchorages by day and be somewhere secure at night. The local population is generally very pro-yachting-visitor and anti-pirate, and help when they can. Venezuelan boats have

Top photo, El Oculto, this photo, Bahia Manare

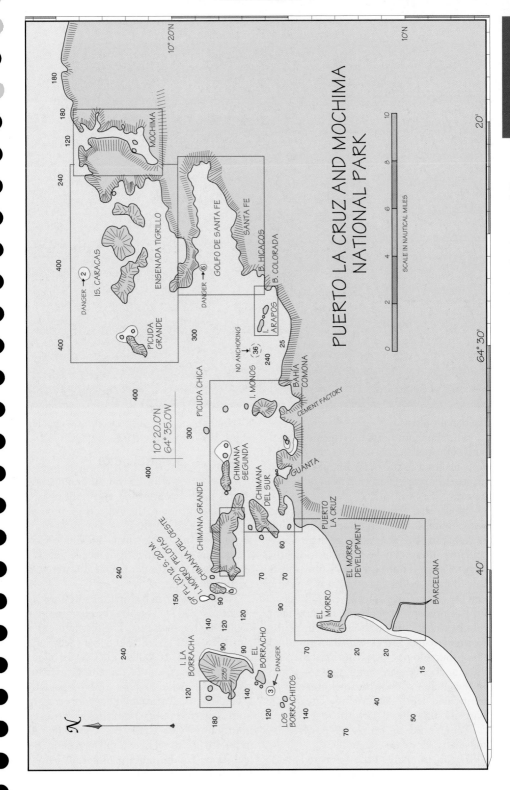

PUERTO LA CRUZ AND MOCHIMA
NATIONAL PARK

SCALE IN NAUTICAL MILES

0 2 4 6 8 10

10° 20.0'N
64° 35.0'W

Mochima, looking in from the entrance

also had problems.

The abundant rainfall in the mountains south of the park reaches as far as the coast. It rarely makes it to the outer islands, and you can see the abrupt transition from rainforest to desert.

Much of the rocky terrain is soft and unstable limestone. Landslides and erosion are reshaping the area little by little. Consequently, there may be changes in depths close to land. There are rocks and shoals close to shore, and some of them are missing from the charts. The water is generally clear, and it is prudent to approach in good light and not to cut corners. Some of our charts are small scale. Rocks within a hundred feet of shore do not show on this scale, and where anchorages are small, we have often put the anchor outside the anchorage so we can include depth data within. The sketch charts should be used with the text.

When walking on cactus-covered islands hefty shoes are essential.

Diving in many of the protected areas, especially on the offhsore rocks and islands, is spectacular, with more than 100 species of fish having been identified.

Regulations

Yachts are allowed to visit and anchor in the park. Spearfishing and hunting are not allowed, nor is the collecting of coral or shells, dead or alive, or any flora from shore, for that matter. It is equally forbidden to buy such things from locals. Jet skis and all forms of similar personal watercraft are not allowed.

The park is run by Inparques in Caracas (0212 273-2741). They are the charging and collecting the park fees. The fees to use the park are: 58,000 Bs (28 $U.S) for yachts under 45 feet and 96,000Bs (45$ US) for larger yachts. This is good for three months. You get to buy a sticker to show you have paid. In Mochima, the Inparques office is open daily from 0600 to 1900. You can also buy a sticker from Transpacific (0281 263-5248 VHF: 72) in Puerto la Cruz. There is talk of raising the fees soon. You must get your permit before you anchor in the park.

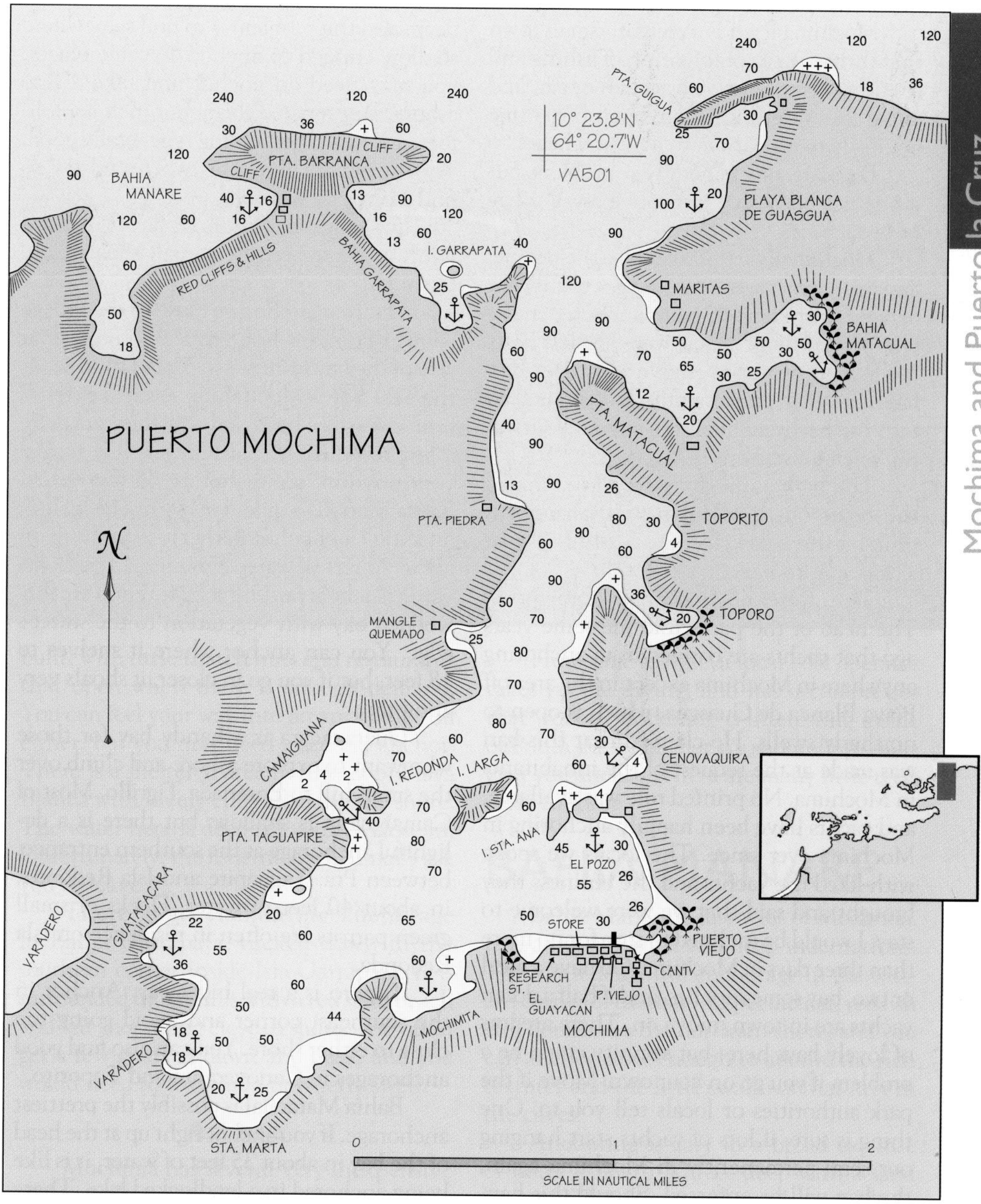

Map labels (nautical chart):

10° 23.8'N
64° 20.7'W
VA501

PTA. GUIGUA

PLAYA BLANCA DE GUASGUA

BAHIA MANARE

PTA. BARRANCA

CLIFF

CLIFF

BAHIA GARRAPATA

RED CLIFFS & HILLS

I. GARRAPATA

MARITAS

BAHIA MATACUAL

PUERTO MOCHIMA

PTA. MATACUAL

PTA. PIEDRA

TOPORITO

MANGLE QUEMADO

TOPORO

N

CAMAGUANA

I. REDONDA

I. LARGA

CENOVAQUIRA

PTA. TAGUAPIRE

I. STA. ANA

EL POZO

GUATACACARA

STORE

PUERTO VIEJO

VARADERO

RESEARCH ST.

EL GUAYACAN

P. VIEJO

CANTV

MOCHIMITA

MOCHIMA

VARADERO

STA. MARTA

0   1   2

SCALE IN NAUTICAL MILES

MOCHIMA

It is thought that Mochima is a sunken valley, making it long and deep like the fiords. It extends four miles into the surrounding hills. It is a magnificent natural harbor of green hills and red rocks. Sailing in and out is much of the pleasure, while watching the ever-changing hill contours.

Inside, the southern part is deeply wooded, and during the rainy season there are frequent afternoon thunder showers. The entrance is much drier, with red rocks and cactus-covered hills. Apparently several hundred years ago, there was another exit, into Ensenada Tigrillo. This made it an ideal hideaway for pirates, and rumor has it that one or two stashes of treasure have been found. There is abundant bird life, including flocks of small green parrots.

El Oculto, I. Venados on the right

ENSENADA TIGRILLO AND ISLAS CARACAS

This area is made up of a series of islands and bays with many delightful, away-from-it-all anchorages that you can have to yourself. Observe a couple of park restrictions here: Anchoring is forbidden anywhere around Picuda Grande, though you are welcome to sail by it. There is a coral reef about 25-40 feet deep right in the middle of the channel between Caracas del Sur and I. Venados. Anchoring is forbidden on this reef.

Snorkeling is often excellent, with lots of coral brightly decorated with Christmas tree and feather duster worms. Try snorkeling wherever you anchor, and if it is not good, take the dinghy round the next corner and try again.

Bugs are only an occasional problem. If they get to you, move to the next bay. It is just round the corner and probably bug-free.

Navigation

Bajo Caracas, just over a mile north of Caracas del Oeste, has several rocks just below the surface. Since this is out in the middle of nowhere, it is a serious navigational hazard and should be avoided. Local dive groups use it as a dive site, though the boat watcher usually gets seasick. Apart from this, the water is steep-to close to shore almost everywhere.

Underwater rocks often extend about 150 feet from the shore, so when coast-hugging or coming into anchor, keep a good lookout.

The wind is constantly shifting in this area, and you will probably point every which way. Danforth-style anchors often trip themselves in these conditions, so better set two.

NORTHEASTERN ENSENADA TIGRILLO

El Oculto (Hidden Bay) is a delightful, well-protected bay. On the north side are two islands. One is sizeable, the other is not much more than a rock about 12 feet high that almost touches the shore. Both have good anchorages.

The larger island is to the northwest. Between this island and the shore is a good-sized bay with an ample 25-30-foot anchor-

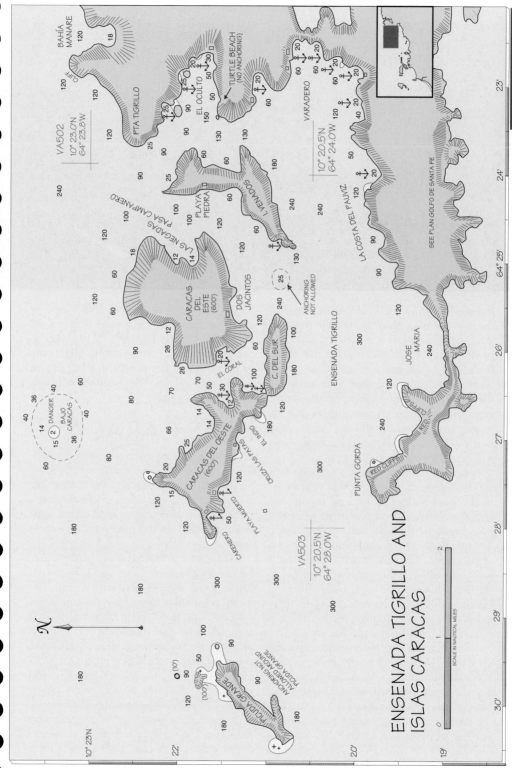

ENSENADA TIGRILLO AND
ISLAS CARACAS

VA502
10° 23.0'N
64° 25.8'W

VA503
10° 20.5'N
64° 28.0'W

10° 20.5'N
64° 24.0'W

BAHÍA MANARE

PTA TIGRILLO

EL OCULTO

TURTLE BEACH
(NO ANCHORING)

VARADERO

SEE PLAN GOLFO DE SANTA FE

LA COSTA DEL PAUVZ

LAS NEGADAS

PASA CAMPANERO

PLAYA PIEDRA

I. VENADOS

CARACAS DEL ESTE
(600)

DOS JACINTOS

ANCHORING
NOT ALLOWED

EL CORAL

C. DEL SUR

ENSENADA TIGRILLO

JOSE MARIA

BAJO CARACAS

DANGER

CARACAS DEL OESTE
(600)

EL INDIO

CRUZA LAS PATAS

PLAYA MUERTO

CARENERO

RED CLIFFS!

RED CLIFFS!

PUNTA GORDA

PICUDA GRANDE

ANCHORING NOT
ALLOWED AROUND
PICUDA GRANDE

SCALE IN NAUTICAL MILES

N

Islas Caracas
Caracas del Este on the right, Caracas del Sur in the
foreground, with Caracas del Oeste behind

ing shelf off the little beach at the head of the bay. The fishermen may want to net, and if so, they may ask you to move. You would probably not be in the way in the other anchorage in this bay, which is close to the island. From the northwest, you approach the gap between the island and the shore, edging in until you get water shoal enough to anchor. This is a pretty spot right close to the island, but the space is limited, so you will need two anchors.

A little further to the southeast is a good, 25-foot shelf just off the smaller island. Those willing to use both a bow and stern anchor can find room between the island and the shore in front of the beach. The anchorage here is unbeatable for one or two boats. You cannot see the sea at all, just pretty hill lines in every direction giving the impression you are landlocked. The pink beach is perfect for a barbecue, and the little red island makes it picture-perfect. To top it off, snorkeling is bright and colorful.

The eastern end of the bay has a wide shelf with 20-30 feet of water over it, though you have to watch for a few shoals close in. You can anchor anywhere on this shelf and have plenty of swinging room.

Between El Oculto and Varadero there is a large, deep bay surrounded by hills (10°21.32'N, 64°22.85'W). There is a small fishing camp on the north side and few small mangroves along the shore. This is an easy and good anchorage, as there is a large shelf at the head of the bay with 20 feet over it. Eyeball your way in to a spot that suits you, or if the water is murky, feel your way in toward the middle of the bay and anchor in 25-30 feet of water.

ISLAS CARACAS

There is a tiny anchorage in the southwestern corner of Isla Venados with room for just one boat to anchor, bow facing out and stern facing the beach. Since there is a fishing camp here, you should check with the fishermen to see that you are not in their way.

The best overnight anchorages are between Caracas del Este and Caracas del Oeste in an area known as El Coral. The most protected of these is on the southwest side of Caracas del Este. Here you have a large bay with two small beaches. There is an adequate anchoring shelf in 20-30 feet of water off either beach. Watch out for rocks close to shore. The snorkeling here and throughout this area is delightfully bright and colorful, though the water can be cold.

West of this anchorage, over on Caracas del Oeste, is a deeply indented bay where anchoring is very easy, as there is a large area of water that shelves gently from 30 to

12 feet. It is generally well protected, though it could be exposed to northerly swells or strong northeasterly winds.

Another lovely and well-protected anchoring area is off the eastern side of Caracas del Oeste, just where Caracas del Oeste is joined to Caracas del Sur. You get protection here from the northeast from Caracas del Este. The water here is very deep so you have to anchor off and find something on shore for a stern line.

Carenero, in the southwest corner of Caracas del Oeste, is a picturesque bay surrounded by dramatic red hills and rocks on which a few green shrubs manage to eke out an existence. There is a good anchoring area at the head of the bay in 25 feet of water, though the bay is very narrow, so two anchors may be necessary. There are two fishing camps in this bay, and anchored yachts are in the way when fishermen are netting. Therefore, it is probably best to treat this as a lunchtime stop. If there are no fishermen about, or if you talk to them and they say it is OK to stay, it makes a good overnight anchorage. Fine snorkeling can be found all around. There is also room to anchor in Playa Muerto and Cruza La Patas, but these are also used by fishermen.

SOUTHERN ENSENADA TIGRILLO

Varadero (Boatyard Bay) is a big double bay, and Mochima is only a few hundred yards away on the other side of the hill. There are anchoring areas in 20 feet of water in both the northern and southern part of this bay.

The next bay south has a small fishing camp and a shoal that sticks out from the far headland. You can find a one-boat anchorage amid pretty rocks in 20 feet of water.

Moving south round the next headland brings you to the southeasternmost bay in Ensenada Tigrillo, which is quite delightful (10°20.23'N, 64°22.78'W). The area is well covered in vegetation, with some good-sized trees close to the little beach. On the shore to the west of the beach is an area of colorful rocks. This anchorage is well protected, with a large shelf on which to anchor in 20-30 feet without getting too close to shore.

If you head a little west, you come to a long bay (10°20.20'N, 64°23.13'W). There is an excellent anchorage in the eastern half of this bay, with ample room to anchor in 20-25 feet of water. Ashore there are green hills and a tiny beach.

About halfway along La Costa del Pauviz there is a fairly deeply indented bay (10°19.93'N, 64°23.92'W). It is a peaceful place surrounded by green hills and has a little beach. There is an anchoring shelf off the beach, 20 to 30 feet deep. It is fairly narrow, so anchoring stern toward the beach with the bow facing out to sea is probably sensible. This bay is exposed if it really blows from the northeast.

From La Costa del Pauviz to Punta Gorda, the shoreline is a bit exposed to the

Opposite:
Santa Fe

northeast, and it is deep close to shore.

GOLFO DE SANTA FE

Golfo de Santa Fé is about five miles long and from one to two miles wide. You often see dolphins swimming here. Many excellent anchorages lie along its shores. A road runs all along the southern shore, so the most secluded anchorages are in the northern part. Most anchorages offer peace, interesting animal and insect sounds, fair snorkeling, and small beaches. After heavy rains, the water can be murky.

Distances between anchorages are short, so you can poke around until you find one you like. There are so many that you will find one to yourself, even on the busiest weekend. We mention the anchorages that seem the easiest and most attractive. However, the weather is often calm, the area is sheltered, and adventurous sailors can anchor wherever they choose.

Navigation

There is one hidden danger called Coralie Rock (10°18.47'N, 64°26.46'W) about 300 yards south of a conspicuous point (see our sketch chart). This is a very nasty rock with a double point, one about seven feet deep, the other about six feet. It is not marked on all charts. It claimed a significant part of the bottom of the steel S.Y. Coralie in 1989.

Bahía Valle Seco

In the northeastern corner of Bahía Valle Seco, there is a small bay with a beach at the head, which has been planted with coconut palms. The water is deep, but you can find anchorage close to the beach in about 20-30 feet of water.

Chapín

Chapín has a very clean, well-maintained beach with a couple of houses in the western corner. Anchoring is very close to the beach in 20-30 feet of water. The area is narrow so you will need two anchors. You might prefer to anchor a little farther out and take a line in to the rocky part of the shore.

La Petaca

The eastern part of this bay is shoal, with lots of coral heads and long seaweeds that sometimes rise 20 feet to the surface. This makes for excellent snorkeling. Anchor in the western part of the bay, where there is 20-30 feet of water off the beach with no weed. It is narrow, so two anchors will be necessary.

Bahía Petare

This is the large bay at the head of Golfo Santa Fé. It has several excellent anchorages. Right up in the northwest corner are two lovely little coves next door to each other, with fair snorkeling between them. The westernmost one has a beach, and you can anchor close to shore in 20-30 feet of water.

The other does not have a beach, but it is still charming with rocks and hills. It has an anchoring area about 30 feet deep and is large enough for one anchor to suffice.

As you proceed eastwards up the bay, there are two beaches, one with a sizeable village and the next with several houses. Beyond that, as far east as you can go in the northern part of Bahía Petare, is a gorgeous, long, wild beach, backed by palms and heavy vegetation. The water is very deep close-to, so you will need to go bow-to the beach or use an anchor in the deep and one in the shallows.

In the southern part of the bay, there is a private beach, the water is shallow in the eastern part and deep in the western part, so anchoring with two anchors, one in the shallows would be essential.

In the southwestern corner of the bay there is a delightful anchorage in the little cove south of the small island. There is room to anchor in the head of the bay in about 26 feet of water. It is very jungly and wild. The road and human habitation are just far away enough not to intrude.

The coastline between Bahía Petare and Esteba is alluring, with many luxurious private homes and pretty beaches. You can feel your way into an anchorage on the beach at the easternmost part of this coast. The rest of this shore is unsuitable for anchoring, as the water is either very deep or shoal with lots of coral heads.

Esteba

Esteba is just round the corner east of the village of Santa Fé. Watch out for the three-foot shoal way out in the middle of the bay. There is a very wide shoal off the southern part of this bay. The shoal comes up slowly, allowing you to find a large anchoring area in 10-25 feet, well offshore. This makes a pleasant contrast from the other anchorages in the area, where you are usually nose into the beach. Here you get a feeling of space, with pretty views of beaches, palms and hill lines.

Santa Fé

When the peace gets to be too much, try anchoring off the little village of Santa Fé. The eastern part is a fishing village, and the water is very deep close to shore. The western part is a cheerful area of brightly painted holiday homes and restaurants. You can find a good, wide anchoring area in 16 to 20 feet off the western part of the town.

Playa Santa Cruz and Playa Los Hicacos

Playa Santa Cruz is a popular public beach lined by a fleet of fishing boats. The village ashore has a restaurant. It is well protected, but is at least 30-40 feet deep close to shore, so you need a stern line to the beach

Playa Santa Cruz

or a second anchor in the shallows.

Playa Los Hicacos is a delightful secluded little bay edged with coconuts and
mangos. A little spring sometimes provides
fresh water out of a pipe that has been rigged
up. There is an excellent and ample anchoring area right in front of the beach, 15 to 25
feet deep. Do not anchor north of the beach,
as there is a shoal there. If there is a slight
swell running, you may need to hold yourself

bow out to sea. In a bad swell, you may prefer
to be farther up in Golfo Santa Fé.

The beach is part of a private club.
There is a restaurant that is sometimes
open.

Playa los Hicacos has a small diving
shop run by an Italian Franco Padda. He does
not speak English but can be very helpful
(0414 820 8758 / 0414 806-3744).

Arapos

ISLAS ARAPOS AND PLAYA COLORADA

Islas Arapos are two delightful little islands, well populated with holiday houses. At the western end of the western island, there are some conspicuous white rocks. This is a bird sanctuary, and anchoring is not allowed from the western end of the island to well beyond the rocks.

The easiest anchorage is in the big bay on the south side of the western island. The water is deep, so you will need a stern line. You can also use a mooring if one is free. Ashore, you will find a good dinghy dock and a restaurant.

The area between the two islands and well beyond to the north and south is dotted with reefs. Approach on the south side, where the water is very deep between the southern reefs. Eyeball your way between the reefs to find delightful anchoring areas on either side of the small island with a house on it that separates the two larger islands. The water here is from 12-25

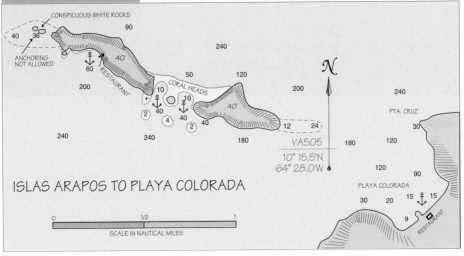

ISLAS ARAPOS TO PLAYA COLORADA

SCALE IN NAUTICAL MILES

Playa Colorada

feet deep, and anchoring room is tight, so if you are staying long, you will need two anchors.

These anchorages offer some of the most colorful snorkeling I have seen. There is a superabundance of Christmas tree and feather duster worms. They cover all the coral and glow like precious gems. Among them swim reef fish, including baby barracudas, pufferfish, and moray eels.

Playa Colorada is on the mainland about a mile from Islas Arapos. There is an ample anchoring shelf in 15 feet of water. The beach is attractive and very popular, so the restaurant here is nearly always open. A main road runs right behind the beach.

BAHIA COMONA

Bahía Comona is a quiet bay with pretty beaches. Some mining has been done on the surrounding hills, but you can anchor out of sight of the scars. There is a neat anchorage behind Isla Comona. A large shoal extends from the middle of the island to the shore and northwards, so you must enter on the south side, where the water is 30-40 foot deep. It gets busy at around 0700, when boats land people who are working in the factory.

Playa Cominita is a lovely beach backed by jungle from which one can hear the strident sounds of exotic birds. At odds with this untamed atmosphere are the trash cans and "Don't litter" signs. Playa Cominita is a public beach, but it is often deserted on weekdays and not too crowded on weekends. The water is deep close to shore, so a second anchor in the shallows is required. If you edge right up into the eastern corner and tie stern-to the mangroves north of the beach you have an excellent anchorage even in northerly swells, when the rest of the bay is untenable.

Bahía Comona

BAHIA BERGANTIN TO BAHIA PERTIGALETE

Heading west along the coast to Puerto La Cruz, the first bay is Bahía Pertigalete. A large cement factory dominates the eastern side. In the middle are two little islands called Islas de Plata. Because they are close to shore, the ferry ride is cheap, and on weekends, they become packed with people, making them lively and colorful. In the old days, yachts used to anchor here because there was a marine railway on the southern island. This has been cleared as part of the conversion to a park, and now the only reason to come is

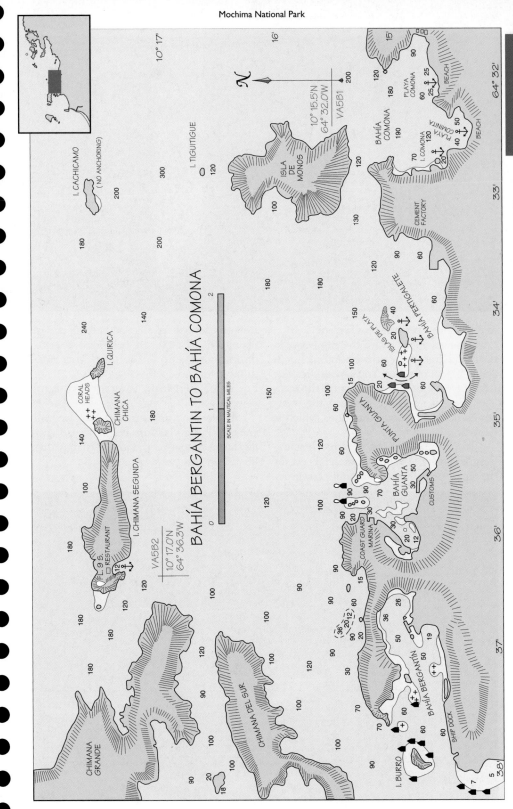

BAHÍA BERGANTIN TO BAHÍA COMONA

Mochima and Puerto la Cruz

Playa El Faro, Chimana Secunda

to check out a popular beach scene.

You can edge toward the gap between the islands from the southwest and anchor in about 30 feet of water. You can also anchor stern-to the southern island or off the reef.

There is a passage between the western end of the reef and the shore, which is buoyed.

Bahía Guanta is the next bay heading west, and it is the main commercial port for the area. A small marina is under construc-

tion on the western side, and part of it is in operation. However, it is beyond walking distance of Puerto la Cruz, and so is more suitable for those with cars.

Bahía Bergantín is owned by an oil company and is private.

If we head any further west, we will come to Puerto la Cruz. Before we get that far, let us detour to the lovely islands that lie just off this coast.

Islas de Plata

Playa El Faro, Chimana Segunda

ISLA CHIMANA SEGUNDA

There is a delightful anchorage on the western end of the south coast of Isla Chimana Segunda called Playa El Faro. Soft, multicolored cliffs surround the bay. They have been sculpted by the elements into attractive shapes. At the head is a broad beach. Ashore, Kike's Chimana Segunda restaurant is open daily till 1800, though if not much is happening, they sometimes go early. Kike encourages the local iguanas and tree boas to come for food, and they are easily seen. He serves good seafood and paella. Kike commutes daily from Puerto la Cruz, and he is willing to bring good customers the odd necessity or sell them a little gasoline or diesel. He will also take well-wrapped garbage for a small fee.

The park rules say that you are not sup- posed to stay here more than 24 hours, but if things are quiet, you probably can stay an extra day.

The red-and-white lighthouse up the hill flashes every nine seconds, and the walk up will get you a bird's-eye view of the bay.

This bay is quiet and peaceful during the week, jolly and busy on weekends and holidays.

Isla Cachicamo, two miles east of Isla Chimana Segunda, is under special protec- tion of the park, and anchoring is not al- lowed anywhere around it.

CHIMANA GRANDE

Chimana Grande is just four miles from Puerto la Cruz but it is a thousand miles away in atmosphere, with peaceful bays, pretty red-brown hills, mangroves, parrots,

165

El Saco

Cienega

Cieneguita

Chimana Grande

and seabirds.

It is so dry here that bugs are not usually a problem, and the water is clear, so you can find some fair snorkeling.

The two best anchorages are Ciénaga (Mangrove-lined Bay) and Ciéneguita (Small Mangrove-lined Bay). These are both well-protected bays with easy anchoring areas that are breezy enough to keep them cool.

Ciénaga

This large bay has mangroves at both ends and a small beach in the middle. Fishermen camp in the western half. A large coral bank extends from the southern shore of the eastern part (see our sketch plan). Occasional coral heads on this shoal rise within a foot of the surface here, so it is best avoided. Anchorage is off the northern shore. Anchoring deep is safe, if you anchor in 12-18 feet of water, watch out for coral heads. There is plenty of room in this bay and you should check out the mangrove passage to Ciéneguita (see Ciéneguita).

Ciéneguita

Ciéneguita is a splendid hideaway. You enter down a narrow channel with steep hills on both sides. This gives way at its head to a larger mangrove-lined bay with an excellent anchoring area 9-16 feet deep. There is room for just a few boats whose crew are friends. At night, Puerto la Cruz glows between the hills guarding the bay, providing the ideal background for your after-dinner drink.

There is an intriguing mangrove channel between Ciéneguita and Ciénaga. It is a tiny, pull-yourself through affair that will not take a dinghy with a beam much over four feet. It takes faith to find it, because it is so hidden you have to turn the first bend before you are sure you are in it.

Those with a taste for a prickly, dangerous climb on loose rock and soft earth can try to make it to the top of the southwest hill for the view.

Playa el Saco

On the western side of Chimana Grande, Playa el Saco is protected from the west by Chimana del Oeste. The beach is divided in two. The northern part has a concession with a seafood restaurant that is open on weekends and busy times; the prices are reasonable and the food good. The southern

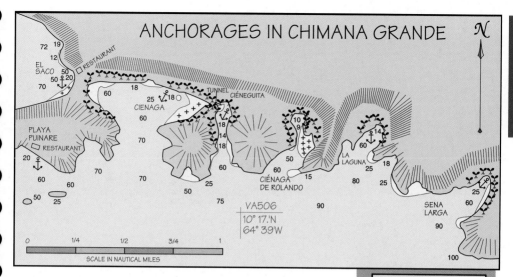

ANCHORAGES IN CHIMANA GRANDE

Mochima and Puerto la Cruz

part is in a more natural state. Anchoring is not easy, as the water is deep close to shore. With two anchors, you can get yourself safely anchored off the southern part of the beach, where there is a shelf about 20-30 feet deep. You may need to snorkel to get your anchors laid in such a way they are not damaging the coral heads. This is a popular spot on weekends and holidays.

Playa Puinare

This popular weekend, white-sand beach is good as a day stop. There is a shelf about 20-30 feet deep to anchor on. You may need to set two anchors. Be careful of the swimming

Chimana Grande
Sena Larga

buoys. Ashore is a weekend restaurant run by Miguel Vargas and Joseito, where you can get seafood, they speak some English. This is a popular fishing and snorkeling spot for locals.

Ciénaga de Rolando

Ciénaga de Rolando is a great place to explore by dinghy. There is a secluded anchorage in the western tongue suitable for shallow-draft boats. The channel is close to the mangroves on the western shore and is about seven feet deep, but there are so many shallow coral heads that you need to check it out with a dinghy first.

La Laguna

There is an anchorage at the head of La Laguna Bay in about 25 feet of water. The swinging room is limited, so you may need two anchors or a line ashore. This bay is sometimes buggy.

Sena Larga

The island's most dramatic cliff and rock formations can be found at Sena Larga. The water is deep close to shore, so it is best to drop one anchor and take another into the shallows or up on the beach.

ISLA LA BORRACHA

Isla La Borracha (The Drunk Woman) is a dramatic and prominent island just over 1,200 feet high. South of Borracha is El Borracho (The Drunk Man), and southwest of him are Los Borrachitos (The Little Drunks). If you are sailing between El Borracho and

On the hill east of Cieneguita, looking over Cieneguita and Cienaga
In the midst of the mangroves between the two is a tiny hidden dinghy channel.

Isla La Borracha

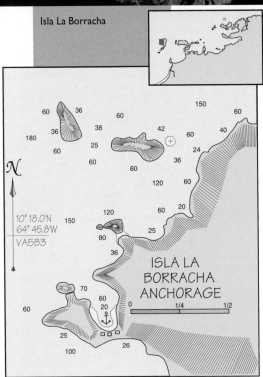

ISLA LA
BORRACHA
ANCHORAGE

10° 18.0'N
64° 45.8'W
VA5B3

Los Borrachitos, watch out for the elusive, three-foot shoal that is said to lurk somewhere in the middle (see sketch chart page 147). The anchorage at Isla La Borracha is scenic, with dramatic cliffs on the eastern side. The anchorage is rather small, and you need to get out of the deep water onto the 9-20-foot shelf in front of the village. To the northeast of the village is a clearly visible rock. The anchorage is west of this, in the middle of the bay. There are reefs extending out on all sides, but the water is usually clear enough to make them visible.

Diving is excellent around the western entrance to the harbor, and snorkeling is worth a go anywhere. Climb the cactusy hills for a spectacular view.

Over the years, many people have anchored in Isla La Borracha, most of them without a problem, but a few have been attacked by vampire bats (see "Dangers" at the beginning of this book). The villagers also mention occasional bat attacks. Be on the safe side: use screens! I also know also of one pirate attack here.

Paseo Colon,
- Oscar Hernandez photo

Puerto la Cruz

Puerto la Cruz is the center of yachting in Venezuela, with eight marinas in operation. You can find good haul out facilities, excellent chandleries, a sailmaker, and several people who are happy to help you get things done. Nearly everyone in the marine industry speaks English. If they don't, they are adept at communicating by sign language. The coast and offshore islands from Puerto la Cruz to Mochima constitute the Mochima National Park and offer outstanding cruising, starting just a couple of miles outside the city.

Safety is not yet as most Venezuelans and visitors, including sailors, want. Despite the efforts the Guardacostas and Inparques, incidents were reported in 2005/06 in La Borracha and Playa El Guaro. To increase security, three permanent, 24-hour police posts with boats and VHF radio have been placed at Playa Puinare in Chimana Grand, at Playa El Faro in Chimana Segunda, and at the anchorage of Paseo Colon in Puerto la Cruz. The emergency channel is VHF: 16.

Safety also comes with a price. The Guarda costa has been cracking down on speeding dinghies in the canal (speed limit five knots). When they stop you, you will need to have with you a light, PFDs, and papers that prove you own the dinghy and engine. (If you don't have one, go to an imaginative computer lab and make a bill of sale; make sure you include the engine and dinghy serial numbers.) Otherwise they confiscate

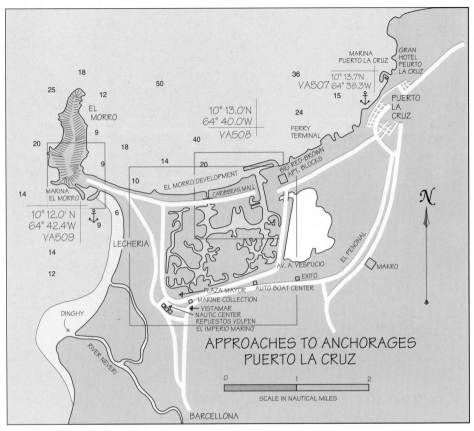

18
25
12
50

EL MORRO

10° 13.0'N
64° 40.0'W
VA508

36
10° 13.7'N
VA507 64° 38.3'W
15

MARINA
PUERTO LA CRUZ

GRAN HOTEL PEURTO LA CRUZ

PUERTO LA CRUZ

24

FERRY TERMINAL

20
18
9

14
20

10
EL MORRO DEVELOPMENT

BIG RED-BROWN APT. BLOCKS

14
MARINA EL MORRO

CARIBBEAN MALL

10° 12.0' N
64° 42.4'W
VA509

6
9

LECHERIA

14

12

EL PENONAL

AV. A. VESPUCIO

MAKRO

EXITO

PLAZA MAYOR   AUTO BOAT CENTER
MARINE COLLECTION
VISTAMAR
NAUTIC CENTER
REPUESTOS VOLPEN
EL IMPERIO MARINO

DINGHY

RIVER NEVERI

N

**APPROACHES TO ANCHORAGES
PUERTO LA CRUZ**

0   1   2
SCALE IN NAUTICAL MILES

BARCELLONA

the dinghy till a hearing at the port captain's office, which usually results in a fine of about 170$US.

Puerto la Cruz is a great center with excellent shopping, and Paseo Colon is famous for good restaurants, travel agents, shops, and nightlife. Caution while wandering ashore is recommended, especially late at night.

Puerto la Cruz is an excellent place to leave your yacht and make a trip inland. It is well located, there are plenty of places to leave your boat, and there are excellent travel agents, flight services, and taxi drivers, plus a ferry that travels to and from Margarita four times a day.

Police checks are rare, but keep at least a photocopy of your green entry paper and your inside passport page with you just in case. When traveling out of the city, take your passport. There is a guy in Plaza Mayor who will photocopy your passport and make it into a plastic card you can carry with you. He is upstairs in a little booth behind Unicasa.

Navigation

You can approach Puerto la Cruz from any of the passages between islands. Avoid sailing between Borracho and Los Borrachitos, and avoid the eastern end of Isla Chimana Segunda. The other passages are very straightforward.

The anchoring area is just west of Marina Puerto la Cruz (Marina Paseo Colón). There is currently no convenient dinghy dock, and you have to haul yours up the beach, so observe where the other dinghies are tied. You can load and unload at the small docks used by the lanceros, or water taxis, at the north end of the beach. At night, it is recommended that you hoist your dinghy on board and lock yourself in. It is safer to be in a marina while here. Some taxi drivers who value cruisers were working on the idea of a mooring area off Playa Muerto to include a dinghy dock. For more information contact Raphael Campos 0414 808-2396, or racecampos@cantv.net.

Marina Paseo Colon and Puerto la Cruz

Regulations

When you come into Puerto la Cruz you are going to have to clear in. The authorities here are pretty straightforward, but the process, while costing very little, is time-consuming. They now have a one-stop check-in at the Capitaneria, but customs and immigration are not always there, and you will still have to make payments into the bank. I highly recommend letting the agents do the clearance. TBS or Transpacific Travel and Services will check you in; they are in Bahia Redonda Marina.

Communications

For local information, listen to the cruisers' net on VHF: 72 at 0745 (except Sundays). It is sometimes hosted by local businesses; for example Victor Diaz from Aqua Vi has been doing the Thursday net.

VHF: 72 is also the general calling channel for businesses except marinas. (We give other marina calling channels under *General yacht services*).

Communications (except mail) are good. If you like to phone, get a Digicel cell phone while you are here.

Transpacific Travel and Services is in Bahia Redonda. Keigla, the manager, is hyperactive and speaks perfect English and French. She can do check-in check-out, and airport transfers, and can organize trips to Merida, Angel fall, Canaima and

173

any other trips around the country, as well as sell you your Mochima park pass. Keigla knows cruisers' needs and it is very friendly and helpful.

TBS has an office in Bahia Redonda run by Sereg. They offer all types of office services, including email, fax, phone, and mail, along with some tour flights.

You will find plenty of inexpensive internet cafes in the giant Plaza Mayor supermall, accessible by dinghy from any of the marinas in the El Morro complex.

There are plenty of places in Puerto la Cruz for communications, including most marinas. You will also see centers all around the city. Look for the sign: Centro De Comunicaciones Cantv. This is the place to do emails, faxes, international calls, pho-

tocopies etc., and it is very inexpensive. (By the way, a special note to any voyeuristic cruisers: in Venezuela, it against the law to navigate porno web pages in public places, like internet cafes, so if you do, you might be arrested.) Wifi should be coming soon to most marinas.

General Yacht Services

Servinauti, also known as Marina Paseo Colón or Marina Puerto la Cruz (VHF: 71), is right in the center of town. The security here is very good. They do not have many slips for cruisers and do not take advance bookings, but as they work on a first-come, first-served basis, you can usually get in if you wait a few days. Facilities include showers and toilets. There is water and electricity (110/120-volt 60-cycle) on the dock. Their fuel dock is open daily 0800-1200 and 1400-1700. Before you come in with your boat,

Marinas area, Marina Amerco Vespucio in foreground

dinghy over and make sure there is enough depth for it.

Also bear in mind that due to an antiquated law, marinas and shoreside facilities pay 10 times the cost that others pay for water, so check with them before you take water. The dockmaster, Jose Mendez, speaks English. Ice, beer, and soft drinks are available during working hours. Marina Puerto la Cruz only takes local currency.

The other marinas are to the west of town. Most are part of the huge new El Morro development. The entrance to El Morro is easy for boats with up to a 10-foot draft. Those of 11 or 12 foot should check it out first or go in gently on high tide. Once inside the wall, the deeper-draft boats will have to turn east immediately, into the Bahía Redonda Marina. The reason for this is a shoal on the west side of the entrance to the main channel. This shoal is not marked, but there is a center channel mark, and it is recommended you pass on the east side of this mark. Stay in the eastern side of the channel, where the maximum depth is nine feet at low tide. Yachts with a draft of 10 feet can squeeze through by working the tides. A submerged rock lies mid-channel just past Aqua Vi Marina, and it is not marked at this time, so favor the east side of the channel. (See our sketch chart.) Once past the rock, there is 12 feet through much of the complex.

The fuel dock is on the inside of the main wall just before the Bahía Redonda Marina.

Bahía Redonda Marina (VHF: 71) is the largest docking facility to date in the country. It is a world-class, full-service marina. It has a capacity for 150 boats up to 100 foot long, with all the amenities to make you feel relaxed and secure.

Oscar Hernandez photo

Several shower and toilet facilities are scattered around, so one is always close to your boat. There are a couple of swimming pools, a restaurant, laundry, phones, and a small grocery store with easy dinghy access. Cable TV and telephone hook-ups are planned. Free wifi is in place and should cover the entire marina by the time you read this. They are also installing electronic surveillance. On Monday evenings, they fire up the barbecue pit and invite yachties from all over Puerto la Cruz to come cook their dinner and intermingle. This is a perfect place to leave your boat in the care of Arnaldo, the dockmaster, and head into the interior of Venezuela for a few days. They have a good list of experienced people authorized to work on boats at the dock as well a several services including Restaurant El Ancla and a beauty salon. Pier Roland, who was managing the marina, was killed with his wife while this edition was being prepared. He was a good friend to cruisers and a supporter of sailing activities in Puerto la Cruz. He is missed.

Bahia Redonda has an annual race in mid-October. It takes place in Bahia Pozuelos. Some 40 boats raced in each of the last few years.

For taxi service on the premises of the marina, you can contact Andres, Raul, Arnaldo, Roger, or Walter. The marina also offers a free shuttle that takes visitors to the supermarkets at 0900.

Dr. Carlos Salavarria (416 846-6643), an English-speaking doctor, visits two days a week to serve cruisers staying in the marina.

PR Yacht Service, in the same area, has a 60-ton marine hoist in addition to a ramp with a trailer capable of hauling multihulls with a beam of 9.5 meters, with a capacity for about 50 boats for work and storage. They can do all types of painting, fiberglass repair, carpentry, S.S. and aluminum welding, sandblasting, rigging, and mechanical work. They can design and build boats as well.

Puerto del Este is a condominium and hotel marina complex on the left as you enter the canal into the El Morro waterway. It is easily recognizable by the lighthouse structure at the north end of the dock. Dockage is stern-to in about 10-feet of water with room for about 20 boats. They have 110- and 220-volt power, and water. There is a small market selling ice, drinks and basic foodstuff. Bathrooms with hot showers as well as the use of the pool and tennis courts are available to those at the dock. They have a couple of washing machines and driers, and

177

Puerto la Cruz from El Morro

a restaurant is planned.

Proyectos Marinos Orientales (VHF: 80/78 usa) is more often known as PMO. This is an impressive marina: it has about 62 berths, dry storage for 155, and every kind of workshop. They even build boats here, in modern wood/epoxy laminates, traditional planking, and fiberglass.

Docking is mainly stern-to, with a few alongside berths. If you draw six feet or more, berth along the main canal wall, as the cut to the east is shallow. There is water alongside and electricity (110- and 220-volt, 60-cycle). Ashore you will find good security, showers, toilets, laundry, and a coffee shop. If you call on the telephone, the operator speaks English.

PMO has a 70-ton Travelift that takes up to a 22-foot beam and a special trailer for hauling multihulls of almost any size. Boats left in dry storage are fenced off with closed circuit TV, and guard dogs are let loose. Each time an owner comes down, the dogs are fed, so the owner can get the boat out. A separate storage area is set aside for sandblasting to

contain the flying sand. For refitting boats, they have a machine shop, as well as paint, mechanical, electrical, refrigeration and up-holstery workshops. It is not a do-it-yourself yard, but arrangements can be made in spe-cial cases, and they have qualified people for all your needs. Service is best when they are not overwhelmed with business. PMO also has a coffee shop, called Compass Rose.

Aqua Vi (VHF: 72) is just next door to PMO, on the other side of the ferry landing. It is as hotel/marina facility with 39 stern-to marina slips with a draft of 10 feet, with water, electricity, cable TV, and telephone. Use of the pool and other hotel services is available to those tied up at their docks. They offer 24-hour assistance. They also have a 50-ton marine hoist and space for about 28 boats on the hard for repairs and maintenance; long-term storage is limited but available. Víctor Díaz de León is the yard manager, with 21 years of experience in the industry, having previously been at Marina Americo Vespucio. Victor is a very helpful person who speaks perfect English, and his work is excellent. They can apply antifouling, and do Awlgrip and Imron topcoats, as well as osmosis treatment and fiberglass repairs. Other mechanical and electronic repairs can be organized through them. Victor recommends Pedro Loyola for diesel repair. Aqua Vi is also the home of Orient Canvas (*see Sailmakers & Canvas*).

You can join the Aqua Vi members' club for about $150. This can give you special discounts and access to facilities while you visit the marina, including 20% discounts in docking, restaurants, and rooms, among other advantages. For a long-term stay it is really worth it.

For taxis in Aqua Vi, Arnaldo and Leopoldo Felicer are very helpful. They speak English and stand by on VHF: 72.

Those with a yen for a touch of luxury at an economical price will opt for Marina Maremares (VHF: 71, SSB: 2738.0). Marina Maremares is part of a large hotel complex with restaurants and an exotic pool, and it has excellent security. There is room for 50 boats stern-to and four alongside. Electricity (220/120-volt 60 cycle), phone, internet, and cable TV, are all supplied to the boat. When you check in, it is like checking into their hotel, and you are treated just like a guest. You sign your credit card slip and the register, and after that, you can order anything and just have it put on your bill. Room service is available to the yacht. They will watch your boat if you want to go on a trip or watch your kids if you want a night on the town. Tennis and golf are right there, too, as well as exercise rooms, spa, and massage. The emphasis is on service. This starts when you call them on the radio before you come in. They will send out a boat to guide you in and to help you get correctly hooked to the mooring for stern-to berthing. If you need clearance, they can arrange it for you. Manager America Perez and her assistant Xiomara Langaine, speak English. On Wednesdays, they have a managers' happy hour and provide free drinks for visiting yachts from all the marinas.

The ownership was changing as we went to press. We can only hope the standards will be maintained; time will tell.

Just outside Maremares, on the main

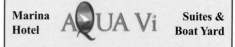

road, is the giant Caribbean Mall, which has many restaurants, shops, and internet services.

Marina Americo Vespucio (VHF: 72) is opposite PMO. This marina is almost in two parts. The inside part is for Venezuelan boats or long-term dockage, and stern-to the outside wall is for visiting yachts. The outside is the more pleasant place to live, as it is more breezy. On the other hand, it is open to the public, so you should ask about current security. There is water, electricity (220/110-volts, 60 cycle), toilets, and showers. A small minimarket and a restaurant, Aguamarina (open for breakfast, lunch and dinner), are on the grounds.

Marina Americo Vespucio also has a 50-ton Travelift run by Jorge Rondon. They do repair and paint jobs of all types, as well as diesel repair, carpentry, and upholstery, but they do not have room for long-term storage on the hard.

Marina Club Nautico El Morro (VHF:

Marina el Morro

MARINA EL MORRO

SAILING SCHOOL

OUTBOARD REPAIR

OFFICE

FUEL

N

SCALE IN NAUTICAL MILES

0   1/8

10° 12.0'N
64° 42.4'W
VA509

71) is sometimes known as Marina Imbuca. It is not in the El Morro complex, but over on the south side of the El Morro headland. It is quiet, pleasant, open to the breeze, and well-protected with good security. The only drawback is that it is rather a long way from town, but there is a good bus service and por puestos. It is an excellent place for anyone renting a car, for those who want to leave their boats while going off into the interior, and for those working on their boats.

The marina entrance is about 12-foot deep. Along the edges of the wall where boats come bow- or stern-to, it shelves to five or six feet, depending on the spot you choose. They have a fuel dock, which has been rebuilt with a new essentials shop. The fuel dock had about nine feet at the deeper end, shelving rapidly toward the marina offices to about six feet. Possibly, with the rebuilding the new dock, it may be deeper. There are showers, toilets, water, electricity at 110-220 volts, 60 cycles. In the same complex is a small coffee shop and a couple of outboard repair shops. There is a marine hoist that is adequate only for powerboats. There is talk of expanding into a haul-out facility for storage and work on multihulls.

There is another marina, Yacht Club Marina de Guanta, over in Guanta, the big commercial port a couple of miles

Mochima and Puerto la Cruz

east of Puerto la Cruz. A few boats are in the marina, though it is only partly finished. This is a little out of town for easy access, but there is a restaurant.

If you need a little extra help in finding parts, filling gas tanks, or other things, you will find some willing people. Kings Services (VHF: 72) offers taxis, laundry delivery, propane gas refills, finding of spare parts, chain galvanizing, and more.

Jose is from Costa Rica, has good local knowledge, and is good at procuring parts.

You can also take your laundry to Altagracia, drop it off in the morning after 0700, and pick up before 1830. They pride themselves in using good-quality detergents and being careful about not mixing colors with whites, all at a good price.

Jaime Callejon Gimenez is a local veterinarian with an office on Av. Bolivar # 409. He speaks some English and will come to the boat to take care of your pet's needs and to give shots. Note that the Inparques forbids having pets on the beaches.

Carolos Gonález, otherwise known as Charlie Alpha Yacht Services (0412 859-

7070, VHF: 72 "Charlie Alpha," or email charliealphams@hotmail.com) is a good contact and a general help in Puerto la Cruz. He will arrange everything from boat repairs and marina reservations to tourist trips or getting medical attention, and he will get you there on time.

Chandleries

Xanadu Marine (VHF: 72) is an excellent chandlery. It is run by Patti from the U.S. who cruised the Caribbean for 20 years with her late husband John in their Tayana 37, called *Xanadu*. They found themselves coming back to the beauty and culture of Venezuela year after year. The shop contains a wide range of gear, from boat alarms to the popular AB and Caribe dinghies. Patti understands all her products, from a GPS to antifouling. She will save you much pain by making sure you have the product you need. This is the first place to come for good information on paints and antifoulings. They carry a good selection of charts, guides, and books. And if it's the weather you want, this is the place to come for an updated picture.

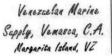
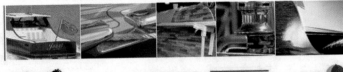
Children's Service League Christmas and note cards are sold here for a very small price but a big cause.

Patty designed the most-used map of Puerto la Cruz (you can get them free all over the place).

At Bahía Redonda Marina in the same building towards the back is Caribbean Marine Corporation, run by Morris Gouverneur. They have zincs, caulking, bearings, antifoulings, lubricants, cutlass bearings, and general paint supplies and epoxies. They represent Woolsey, Z Spar, Schaeffer, Pettit, and Boatlife. They specialize in all supplies for below the waterline.

Vemasca, the big general marine chandlery, from Margarita, also has a branch in Bahia Redonda. If you cannot see what you want on the shelves, ask for Miguel Perez.

There is also a chandlery at Marina Americo Vespucio, which is convenient to those in that area. It is called Rich Electronics, and they stock yachting accessories, electronics and fishing gear or will order for you from West Marine. They also do installation and repair of electronic parts.

From any of the marinas in the El Morro complex, you can get to the giant super-mall Plaza Mayor by dinghy. Just outside this complex are a couple of marine stores. Nautic Center (VHF: 68, Av. Principal de Lecherias, C.C. Classic Center), stocks Uniden VHFs, GPS and other electronics, ground tackle and ropes, a good stock of fishing and diving equipment, as well as fastenings and some sports clothing.

Repuestos Volpen C.A. is close by in the same commercial area. They are the agents for Volvo Penta, Yanmar, Kohler, and Westerbeke; they have some stock and will order specific parts for your engine.

El Imperio Marino, across the street from Arturo's, is close to Nautic Center. They are the Yamaha distributors and carry a good supply of parts as well as electronics, water pumps, S.S. fastenings, and marine-grade fabrics. They can also special order for you.

Auto Boat Center (next to the Toyota dealership) is a huge shop specializing in auto and boat parts. They carry AB dinghies, electronics, marine fabrics, impellers, batteries, ground tackle, snorkeling equipment, and much more. They are Mercury dealers and have parts and repair services for that brand.

Pintacasa is the International, Sherwin Williams, and Sika paint store in town, with a good range of paints and accessories. You can get many types of antifouling and hull paint here. Also for paints and varnish, check Todo Para El Pintor and the junction of Calle San Juan Bosco and Calle Anzoategui.

Sailmakers and canvas work

Orient Canvas is run by brothers Hernan and Edin Moncada (0281 263-5544). They are in the haul-out area of Aqua Vi Marina and speak English. They do all types of upholstery and fabricate and bend alumi-

num and stainless steel structures for dodgers and biminis. They can recover cushions as well as make them from scratch. They now also make sails under the Orient Sails brand. The clients we talked to were very happy with their sails, which offer good quality for an excellent price.

Venezuela is a good place to recover cabin cushions or make new awnings. Michael Mitera, a German who has been married to a Venezuelan for many years, has his shop in Bahia Redonda Marina. Michael is a real artist, and he does the best-quality work, as well as being businesslike and able to deliver on time. He not only does great upholstery but also is the person to see for decorative leatherwork, including unusual snakeskins. He can cover your wheel to give the cockpit a great new look.

Mauricio Costanzo runs a first-rate sail loft in Bahia Redonda Marina. It is called Kostan Sails (VHF: 72). Mauricio speaks perfect English and Italian. He can build good sails for yachts of any size, or, if you prefer, you can order the North Sails

brand through him. In addition to making and repairing sails, Mauricio does awnings, biminis, and dodgers complete with frames that he custom-makes. He is also an agent for Norseman and Stalok. You can get a new mast and rig or just a new stay or roller furling; he also has Harken gear in stock as well as New England ropes. He sells lifelines and rigging and swages up to a quarter-inch. If you call him on the radio, he will come to your boat to collect your torn sail or to measure up for that new one. He can also

wash your sails or awnings.

Check also Tapimar (VHF: 77) on Calle Freites # 108, El Pensil. Luis Marcano and his wife, Moraina, can make and repair awnings, biminis, and dodgers, including the metal frames in aluminum or stainless steel. They have Sunbrella and other materials in stock, including clear window material, weblon, and vinyls. For covering cushions, they have access to a large selection of materials such as Textiline and local or imported leathers. Also, interior overheads can be redone. Their service includes pickup and delivery.

Technical Yacht Services

Dinghy Hospital (VHF: 71.), now 10 years in the business, is on the side of the boat storage yard at Bahia Redonda Marina and is run by Linda Lanzon, who previously worked with Caribe inflatables for 13 years and knows all about inflatables. Her team does warranty work for Caribe dinghies. They can also repair all types of hypalon inflatables as well as PVC boats. They will also work on small outboards of all makes. Picking up your dinghy and delivering it back to you by sea or land is part of the service. Check them out also if you need a new or used inflatable or accessories.

For quality metal work, see Serviboat, La Fé #30, Puerto la Cruz, near the Rasil Hotel. Jose de Veer, the owner, speaks English. His machine shop can do all types of work with SS 316, aluminum, steel, and bronze. He often does tubing for dodgers, biminis, stanchions, etc. He can build davits and solar panel frames and will repair water pumps or turn new parts for bearings, shafts, and motors, or fabricate a new cleat or fairlead to match the rest on your boat. He can work on your boat or move the work to his shop.

Seatronics 2000 (VHF: 5A), a marine electronics facility, is in Bahia Redonda and run by Martin Garcia, who learned from his father who worked in the electronics repair business for 35 years. He can service and install all kinds of marine electronics, and is the Furuno agent for radars, echo sounders and GPS. We have had good reports on Martin and have also heard of the store referred to as Maritime Electronics Technologies.

Evinmotors, Oriente, C.A. (0281 286-0086), the dealer for Evinrude/Johnson/Bombardier, has a good stock of parts and is located on Av. Intercomunal Barcelona, Centro Com. Las Garzas, Loc. J, Lecheria, across from the Polar plant and behind the Banco Provincial.

Joshua Brazil (0414 820-0623) will repair refrigeration systems and air conditioners.

Juan Guerrero (0414 824-7832) is a diesel mechanic. He

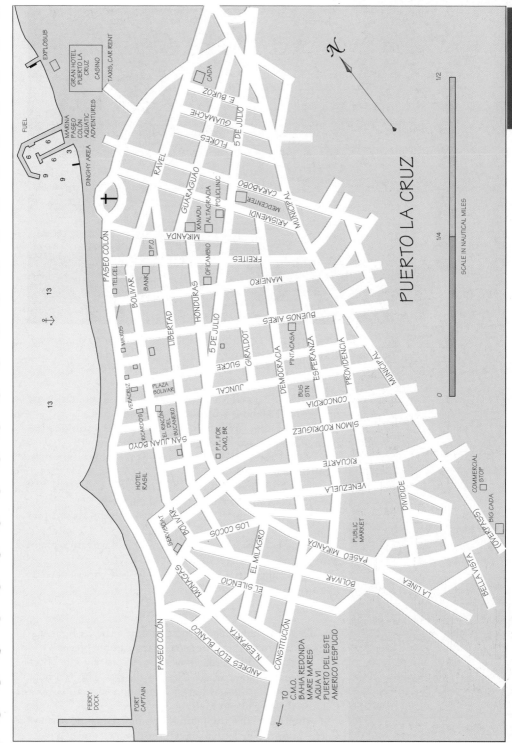

PUERTO LA CRUZ

SCALE IN NAUTICAL MILES

Marina Paseo Colon - Oscar Hernandez photo

completely rebuilt a Perkins for the Robinsons on *Skybird*, and they were very happy.

Alfredo (0416 884-3589) operates a taxi and speaks some English

Chris Robinson (0281 281-4912) rents air-conditioning units for boats and is a Lloyds qualified surveyor.

Jesus Guerra (0414 818-2016) does A/C repair and has been recommended by readers.

Angel Perez (0414 824-0968) works with electronics, mostly out of CMO.

Carlos Villanueva (T: 0281 265-2368, Cel: 0414 818 4783) is a qualified marine electrical engineer.

Agustin Salazar (0417 813-7610) is an outboard mechanic.

Urma la Deuce Marine (VHF: 72) will galvanize chain with pickup and delivery in about two days.

Joel Campos (0414 813-9457) is well experienced at painting Awlgrip.

Provisioning

To get money from a credit card, use the 24-hour machines scattered around, or some of the cambio offices.

Unicasa in Plaza Mayor is the cruisers' favorite shopping place, and you can get there by dinghy. This is a huge supermarket that should have everything you want. Check out also the Caribbean Mall.

After the malls, the main shopping area is the town of Puerto la Cruz. The local market is the cheapest and best place for fresh produce. You can also get meat and fish. It is open seven days a week from 0700, and the earlier you get there the

Puerto La Cruz fom the sea

better. It is all over by noon. There is a fish market beside Conferry, at the beginning of Paseo Colon coming from the marinas.

Otherwise, Enrique Cordenons Automercado Veracruz offers a good stock of the usual supermarket items, including wine, beer, and liquor, as well as European cheeses, deli goods, imported caviar, and grade-A meat cuts. They will deliver large orders to your boat, and both English and Italian are spoken.

For more good meats, check out Comercial Las Flores. They have a wide selection of meat cuts packaged to order. Orlando, the butcher, has a beef chart that is easy to understand and point to for selecting cuts. They also stock vegetables and other foodstuffs.

There are two Cada supermarkets good for a big provisioning, but the one that is furthest away on Municipal is the biggest.

Makro is the largest of these supermarkets and good for major provisioning; it is not far from Plaza Mayor and any taxi will know. They do not accept credit cards, but the prices are very good.

EPA is a huge Home Depot-like place for household items and hardware.

Exito is like a Kmart with a good grocery store that has fresh produce.

Fun Shopping

In Puerto la Cruz, the main street is Paseo Colón, an attractive, broad street with a large walkway by the water. It becomes lively in the evenings, when people wander up and down and street sellers, artisans, and entertainers set up along the walkway westwards from the big roundabout. Since

this street was rebuilt into a wide boulevard, some of the old waterfront restaurants were removed to make enough room.

There is a newsstand in the middle of Paseo Colón that stocks the *Daily Journal*, an English-language Venezuelan newspaper with much international news, and a wide selection of magazines in both Spanish and English.

If you have prints to process, then Fotolisto is one of the quickest and best places.

From any of the marinas in the El Morro complex, you can get to Plaza Mayor by dinghy. This newly opened super-mall is worth a visit just to see it, and you might just spend the day there and never have to take a taxi again. Several restaurants face the dinghy dock, among them, Chinese, Italian, Subway, and of course local dishes. Beyond, every kind of store, shop, or office exists. Amphitheatres, banks, bookstores, boutiques, bakeries, clothing shops, travel agents, family centers, optometrists, perfume shops, you name it, they've got it, and it is all beautifully laid out and landscaped. There are five movie theaters and several internet cafes, including one on the third floor. A huge supermarket called Unicasa is located on the west side of the Plaza.

If there is an American movie you want to see, check out the cinemas; the films are in the original language with subtitles in Spanish. Only the animated cartoon type movies are dubbed in Spanish.

Restaurants

Eating out is no problem. There are

countless restaurants, many of them along Paseo Colón. The wide variety includes Chinese, Japanese, a lot of Italian, and Arabian (try their main dish served wrapped in a tortilla-like patty rolled up with a variety of meats and vegetables).

El Rincón Del Bucanero (Pirate's Corner) is a good, traditional, Spanish-style restaurant with snappy service and good food at reasonable prices.

When you want a change from the usual menus, try El Faraón (The Pharo). They serve good Arabian food in an exotic and gaudy atmosphere.

El Amir Palace on Paseo Colón has sidewalk seating as well as seats inside and serves Arabian as well as international food.

Gran Hotel Puerto la Cruz has an expensive restaurant on the outside called Tascamar, but there is a good and less expensive

restaurant inside by the pool where you can get a good meal at a reasonable price. They tend to close a bit on the early side, so don't expect to get a meal at 2100.

Neptuno, a top-floor restaurant on Paseo Colon, serves good meals at a reasonable price with a great view.

Riccardo's is small but with very attentive service and specializes in pizza but also has a varied menu, including a giant salad. It is owned and operated by Ricardo, a Brazilian, and his Canadian wife Carol.

The Mediterrane ($B) is an American grill, sushi, and teppan restaurant on Américo Vespucio Av. across from the new Caribbean Mall, close by Maremares.

Exploring and travel

Most por puestos travel along Av. 5 de Julio. We have marked the most important

Beach view of Chimana - Oscar Hernandez photo

por puesto stop. Peli Express Buses to Caracas leave from the bus station on the Intercomunal, near the pedestrian overpass and Yamaha dealer. They go to Parque del Este in Caracas. They are quite luxurious, with DVDs, but pack a sweater for the ferocious air-conditioning.

You can rent a car from Budget at the Gran Hotel Puerto la Cruz or call Budget in Lecherias (see our directory).

For inland and overseas travel, check out Keigla at Transpacific Travel and Services in Bahia Redonda. She speaks perfect English and French and will arrange airport transfers, organize trips to Merida, Angel Falls, Canaima, and any other trips around the country, or get you a ticket home.

It is also worth visiting the website of Jakera Tours (www.jakera.com), run by Chris Patterson from Scotland and his Venezuelan wife. Their main office has moved from Puerto la Cruz to Plaza Las Heroinas, Merida. They are worth knowing about as they do some fairly exotic trips into the far reaches of the jungle to meet and live with the Amazon Indians. As experienced jungle

travelers, they are well prepared, taking care to provide health precautions in the form of malaria, yellow fever, and anti-venom medications. They also have a special traveling classroom for students that takes them on a six-month exploration of the interior, providing invaluable cultural and physical experiences. Chris is also happy to provide information of a general nature.

If you happen to be in or near Marina El Morro, there is a super dinghy trip you can take a long way up the River Neveri. Enter where we indicate on the sketch chart and explore. You can go all the way to Barcelona on the river and be treated to views of wildlife including alligators, egrets, cormorants, herons, and parakeets. Arboleda, a restaurant on the river, makes a good destination. When you visit Barcelona, check out the old church and museum. For more information consult Patti at Xanadu.

Another point of interest around Puerto la Cruz is the remaining big lagoon on the east side of the new El Morro development. This is not a particularly beautiful lagoon, but the bird life here around sunset can be

El Morro view - Oscar Hernandez

Orient Canvas at work

spectacular. La Sirena waterfalls are set in a park about 40 minutes east of Puerto la Cruz. The park closes at 1600. The bus ride to Cumaná is delightfully scenic.

Barcelona is worth a visit for its historic value. One of the oldest towns in the area, founded in 1671, it is the capital of the state of Anzoategui. Plaza Boyoca has on one side the Cathedral, where the glass-encased remains of Saint Celestino and other venerated objects are to be found. The Museo de Anzoategui is housed in the restored and oldest building remaining in the town, which also borders the square. A couple of blocks away is the Ataneo de Barcelona, with a collection of Venezuelan paintings from the early 1900s. For more arts and crafts, check out the Galeria de Arte and Gunda Arte Popular.

Water Sports

Just on the other side of the headland from Marina Club Nautico El Morro is the Americo Vespucio sailing school, founded 18 years ago by Umberto Constanzo. He has been teaching youngsters not only how to sail, race, and maintain their boats, but how to do it exceptionally well. In 2000, one of his pupils, 29-year-old Eduardo Cordero, retook the title of World Sunfish Champion making him the only one to hold that title five times. And 17-year old Hector Vidal in 1996 brought home both the World Junior Sunfish and the North

Caribbean Mall

American Junior Sunfish titles. This enthusiastic group is also the heart of the annual yachting event called the SCOR (South Caribbean Ocean Regatta), a three-week event in June that races in Margarita and then moves on to Puerto la Cruz for more racing. This event is not only for serious racers, but special classes accommodate live-aboards, and one of the big benefits is free dockage for all participants during the whole event. So think about intermingling with your Venezuelan hosts, and learn to make that tub go a little faster while you prepare to wait out the hurricane season.

Diving here is rather special, as the rock formations around Puerto la Cruz are exceptionally dramatic.

There are three distinct island groups each a little different from the next: the Chimanas, Borrachas, and Caracas Islands, besides many smaller individual islands.

They are rich in flora and fauna. Soft and hard corals, more types of anemones than anywhere else in the world, sponges, many kinds of tube worms, a great variety and quantity of all reef fish, spotted morays, often large snappers and groupers, cleaner shrimp stations, large hermit crabs, occasionally a ray or turtle can be found.

One interesting dive is the Cathedral, which is located just outside the western headland of the anchorage in La Borracha. It is a cave with an entrance like a cathedral, some 40 feet tall. Inside are three chambers. In one of them there is a hole in the roof. If you time it to be there between noon and 1300, a shaft of sunlight comes through the hole and shines on the bottom of the cave. This gives the illusion that the bottom of the cave is actually the surface. This fools the fish, and they all swim upside down. If you shine a flashlight on the wall of the cave, the quartz in the rocks gives brilliant reflections. However, for the best reflections, go to the Manhattan cavern in Los Borrachitos. This is a dive for a maximum of three experienced divers. You step out of the boat over a rock wall and drop into a pool. You go straight down a well-like hole about 30 feet until a chamber opens out on one side. Inside the chamber, you must attach a chemical light to the wall so you can find your way out again. In the chamber, you turn on your light, and the reflections from the quartz rocks are both beautiful and dazzling. There are lots of sharp pinnacles that stick up from the bottom and down from the top, so you have to proceed with caution.

Those who have a horror of caves will prefer the Manta Wall Dive, around the corner from the Cathedral. This is a vertical wall some 90 feet deep with lots of soft corals and brightly colored Christmas tree and feather duster worms. There are many arrow crabs and small reef fish. At the bottom of the wall is a cavern that is used by thousands of baby fish, which hang out in a huge group. You can come up a slope beyond the wall if the current is not too strong. Here, you see a profusion of hard and soft corals

and angelfish. There is always a chance of seeing a manta ray.

The Twin Tunnels, or Cachua, is a dive that starts between two rocks near the southwest corner of El Borracho. You can see the tunnel going into the rock on the left. Swim through it (it is only about eight feet long). As you come to the far end, there is a great view of thousands of small fish clustered in the entrance. Follow the reef around to the right at 40 feet. There is an abundance of hard and soft corals and colorful reef fish. You finish by passing through another tunnel through the other rock and this brings you back to the boat.

There are several wrecks in the Borrachos. The *Galeon* a sailboat recently sunk at 30 meters, is already attracting big snappers, French angelfish, and Atlantic spadefish; at Cachua, there are two small sailboats; north of Chimana is a 40-year-old, dynamited cargo ship from the cement factory with mounds of square reef from the sacks of cement; and over in the Caracas islands is the skeleton of a 90-year-old steam boat.

Six submerged banks, or bajos as locals call them, play havoc for ships and sailing vessels but are great spots for diving.

Over near the Caracas Islands is a bubble dive, with bubbles and thermal waters the main attraction on a reef that is very

different form others in Mochima. Believe it or not, new species are still being found.

In Marina Puerto la Cruz, you will find Aquatic Adventures. It is run by Jenner Rodriguez and Gina Malpica, a nice lady from the U.S. who has been living in Venezuela for 35 years. They teach from discovery to instructor level. They also repair equipment, fills tank, and have a retail store. They have a 33-foot boat with new engines and know where to dive in the Mochima Park.

Explosub (VHF: 71) is on the beach in front of the Gran Hotel Turistico Puerto la Cruz and has its own dock. Vinicio Albanese is Venezuela's first instructor whose number is 001, and probably one of the most experienced. He speaks English, Italian, and French, fills bottles, and will take you on dives to a dozen locations between Puerto la Cruz and Mochima.

Horisub (VHF: 71) is located at Americo Vespucio Marina and is owned and run by Arturo Barrios, a welcoming Venezuelan who speaks English like an American, which he learned while he taught diving at Texas University. His is a full Padi shop that has two 30-foot dive boats. You can go diving and take resort or certification courses, and they sell dive gear and fill tanks as well as doing hydrotesting and maintenance.

Islas Píritu to Chichiriviche

AREA 6

Oscar Hernandez photo

Bahia Cato-Edo

Píritu to Chichiriviche

*I*slas de Píritu lie just 18 miles west of Puerto la Cruz. From here west are some lovely anchorages, but they are well spread apart. As usual, heading west is downwind and easy, returning is against the wind and harder, though not that hard. In this chapter we are only discussing the coastal route, which is fine both ways, but 60 to 100 miles offshore you also have Venezuela's offshore islands, and you can use these to vary your cruise. For example, if you are not that interested in the coast around La Guaira, you could sail from Carenero to Los Roques and then back to Puerto Cabello or Chichiriviche. We cover these offshore islands in the next chapter.

Of special interest in this area is Carenero, which has beautiful mangroves with good anchorages and dinghy exploration. And the Morrocoy National Park, which again has great anchorages amid mangroves. Both places have lots of bird life.

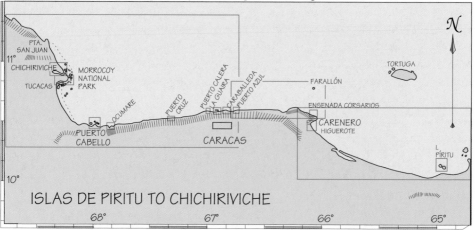

ISLAS DE PIRITU TO CHICHIRIVICHE

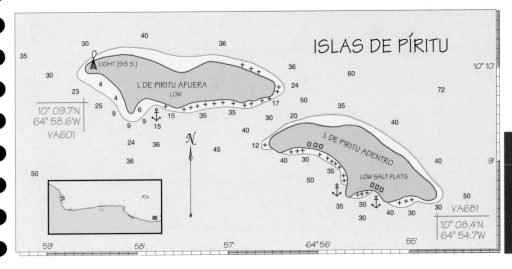

ISLAS DE PIRITU

These islands are good for a day away from it all on the beach, and an easy 12-mile day-sail from Puerto la Cruz. They are a handy stepping stone between Puerto la Cruz and Carenero, shortening the passage. It is also a comfortable day-sail from Píritu to Tortuga.

Islas de Píritu are very low and scrubby, with beaches that look delightful in bright sunlight. The islands are surrounded by reefs that make for acceptable snorkeling.

The easiest anchorage is in Isla de Píritu Afuera, in the area shown on our sketch chart. Approach from the south toward the eastern end of the bay, where the water is deepest. You will find a good anchoring area in 15 feet of water.

Anchoring in Isla de Píritu Adentro is more of a challenge. The water is usually too deep or too shallow for anchoring. There is an anchoring area in the southwestern bay in 30-40 feet of water, but getting the anchor to hold can be a problem.

A scenic alternative is to anchor bow or stern-to the sand spit at the eastern end of this bay, taking an anchor ashore. It is possible to do the same at the eastern end of the next bay.

Islas de Píritu, Afuera in the foreground

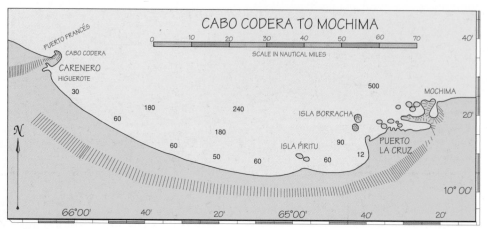

ISLAS DE PIRITU TO CARENERO

It is a 70-mile haul from Islas de Píritu to Carenero, and it is usually pleasant in either direction. The winds in the morning are often south through to west. By mid-afternoon they are often northeast and blow at their hardest. After dark, they tend to drop. If your boat is good in light airs, you can make it under sail. Otherwise, if you motor-sail well, you can probably do the 70-mile haul as a long day-trip.

You can also break your trip by visiting Tortuga (see the next chapter on Venezuela's offshore islands)

When you are sailing east from Carenero, Islas de Píritu are very low-lying and you cannot see them until you are about five miles away. Isla la Borracha will usually appear long before.

CARENERO

Carenero (The Carenage) is a large, well-protected harbor with many anchorages and mangrove channels. There is an impressive, three-mile dinghy passage all the way through to the town of Higuerote. Bird watching in this passage is always good, but is spectacular at dusk and dawn. You can anchor anywhere you like, but the most convenient anchorage is near the yacht club and Club Bahía de los Piratas.

As you approach this area, you will see both Higuerote and Carenero. The entrance is straightforward, though you do not want to go aground on Bajo La Crucesita, which is marked by a red buoy. This buoy is on the shoal and should be given a wide berth. There is also a four-foot shoal off Astillero de Higuerote, which is marked by a green buoy. People usually have problems when they are approaching from the east, so this is worth a special mention. As you round Cabo Codera and head south, the first buildings that you see will be those of Higuerote, which has several high-rises. Southwest of Cabo Codera are some tanks partly hidden in mangroves. Tankers lie off here and there are some moorings. It is best to go outside them all. At night, the area is demarcated by four buoys: two white flashing ones on the seaward (southeast) side and two red flashing ones on the landward (northwest) side. Stay well clear of them all. Carenero looks smaller than Higuerote, though it has a couple of high-rise buildings and you can see stacked boats from a fair way off. If you head for the white high-rise toward the right hand side of the building group on a bearing of 310° magnetic, this will bring you to the edge of Bajo La Crucesita (Small Cross Shoal). When you get near Pta. La Crucesita, go southwest of our bearing to avoid this bank, then, before you get to Astillero de Higuerote, head back over to the east side of the channel to avoid the four-foot shoal, which is harder to see.

The area includes two separate harbors, Carenero and Bahía La Buche.

General yacht services

There are two fuel docks where you

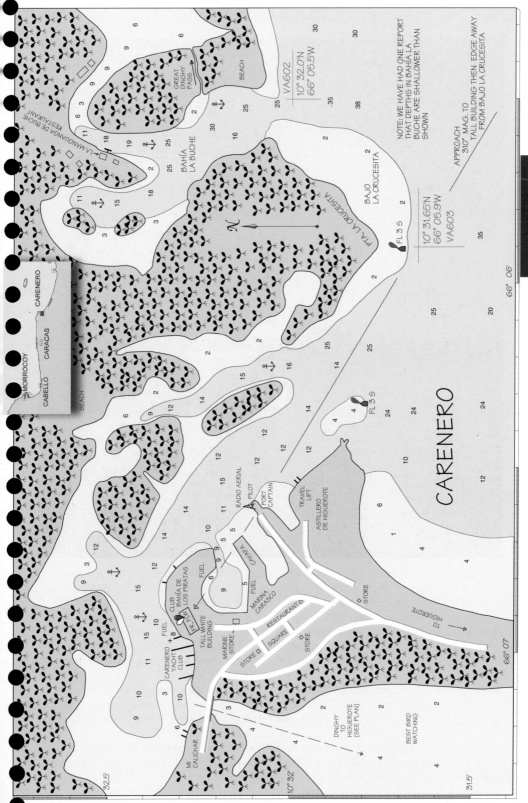

CARENERO

BAHÍA LA BUCHE

PTA. LA CRUCESITA

BAJO LA CRUCESITA

LA MANGNANAGA DE BUCHE RESTAURANT

GREAT DINGHY PASS

BEACH

NOTE: WE HAVE HAD ONE REPORT THAT DEPTHS IN BAHÍA LA BUCHE ARE SHALLOWER THAN SHOWN

APPROACH 310° MAG. TO TALL BUILDING THEN EDGE AWAY FROM BAJO LA CRUCESITA

10° 32.0'N
66° 05.5'W
VA602

10° 31.65'N
66° 05.9'W
VA603

FL 3 S

FL 3 S

RADIO AERIAL

PILOT

PORT CAPTAIN

TRAVEL LIFT

ASTILLERO DE HIGUEROTE

STORE

TO HIGUEROTE

DINGHY TO HIGUEROTE (SEE PLAN)

BEST BIRD WATCHING

MI CALICHAR

BAHÍA DE LOS PIRATAS

FUEL

FUEL

CALETA

FUEL

MARINA CARASCO

RESTAURANT

SQUARE

STORE

STORE

MARINE STORE

CARENERO YACHT CLUB

CLUB

TALL WHITE BUILDING

FL R

FL R

MORROCOY
CABELLO
CARACAS
CARENERO
CARACAS
BEACH

10° 32'
'32.5'
'31.5'

66° 06'

66° 07'

197

can also get ice. The deepest is the Carenero Yacht Club. There is about eight feet up to the dock. Unfortunately, there is an obstruction very close to the end of the dock. If the wind is blowing strongly from the east, it may be easiest to anchor and come stern-to the dock on its east side toward the outer end. It is open Monday 0800 to 1330, other weekdays 0800-1530, weekends 0800-1730.

The Caranero Yacht Club (0234 323-1624/0234 323-1363) is undergoing significant expansion, with new floating docks for up to 260 boats and a good restaurant and other facilities ashore. Hopefully, it will be possible to get dockage here. If not, you might be able to anchor really close to have a

little security at night. The deepest approach is close by the Carenero Yacht Club. Talk to M. Doris.

If you draw less than six feet, you can make it into the fuel dock at Club Bahía de Los Piratas. You have to enter almost touching the stones on the north side of the channel. There is about nine feet into the basin, but the fuel dock only has about six feet.

There are two slipping facilities. Mi Calichar VHF: 16 is a small yard on the west side of the bridge. Their hoist takes 25 tons, and they are happy to fix your boat or let you do the work yourself. They specialize in antifouling jobs and repairing fiberglass. The limiting factor is depth, and they can haul a maximum of 6.5 feet at high water.

Astillero de Higuerote is a much bigger yard with a 60-ton marine hoist. The head office is in Caracas. It is about eight feet deep in the approach dock. The dock is reported to be 22 feet wide, but it looks narrower. They are not really used to working on sailing yachts, so I would leave this one for an emergency.

Ashore

There is no public access ashore, as all the waterfront is private. However, the guards will let you go ashore at Cavafa and probably also Club Bahía de Los Piratas, if you look smart. Try also the yacht club. Failing that, you can tie to the dock ruins inside the pilot boat station. This is also where the port captain works, but you probably will not need to see him, because Carenero is not a port of entry and you have to clear in somewhere else. If you have the correct clearance, you do not need to check with anyone.

The town has become livelier since a big new road from Caracas makes this whole area accessible, and you will find restaurants and shops.

Club Bahía de Los Piratas (VHF: 70, $C-D) has a good restaurant with strong air-conditioning for the heat of the day. You can tie your dinghy right outside.

Ashore at Higuerote

For more extensive shopping, you have to visit Higuerote. Buses run frequently from near the town square, but the dinghy trip is more fun. Access to the canal is under the bridge. The current under the bridge can go either way and is usually strong. You cross the first bay and go straight down the canal. After a while you will start to see lovely homes along the water's edge. To get access to the town, take the last turn on the left, just before the end of the canal. Hang a right and follow round into a circular area. Here you will find one or two paths that lead to the road from the water between the houses. The mangrove tree we used to lock our dinghy to may still be there. If you see anyone, you can ask permission.

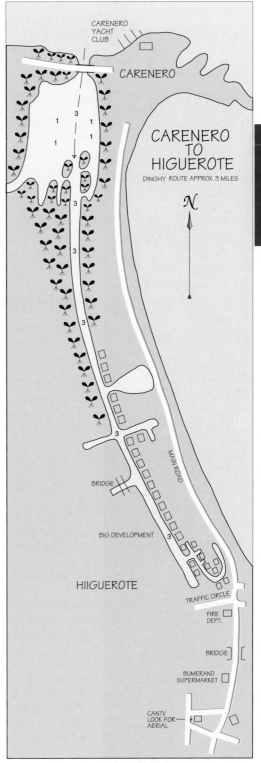

CARENERO YACHT CLUB

CARENERO

CARENERO TO HIGUEROTE

DINGHY ROUTE APPROX. 3 MILES

N

MAIN ROAD

BRIDGE

BIG DEVELOPMENT

HIIGUEROTE

TRAFFIC CIRCLE

FIRE DEPT.

BRIDGE

BUMERAND SUPERMARKET

CANTV LOOK FOR AERIAL

Any path will bring you to the big main road and a traffic circle. (See our plan.) It is about a quarter of a mile down the road to the beginning of the main drag. Here you will find good bakers, butchers, green-grocers and Bumerand Supermarket which opens daily 0800-1900, except Sundays, when it closes at noon. If you need to make a phone call, there is a Cantv, which is open daily 0800-1930.

While in Carenero, don't miss the evening bird show under the bridge in the first lagoon. For the evening performance, go about an hour before sunset and anchor toward the east side about halfway down. (If you go too close to the mangroves, the birds will avoid your spot.) Take cushions, bug spray, binoculars, cocktails, and snacks and wait for all the birds to come in. All manner of herons, cormorants, pelicans, and parrots are the supporting cast for the scarlet ibis, prima Donna of the mangroves. If you are a parrot fan, the early morning show may be better. Hundreds of parrots wake up and squawk to each other before they take off for the day's foraging. When a big flock clears out of a tree, it is like a parrot explosion.

BAHIA LA BUCHE

The entrance to this harbor is about half a mile to the east of the entrance to Carenero. If you are coming from Carenero, you have to pass outside the Bajo la Crucesita.

There are shoals on both sides of the entrance to Bahía La Buche, but in between, the water is 25 feet deep. The breeziest and most pleasant anchorage is right off the beach as you enter. In really bad weather you might want to go deeper into the mangroves up either channel.

Ashore

This is a lovely and well-protected bay in which to anchor and relax. There is great dinghy exploration through all the mangrove channels. The narrow dinghy pass just north of the beach is overhung with mangrove trees. Follow it down until it comes out in a bay almost a mile wide on the other side. The inland lagoons heat up during the day and make for good, warm bathing in the afternoon. Fishing is good, as is the evening bird show, with many herons, parrots, doves, various land birds, cormorants, frigates, pelicans, and a few scarlet ibis flying over. While not as spectacular as in the Carenero-Higuerote dinghy passage, here you can sit and enjoy it from the comfort of your yacht.

On the north central part of the bay, there is a landing ramp, some campers, smart holiday houses, a small first-aid station, and La Manguangua de Buche Restaurant ($D). This pleasant and friendly place is open every day from 0900 to dinner. They serve excellent calamares rebozados and paella. There are also several huts on the beach that serve food on the weekends or whenever there are enough people.

Birds in the Higuerote channel

CARENERO TO PUERTO FRANCES

Puerto Francés is only about five miles from Carenero and makes a change of scene. It is also a good stopping place on your way east or west. Between Carenero and Puerto Francés are some oil tanks along with tanker buoys, and often tankers are anchored out. Give all these a wide berth.

PUERTO FRANCES

Puerto Francés is also known as Ensenada de Corsarios. It was given these names because it was used by French pirates in the olden days.

It is a well-protected bay in all normal conditions. If you are approaching from the east, Cabo Codera has no off-lying shoals, and you can pass around the headland a couple of hundred yards off. If you are approaching from the west, you will notice a small island with a house on it about two miles before the headland. Give this a good clearance, as rocks come a long way out beyond it. The rest of this coast is also rocky and best given a quarter of a mile clearance.

As you approach Cabo Codera, you will see two beaches. The main beach is accessible by road and has lifeguard lookout towers. On weekends, it is full of visitors. For the rest of the week, it is left to a few fishermen. The swells come in around the corner and find their way to this beach, so you want to anchor farther north, anywhere between the small beach and the headland. You can carry 16 feet fairly close to the beach. There are a few rocks close to shore, especially near the tiny beach, but these are closer to shore than most sane people would anchor. You can find good anchorage 100 yards off the cliffs, between the beach and the headland, in about 25-35 feet of water. Fishermen have huts on the beach and keep boats anchored here. On weekends this anchorage is full of powerboats from Carenero. On the summit of Cabo Codera is a light structure that flashes every six seconds and radio masts with fixed red lights.

The water here can be refreshingly chilly. The snorkeling is mixed with some good parts and some barren rock and pebbles. The beaches are fine for a visit. The only one with road access is the main beach, and there are no restaurants or facilities.

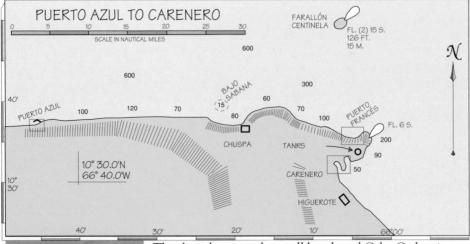

PUERTO AZUL TO CARENERO

SCALE IN NAUTICAL MILES

FARALLÓN
CENTINELA
FL. (2) 15 S.
126 FT.
15 M.

10° 30.0'N
66° 40.0'W

PUERTO AZUL

BAJO
SABANA

CHUSPA   TANKS

PUERTO
FRANCES
FL. 6 S.

CARENERO

HIGUEROTE

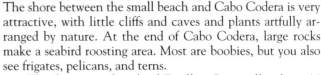

The shore between the small beach and Cabo Codera is very attractive, with little cliffs and caves and plants artfully arranged by nature. At the end of Cabo Codera, large rocks make a seabird roosting area. Most are boobies, but you also see frigates, pelicans, and terns.

The diving on the island Farallon Centinella, about 14 miles north of Puerto Frances, is said to be superb.

PUERTO FRANCES TO PUERTO AZUL

It is about 41 miles from Puerto Francés to Puerto Azul, which makes a good day's sail. If you are heading east from Puerto Azul to Puerto Francés and you want to motor-sail, you are likely to get the calmest seas by leaving around midnight.

Avoid Bajo Sabana in the middle of Bahía Chuspa, even though the charts say it has 15 feet over it. Best stay outside it if you are sailing by night. In good light, the adventurous can eyeball their way inside.

After Chuspa, as you head west, the mountains start to recede behind the coast and there are smaller hills along the water's edge.

To get a better angle to the wind in either direction, you can sail out to Los Roques and back in again. This takes you much farther, but if you are ready for a few extra days in Los Roques, why not?

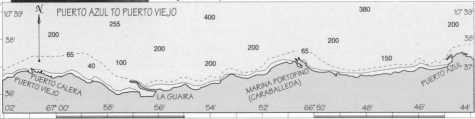

PUERTO AZUL TO PUERTO VIEJO

PUERTO CALERA
PUERTO VIEJO

LA GUAIRA

MARINA PORTOFINO
(CARABALLEDA)

PUERTO AZUL

MARINAS AREA

The 20-mile stretch from Puerto Azul to Puerto Viejo is as close as the coast gets to Caracas and so is a popular marina area. It is also somewhat of a tourist area and famous for sport fishing.

There were massive floods here in '99, as well as some looting. This has left much of the surrounding land in bad shape, but most marinas are fine, and they have heavy security.

We had reports then that there were major changes to the coastline from around Puerto Azul through to La Guaira. Now my information is that navigation has not really been affected. However, I advise caution when navigating this part of the coast. At night, stay a mile or two offshore. Approach the coast by day, when you can see what you are doing.

New rules have come on line for fuel for visitors. Since no one here seems to understand them, this has made taking on fuel sometimes difficult. It depends a lot on the man at the fuel pump.

PUERTO AZUL

Puerto Azul (VHF: 16) is a magnificent and very large private club run by Commodore Anibal Abate. Foreign flag yachts are not welcome inside but there is a perfectly adequate anchorage just outside. The

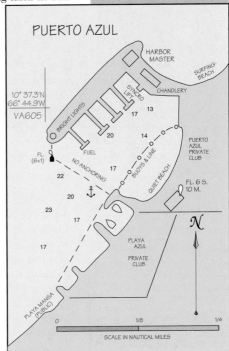

203

10° 37.4'N
66° 50.9'W
VA606 50   120

50

25   16
TRAVELIFT & FUEL   MARINA   OFFICE
                13 11
+ + + +   9
        BIG APT.   BATHING
        BLOCK   SEA
                12   BARRIER

REMOMAR CHANDERLY &
CARABALLEDA GOLF
YACHT CLUB

𝒩   SHOPS, RESTAURANTS

0   1/4   1/2

SCALE IN NAUTICAL MILES

MARINA DE CARABALLEDA

Bird's-eye view of Marina
de Caraballeda

MORROCOY
                    CARENERO
CABELLO   CARACAS

anchoring limitation line runs from the entrance buoy to the small breakwater on the opposite side. The calmest place is right up to the line on the shore side. When you have got your bow anchor holding, put out a stern anchor as the wind switches around. Make sure you do not block the entrance to the small Playa Azul Marina. For security, you want to be anchored very close to the marina boundary.

There is a light flashing every six seconds on top of an apartment block in Puerto Azul. It is about 100 feet high, and the range is over 10 miles.

Services

The fuel dock in Puerto Azul is open to the public and open daily from 0800-1600. (New regulations permitting.) Puerto Azul has an 85-ton marine hoist for their own members only.

Ashore

While this is a good place to stop for the night, getting ashore presents some difficulties. The only public access is Playa Mansa, which is stony and surfy and probably best left to ex-navy Seals.

If you desperately need a new battery or some boat part, there is a good chandlery called Shop Puerto Azul in the marina. Dinghy in and plead your case with a guard. He will probably try to help. They also have a sail repair shop and other facilities ashore. However, all facilities belong to the club and are for club members only. Whether they are willing to offer you any assistance depends entirely on the staff. You will meet the patrolling guards first, and if you need to talk to anyone else, ask to speak to the Commodore.

MARINA DE CARABALLEDA

Marina de Caraballeda, seven miles west of Puerto Azul, can make a good base if you want to visit Caracas, collect people from the airport, or spend time in this area. This marina is suffering from neglect and has been generally very run down. It is currently closed but about to reopen "just now." (If I hear it has opened, I will post it on www.doyleguides.com.)

Just because it is closed does not mean there are no boats here, and in a squeeze you can get fair protection anchored just outside with protection from the seawall.

They have a fuel dock and an 80-ton marine hoist, which is used more for hauling powerboats than sailing craft, though they can manage the latter. Advance arrangements would be advisable.

Marina de Caraballeda

Haulout

Chandlery

Just west of Caraballeda is a deep and well-protected lagoon inside of which is the Caraballeda Golf Yacht Club. This is a fancy and well-maintained marina, but they have no interest in visiting boats. Just in case you have to go in here for some reason, take care going down the first part of the channel by the big apartment block. There is a shoal on the west side of the channel under the apartment. Stay to the east side until you pass the shoal and then stay in the center. There is about nine feet in the deep part of the channel near the shoal. After that the channel deepens to about 12 feet.

The main interest of this yacht club is that they have a good Remomar chandlery, which is open to the public.

Oscar Hernadez photos

Technical yacht services

If you need any work done, you will find good carpenters, namely, Henry Rojas and Johnny Rivero (tel: 0414 250-7809), and a good fiberglass man, Hector Echarrys (tel: 0414 559-0486) in the Caraballeda Marina.

Water sports

The marina is home to Epsilondive diving school, which has sunk several ships and a helicopter to create some interesting dives nearby. You could contact them for any recent information on the marina (0212 993-6081).

The marina is also home to a sailing school.

Dive shop

Ashore

If the marina is open and you manage to get a place, this is a good place from which to visit Caracas. It is about an hour's

Punta Calera

drive away. Taxis are not exorbitant, and buses run from right outside the marina.

Otherwise, you are within walking distance of a shopping area with small supermarkets and restaurants. There is also a bar in the marina.

There is a very good restaurant serving excellent Spanish seafood (speciality caserola de mariscos) in the Hotel Posada Hidalgo. You will need a taxi to get there; it about a 10-minute drive to the west in the direction of the airport.

LA GUAIRA

La Guaira lies just a few miles west of Caraballeda. It is a big commercial port, the main port in Venezuela. It has no facilities for yachts, and I can think of no good reason, except inclement weather, for a yachtsperson to come in here. We include a rough sketch chart in case you do need to enter. Tie up to the fishing fleet. Watch out for the high-speed Margarita ferries: they will pay no attention to yachts and care nothing about wakes.

If you do end up here, the area is not without interest. It has a big market with a famous place to eat local fresh food "El Mosquero" (The Flies). You can see handsome colonial houses, a cathedral dating from 1857, and some forts, including Casa Guipuzcoana, built in 1734. There are plenty of taxis and buses to Caracas.

If you make it to Caracas, check out the big El Capitan chandlery, fishing, and

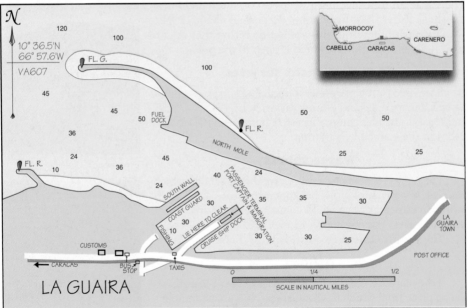

LA GUAIRA

marine store.

Puerto Calera and Puerto Viejo are two more marinas just a few miles west of La Guaira; after this you are back into long hops between anchorages.

PUNTA CALERA

Punta Calera is the home of Playa Grande Yacthing (sic) Club (VHF: 71). This is a private yacht club. Foreign yachts are currently welcome for short visits (up to three days). There is room to anchor in the northeast corner. While you would not be given permission to anchor here, if you did so in really bad weather, it is unlikely anyone would stop you. At the last update, fuel was not available to visiting yachts, but this may change. This is a fancy marina and visiting yachts are charged accordingly (about 3$US per foot per day). They have a 30-ton marine hoist, but it is mainly for their own members.

This port is clean and pleasant and you will find a restaurant and showers ashore. The restaurant sells ice, and the marina office will call a taxi if you wish to go shopping. Captain Gustavo Villamizar is the Commodore and man in charge.

Not far from the marina is a good pizzeria called Il Prezzano.

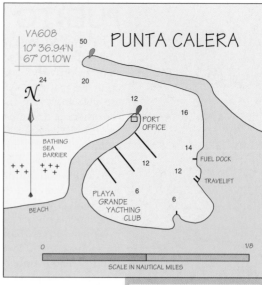

207

PUERTO VIEJO

Puerto Viejo is about quarter of a mile west of Puerto Calera. It is part of Puerto Viejo Resort, a five-star hotel. They stand by on VHF: 68 /16 and SSB: 21820 When you are tied up in the marina you are treated like a guest in the hotel and are welcome to use the three swimming pools, along with all the other hotel facilities. The docks have water and electricity, and the marina has plenty of security. Should you not be getting along with your companions, they have bathrooms for both owners and crew. The marina takes 67 boats and includes a fuel dock with both diesel and gasoline (whether you can buy it will depend on current regulations). They also store about 800 small powerboats ashore in sheds. Foreign-flag yachts are welcomed. This is a fancy marina, and while not inexpensive, it is priced lower than Punta Calera, at about 100$US a day for yachts over 50 feet and about $40 for those up to 50 feet. Puerto Viejo mainly caters to large power yachts, but sailing yachts are welcome.

Navigation

This marina can be hard to enter when swells are running. The plan I give is taken from a satellite photo, and our information was based on a recent land visit, but we have done no surveying here. The information I have is that there is a shoal in the middle and the best approach is towards the west, where the depths are 7-10 feet. However, since we have not surveyed this one, I suggest you approach slowly with your eye on the echo sounder.

Ashore

If you have a Beneteau with problems, Ricardo D'Andrea is the agent and is based in the marina.

You will find several restaurants just outside the marina; the best one is El Meson del Faro, which is one block to the east from the marina entrance. They serve good fish and paella in an informal atmosphere (you could make it in shorts), but do at least wear a sports shirt.

VA609
10° 36.84'N
67° 01.88'W

PUERTO VIEJO

20

SEE GUIDE FOR INFORMATION

N

0   1/8

SCALE IN NAUTICAL MILES

FROM PUERTO AZUL TO PUERTO CABELLO

It is about 60 miles from Puerto Calera to Puerto Cabello, the next large stopping place. This is not a big deal when heading west, but for those who have sailed from the Windwards or Trinidad and have to return, this is the time you start to pay your dues. It is not too bad, as there are a couple of little stopping places along the way.

After Puerto Cabello, Bahía Cata makes a good takeoff point. If you leave Bahía Cata at first light, you probably can make Bahía Puerto Cruz before the wind gets too strong. From here it is also possible to day-sail to Puerto Calera or Caraballeda.

The land from Calera to Bahía Cata is rugged, with dramatic mountains and steep valleys rising from the water's edge. There are many beaches and cliffs. Two antennae and a light make Morro Choroní a good landmark. It also has a beach and a few houses. Civilization continues about five miles west of Calera before it peters out into wild country.

Along the civilized part, a skirt of flatter land lies along the coast, while the mountains just behind get even higher and more spectacular. As you head west from Calera, you soon pass Catia La Mar with some big tanks ashore, a long dock and several big buoys. A little after that is a large, conspicuous power station. These make good landmarks when you are coming from the east and looking for Calera. If you are hugging the coast pretty close, both Calera and Caraballeda stand out as distinctive headlands.

For those going the other way, the westwards trip is an easy passage down both wind and sea. However, it should be noted that westward sailing is much better by Los Roques and Las Aves.

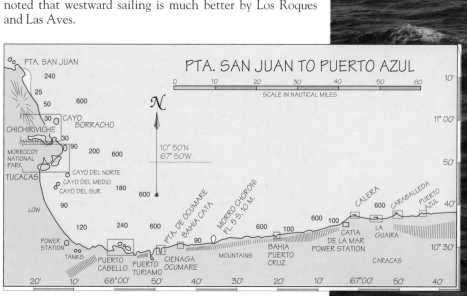

Bahía Cata

BAHIA PUERTO CRUZ

Bahía Puerto Cruz is a little bay conveniently placed about halfway between Caraballeda and Puerto Cabello. From close to the coast, the entrance stands out as a distinctive headland.

It is a beautiful bay with steep hills on both sides and a lush, narrow valley leading into peaky hills and mountains behind. At the head of the bay is a white sand beach backed by palm trees.

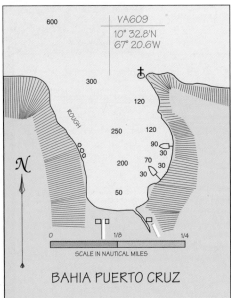

VA609
10° 32.8'N
67° 20.6'W

SCALE IN NAUTICAL MILES

BAHIA PUERTO CRUZ

However, it is a tricky anchorage, usually a bit rolly and untenable much of the winter. If you plan to use this on your way east, have a backup plan in case it doesn't work out. There are crosses on two of the rocks that help identify it, and it is the only bay in this area that looks protected enough to be an anchorage.

The problem with Bahía Puerto Cruz is that the water in the middle of the bay is 240 feet deep, and it stays deep almost until the rocks. The only way to anchor is stern-to the shore, and the best anchoring area (shown on our sketch chart) is not very large. As you come in, the water shelves abruptly from about 70 feet to about 40 feet. You need to drop your anchor over the deep ledge and take a stern anchor into the shallows by dinghy. Taking a line ashore is probably not feasible, as landing a dinghy on the rocks among the waves could be dangerous.

If you come in the rainy season and the river is running fast, it will create a current in the middle of the bay.

Bahía Puerto Cruz was once a coffee estate. There is a stately old road lined with large mahogany trees that leads back to the main village. In the village are a couple of small shops where you can get essentials.

You can return along the other side of the cool-looking river. Many fishing boats are anchored off the beach. The large pipes that go over the hills carry water to La Guaira.

BAHIA CATA

Bahía Cata lies about 23 miles west of Bahía Puerto Cruz. It offers a good, but not totally calm, anchorage up in the eastern corner of the bay, behind the protective island and rocks. In heavy northerly winds and swells, this anchorage could be untenable. However, it is only five miles east of Ciénaga de Ocumare, so if you come with enough time, you can decide whether to stay. It is an easy anchorage with plenty of room to anchor in depths of 16-35 feet over sand and weed. If you want to leave at night, it is an easy exit. (The next port, Ciénaga de Ocumare, could be hard to leave at night.)

The main beach is a popular but surgy holiday beach. There are two tall high-rise buildings which make it easy to identify the bay. There is also a pretty beach on the east shore right ahead of the anchorage.

CIENAGA DE OCUMARE

Ciénaga de Ocumare is about five miles west of Bahía Cata. On the way you pass the town of Independencia. There is a protected eastern corner of this bay, but it is marginal as an anchorage.

Ciénaga de Ocumare is a deep, well-protected bay surrounded by mangroves and steep hills. It is the first really protected anchorage after the marinas near La Guaira. (Puerto Turiamo is military and closed to yachts.)

Ashore you can hear many birds, including cristofues (the Spanish name for the cocrico). At night there are hundreds of mosquitoes. Bats come and try to keep them down, but they do a poor job, and it is best to put up nets or plan on burning a coil. Ashore there are several holiday homes. There is no road, only a two-and-a-half-hour trail to the next village. The people who stay here come by boat. The bay is also used by fishermen from nearby villages. Ciénaga de Ocumare comes under the control of the military, but normally they have no objection to yachts anchoring here.

Although the bay is big, much of it is taken up by a reef and shallows. Enter down the channel and watch out for the reef on the west side of the entrance. The water is 50 feet deep until you get toward the southern end of the bay, where

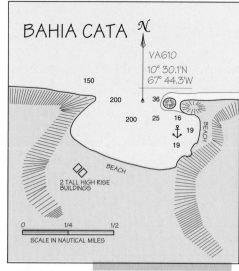

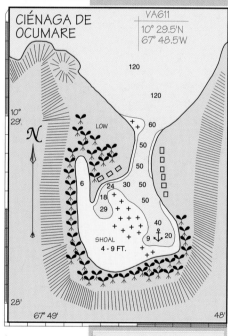

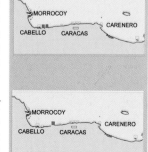

Piritu to Chichiriviche

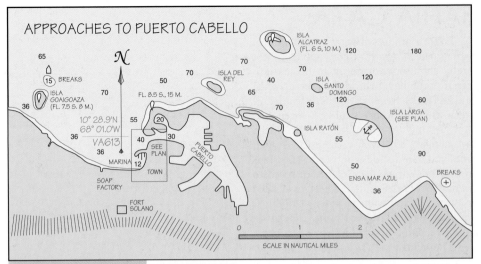

APPROACHES TO PUERTO CABELLO

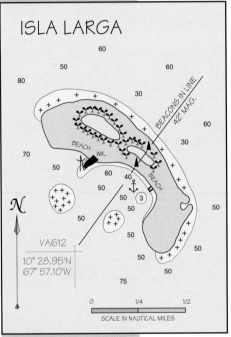

ISLA LARGA

you can find anchoring depths of 10-25 feet before running aground.

There is a very narrow, deep-water passage on the north side of the reef, but the area is a bit small for anchoring. Shoal-draft boats could get back there and anchor. The whole area makes for good dinghy exploration.

ISLA LARGA

Isla Larga lies just off Puerto Cabello, and it is the only one of Puerto Cabello's alluring islands that is open to visitors. The rest are reserved for the military. It is a delightful place to spend a few days. Boats do bring tourists here from the mainland, but holidays and weekends are the only really busy times. Isla Larga has a bay, which is well protected from the normal winds and swells. The easiest way to approach is by lining up the two beacons, which brings you right between the reefs. The reefs are all quite easy to see. There is a conspicuous wreck of an old World War II ship whose mast shows almost before the beacons.

Most of the sand bottom is about 50 feet deep. You need lots of anchoring line, and resist the temptation to anchor in any small, 35-foot patches, as they are probably coral. An alternative is to anchor bow-to the beach, using one anchor in the shallows and a stern anchor to hold you off. This is OK, but you have to find a place to do it where your line will not be chewing up the fringing reef, which is popular with snorkelers.

The snorkeling here is good, both on the reefs and the wreck. Ashore there are pristine beaches.

PUERTO CABELLO

Puerto Cabello is a charming and pleasant town and a good place to stay for awhile. The area around Paseo El Malecón is especially attractive, with well-restored old buildings. Many historic buildings and churches have been renovated. Most of these are within a short walking distance from the marina. Puerto Cabello seems to have come up in the world in the last four years, it feels both clean and vibrant, yet it is less expensive than a lot of other places. Very shortly the new ferry terminal should be completed, offering service to places like Margarita, Bonaire, and Curacao.

Puerto Cabello is a major port and the largest natural harbor in Venezuela. It is said that the name Cabello (One Hair) was given because it was so well protected and secure, you would only have to secure your ship with a single hair to make it safe. Unfortunately, this huge natural harbor has been taken over by the Venezuelan navy, so yachts are not allowed to anchor inside.

Puerto Cabello is also only 40 minutes away from the major town of Valencia and about three hours from Caracas by car.

The main drag in town for shops and restaurants is Avenida Bolívar. Puerto Cabello is a major commercial port and a good place to provision and get things fixed.

Carolos Alvarez,
- Oscar Hernandez photos

213

Puerto Cabello from above. The marina is clearly visible

Navigation

If you are approaching from the east, you can choose a path between the four islands just east of the harbor. Isla Larga, we have just described, you may not land on the others which are used by the military.

When approaching from the west, avoid the breaking shoal just north of Isla Goaigoaza, which is buoyed. The big, semicircular buildings you see to the west of Puerto Cabello are part of a soap factory.

Regulations

Puerto Cabello is a port of entry, and the bureaucracy has not improved with the town. The present port captain wants you to go into the marina. Then you can contact Carlos Alvarez (VHF: 71, 0414 343-2545/0242 361-6466) to do the paperwork for you, as he understands just what the officials want. It can take time.

General yacht services

Marina Puerto Cabello (VHF: 71) is the best place to be while you visit Puerto Cabello. They do not have much spare room, but they usually manage to fit everyone in. Carlos Alvarez is the Commodore and they welcome visiting yachts, but please keep in mind that it is a private club, not a commercial establishment where you can demand services. Water and electricity (110/220-volt 60-cycles) are available on the dock. They have showers, ice, security, diesel, and gasoline, as well as a restaurant and boutique and a helpful staff. They average about 15 visiting yachts a month and would be happy to see a few more.

You do need to use the marina; the anchorage between

214

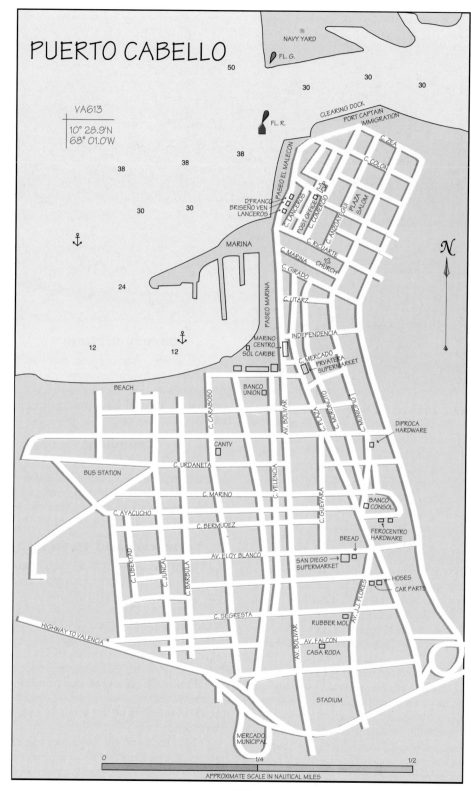

PUERTO CABELLO

50

VA613

10° 28.9'N
68° 01.0'W

NAVY YARD

FL. G.

30

30   30

FL. R.

CLEARING DOCK
PORT CAPTAIN
IMMIGRATION

C. ZEA

C. COLON

38   38   38

38

30   30

D'FRANCO
BRISEÑO VEN
LANCEROS

PASEO EL MALECON

C. LANCEROS
POST OFFICE
C. COMERCIO

C. ANZATEGUI
PLAZA
SALOM

MARINA

C. RICUARTE

C. MARINA
CHURCH

C. GIRADO

24

C. UTARZ

PASEO MARINA

INDEPENDENCIA

12

MARINO
CENTRO
SOL CARIBE

C. MERCADO
PRVATERA
SUPERMARKET

12

BEACH

BANCO
UNION

C. CARABOBO

AV. BOLIVAR

C. PLAZA

C. MORONCITO

C. MUNICIPIO

DIPROCA
HARDWARE

CANTV

BUS STATION

C. URDANETA

C. VELENCIA

C. MARINO

C. GUEVARA

BANCO
CONSOL.

C. AYACUCHO

C. BERMUDEZ

FEROCENTRO
HARDWARE

BREAD

C. LIBERTAD

C. JUNCAL

C. BARBULA

AV. ELOY BLANCO

SAN DIEGO
SUPERMARKET

HOSES
CAR PARTS

AV. J.J. FLORES

C. SEGRESTA

RUBBER MOL

HIGHWAY TO VALENCIA

AV. BOLIVAR

AV. FALCON
CASA RODA

STADIUM

MERCADO
MUNICIPAL

0   1/4   1/2

APPROXIMATE SCALE IN NAUTICAL MILES

N

Piritu to Chichiriviche

Oscar Hernandez photos

the marina and the beach is a very bad area for thefts, especially at night. There are also some security issues ashore, but mainly if you visit red-light areas at night. If you have to wait for room in the marina, I would ask the marina staff about anchoring in front of the marina by day and going to Isla Larga for the night.

Carlos Alvarez (VHF: 71), speaks English and does all the paperwork for yachts. Carlos is good at sourcing anything you may need at a reasonable price and is happy to arrange tours for you in the surrounding countryside. In this he is helped by his wife Maritza Rodriguez, who has been very helpful for women needing advice on laundries, hairdressing, etc. Carlos's daughter, Amibis Alvarez, will look after pets if you wish to leave your boat and go travelling for a while.

Ucocar is a company that will haul and repair boats in the navy yard. They use a 300-ton railway. They are geared more to commercial vessels and will probably not be economical for small cruisers, but they might be a great deal for super-yachts. Talk to Carlos about them.

Communications

The marina does not yet have wifi. In front of the marina entrance towards Banco Mercantil is an internet cafe, which is very reasonable and will also arrange international calls.

Chandlery

Puerto Cabello is a big shipping port, so there are lots of stores catering to the marine industry, allbeit that many of them are geared to ships rather than yachts. Radio Marine is the first one you should check out.

Technical yacht services

There are lots of places to buy gear or get things fixed. Start by asking Carlos. Some of the businesses that used to be here have moved to Valencia. These include Electrotecnio for electrics and Catelmar Representaciones for electronics.

Taller Henriques, in Av. Bolivar de Rancho Grande, beside the medical college, can fix refrigeration and air-conditioning.

Puerto Filter, owned by Sr. Custodio, has every kind of air or water filter you might need.

There are excellent hardware stores all over town, including Ferreteria Erro-centro, with fastenings, tools, and an excellent stock of electrical fittings.

Diproca not only sells hardware but also keeps a good stock of oil and fuel filters, pumps, etc.

Mangueras Oporto is one of several stores specializing in hoses of many types, including all hydraulic hoses, and their fittings. Rubber Mol is another. Casa Roda specializes in all kinds of belts, hoses and seals.

Mr. Benitos (0414 481-6372) fixes outboards. Contact him by phone or through the marina.

Provisioning

Shopping is easily done at Privitera (weekdays 0800-1230 and 1430-1930, Saturdays 0700-2000, Sundays 0800-1200). Privitera is big, close, and well stocked. You can arrange a taxi to get your shopping back. San Diego Supermarket is another supermarket. You will also want to check out Hyper Market at the end of C. Udraneta, close to McDonalds and Puerto Filter.

There are bread shops all over town, including one opposite Marino Centro. Calle Mercado has lots of stalls selling fresh fruits and vegetables. For large orders of beer and soft drinks, talk to any liquor store near Marino Centro. Most will deliver to the dock.

Restaurants

The marina's Cocobay Restaurant is a good place to start: it is open on one side and has air-conditioning on the other. They have a great view of the marina and ships arriving and leaving. It is not cheap, but they serve good international and local food. The staff is nice, and it is very clean. Their main dishes are fish, pasta, and excellent Venezuelan breakfasts.

Armando and Chicho are owners of a boat in the marina, they also have a lovely restored Colonial house dating back to 1780. They speak perfect English, Portuguese, and French and serve dinner by reservation. They are also very helpful and friendly. Talk to them in the marina or call (0412-719-0598).

Right near the marina, Biseño Ven ($D) is an excellent Venezuelan restaurant specializing in local food. Lunch (1000-1430) is the big meal, and they have a wide choice. In the evening (1700-2130), they serve only arepas (the very best) with various fillings.

Notes on heading back east from Puerto Cabello

From Puerto Cabello to Carenero, the average wind is fairly light and usually comes from an easterly direction. It is often strongest from mid-morning to late evening and light and variable from late evening to mid-morning. "Often" does not mean "always," and the wind can blow hard against you day and night. It can also be calm day and night and you can even have light westerly winds for some days. The weather is also affected by fronts that come through. In the winter, when the winds are stronger and the swells larger, the trip will be tougher than in the spring or summer.

People generally make their way east within a few miles of the coast to keep out of the west-setting current. Sometimes you get a weak counter-current in your favor. The coast is steep-to and if you go by day and keep a lookout, you can stay within about half a mile.

Many people prefer to motor when the wind is light. It should be noted that a lack of wind does not mean there is no sea. Sometimes this coast is like a lake; at others, it seems that all those seas you saw out there in the outer islands have come home to roost here, resulting in large and confused swells. If you plan your trip using any of the marginal anchorages we describe, you should have a backup plan to push on should the anchorage prove difficult. Remember, too, if you like long sails, you can always make long tacks out to the offshore islands.

Piritu to Chichiriviche

D'Franco is Italian-owned and serves good pizzas and pasta.

El Bodegon de Antonio ($C) on the corner of C. Sucre and C. Barbula (about a five-block walk) is a local restaurant (the sign just says restaurant). Antonio, the owner, is Spanish and the food is very good.

The Delmar restaurant ($B) in Distribuidor El Palito is very good, but it is a taxi ride away. It is right on the seafront with a good breeze, though they also offer an air-conditioned section. It is very popular with locals and often has music, especially on the weekends. Fish and their famous mariner's soup are their main specialities.

Ashore

You can get buses around town and to Caracas (mornings only) from outside the marina. For other buses, go to the bus station. Taxis are available opposite the marina and at Marino Centro. Valencia is only about 20 miles away from Puerto Cabello.

There are several interesting side trips while you are in Puerto Cabello. Take a taxi, arrange transport with Carlos, or put on your hiking shoes and walk up to Fort Solano, about a mile south of town. Built by the Spanish in 1740 and still in use as a signal station today, this fort offers excellent views over Puerto Cabello.

Just in front of the marina is the Cathedral of San José built in 1852 with a huge bell cupola built out of coral blocks. There is an ancient statue of Christ in the middle of the cathedral, now missing one hand.

In the historical quarter you will find the Museum of Historica Antropologico, which has historical crafts and ancient handicrafts along with a replica of the room where Simon Bolívar died in Santa Martha, Colombia.

The Spa Clinic (Spa Corpus Stetics) is just a one-minute walk from the marina in front of the Malecon, beside the post office, among the colonial buildings. They give massages from eight dollars up as well of other type of treatments. Marisa and Ivan, the owners, speak fluent English. (0242 361-8512.) About 35 minutes away by car are the Aguas Termales (thermal baths), These are very well known natural steam baths. This is a great way to relax, and it is very inexpensive. (0241 808-1502, www.trincheras.com.) In front of the marina, the National Theatre of Puerto Cabello is painted in fancy yellow with red trim. It is a good building to look at, and from time to time they have shows. Cyclists may want to consider mountain biking in San Sebastian national park. This a rainforest area with waterfalls and an ancient Spanish road. The person to contact is Hermann Seijas. (0249 941-1169.) You can also ask about hiking here.

Very inexpensive round-trip tickets to Miami are available from Valencia. Contact Carlos for details on any of the above.

The interesting old railway to Barquisimeto is closed, but may be rebuilt one day.

Water sports

Iris Santana and Juan Hernandez have a diving shop in Valencia and keep their two boats in the marina. They speak English and are great people to go diving with. In addition, Iris is a lovely lady and will help cruisers with other things. Contact her for help if Carlos is not available. Iris and Juan know the best places to dive. These include two sunken German ships off Isla Larga. (0414 941-5981, venezueladiving.com.)

PASSAGE BETWEEN PUERTO CABELLO AND MORROCOY

It is about 25 miles from Puerto Cabello to Morrocoy national park. It is an easy sail in either direction. Even if you are heading east, you can often make it in one tack, and if you are lucky, it will be a close reach. Three small islands lie between Puerto Cabello and Morrocoy national park: Cayo del Norte, Cayo del Medio, and Cayo del Sur. None of them is large enough to have an acceptable anchorage, though local scuba boats visit for diving.

MORROCOY NATIONAL PARK AND TUCACAS

The Morrocoy national park has some wonderfully calm yet breezy anchorages. The whole park covers about 25 square miles and consists mainly of mangrove islands with channels between them. Some outer islands and Cayo Sombrero have lovely beaches. Fishing is excellent and dinghy exploration never ending, with thousands of narrow, twisty channels opening out into hidden lagoons. Some areas are roped off to protect the birds. You have a good chance of spotting a turtle. Before this area was made into a park, there were some 1,700 holiday homes, mostly on stilts. These were all pulled down to make this a park.

Morrocoy national park covers about 25 square miles and consists mainly of mangrove islands with channels between them.

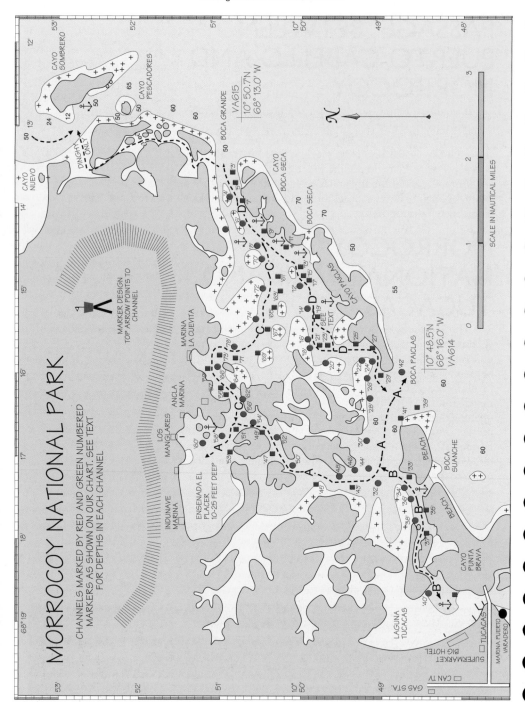

There were no yacht charges as we went to press. This could change; for more information contact Inparques 0259 812-0053.

A national guard unit is posted here and they seem pleasant to cruisers.

This whole area is very popular with Venezuelans, and many Caracas residents keep small powerboats here for weekend camping. It is a very cheerful place to be on the weekends: the beaches are decorated

Scarlet Ibis - Oscar Hernandez photos

with sunshades and tents, and lots of small boats and a few yachts are anchored. Everyone seems happy.

Bird life is varied, with pelicans, herons, egrets, cormorants, stilts, hawks, and some scarlet ibis, which fly by looking like little Father Christmases. The birds like the shallowest water, so the place to see them is way back in the mangroves, and the best time is early morning or late afternoon, when they travel to and from their roosting grounds. Ensenada El Placer is a good place for viewing.

Lanceros take tourists out to the outer islands in small, open boats. They can be useful as water taxis or for visiting Tucacas for shopping. Some cruisers leave their yachts at anchor and use the lanceros to tour around the cays.

Navigation

Morrocoy national park is a maze in endless shades of green. Clues to this puzzle are in the form of three main channels now marked with small beacons whose arrows point into the channel; false clues may still be given by older buoys, which have been left to drift around. The buoyage system is simple, and if you use our plan, which shows where the beacons are supposed to be, and use your eyes to gauge the depth, you can navigate through it without too much problem.

Keep in mind the last time we surveyed this area for depths was about eight years ago. Some of the shallower depths may possibly have changed, so proceed with caution. The two main entrances are Boca Paiclas, and Boca Grande. Both are very deep. If you are coming from Puerto Cabello and the south, the logical entrance is Boca Paiclas. If you stick to

Moroccoy views
- Oscar Hernadez
photos

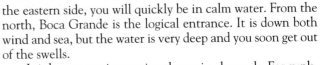

the eastern side, you will quickly be in calm water. From the north, Boca Grande is the logical entrance. It is down both wind and sea, but the water is very deep and you soon get out of the swells.

It is best to navigate using the main channels. For gunkholing and anchoring, look for a deep area outside the channels and eyeball your way in. In many places you have depths of 40-60 feet, making eyeball navigation easy. You can anchor anywhere you like out of the main channels, though for some of the best spots, you should be prepared to anchor in 50 feet of water. To avoid confusion on our small-scale chart, we have numbered the beacons and left out depths. (Reports tell us that the numbers are missing on many of the beacons.) We have also given a letter to each of the four channels. Channel A is the main channel from Boca Paiclas to Ensenada El Placer (Pleasure Lagoon). This has 60 feet at the entrance and 50 feet to beacon #52, from where it shoals slowly to about 35 feet at the entrance to the lagoon. The lagoon has depths from 10-25 feet.

There is an excellent anchorage to the southeast of the two mangrove islands just as you enter Ensenada El Placer. This is a good bird-viewing spot, and sometimes scarlet ibis roost on the mangrove islands, so do not anchor too close.

Channel B runs from the main channel to Laguna Tucacas. Up to Boca Suanche there is about 30 feet of water. There are several good anchoring spots around Boca Suanche. Do not pass too close to beacon #36 as it is shoal, though a little farther south, there is over 30 feet of water. The shallowest part comes between beacons #36 and #35. A boat drawing 6.5 feet can bounce gently over this on a low tide and is fine on a high tide.

Thereafter, depths are 8-13 feet and remain this deep all the way. The twisty, narrow mangrove channel just before Laguna Tucacas is a pleasure to traverse under a minimum of sail with the wind behind. It is best during the weekdays, when there are not too many high-speed power boats with which to share it.

There is a good anchoring area in Laguna Tucacas about halfway between town and the channel entrance. If you go any closer to town, it is shallow.

Channel C runs from Ensenada El Placer and joins the main channel off Cayo Boca Seca. This is an easy channel to follow. The depths jump around a lot, but we found nothing less than 15 feet.

Channel D runs from Boca Grande through to Boca Paiclas. There is between 30 and 60 feet of water near Boca Grande, with many excellent anchorages behind the barrier islands. Pass very close to beacon #13, as the channel is only 100 feet wide and 13 feet deep. The shallowest part comes between beacons #21 and #23. There is only about 6.5 feet of water here at low tide. We found considerably deeper water (about nine feet at low water) fairly close to the north of beacon #19, rejoining the channel just south of beacon #23 (see the sketch chart). Eyeball your way through the deepest-looking water. Once past beacon #23, the channel deepens to 50 feet or more.

One of the nicest anchorages is close by Boca Seca (Dry Channel). The reef protects you from the sea, and you get the full breeze.

In calm weather, Cayo Sombrero, an island northeast of the mangrove channels, is a delightful anchorage. Anchor off the beach on the western side. Along part of the beach, the water is about 60 feet deep almost to the sand. This is the place to anchor, though we have had reports that the holding is difficult here. Beware of the tempting little bay farther southeast. It is used by many powerboats, but there are reefs off it. In a

strong easterly wind, some waves find their way along the shore. In these conditions, you can get a much more sheltered anchorage behind Cayo Pescadores (Fishermen's Cay). The only trouble is the depth. The channel is some 50-60 feet deep all the way through. The shoals on both sides are so wide that taking a line ashore is difficult, so it is best to take enough line to anchor in the deep area.

Yacht services

There is a fuel dock with 10 feet alongside called Los Manglares (VHF: 77) in Ensenada El Placer. It opens weekdays 0800-1300 and 1400-1700, weekends 0800-1700. Owner Alfredo Ceasares sells gasoline and water (diesel is planned), engine oil, and ice and has a marine store and restaurant ($C), which are open weekends only. Alfredo speaks good English, gives information, takes garbage, and offers telephone and fax service.

There are several other small marinas in the area, including Ancla Marina (VHF: 74), where you can get fresh water, and Indunave (VHF: 16).

Marina La Cuevita (VHF: 72) is one of the larger marinas. They do not sell fuel, but they have a pleasant seafood restaurant ($D) and a small shop that stocks large quantities of ice and bug repellent. These are open all day from Friday to Sunday. The restaurant looks out over the water, is active on the weekends, and is a great place to visit for lunch. You can even buy a beer here.

Showers and bathrooms are open to the public all week long. There is dockage with up to 16 feet of water alongside. Boat storage and mechanics can be arranged. (0416 769-2836 and 0414 457-2025).

Tapiceria Frank is run by Jose Francisco Peña, who does upholstery and canvas work for cruisers, who find him inexpensive and good. He also has a sort of taxi and can take people to Tucacas and Chichiriviche. They are on the main national park road close to the marinas.

If you run short of something, you may want to try Tucacas. There is no diesel on the waterfront and there are no taxis, but, if you ask the fishermen, someone may have a

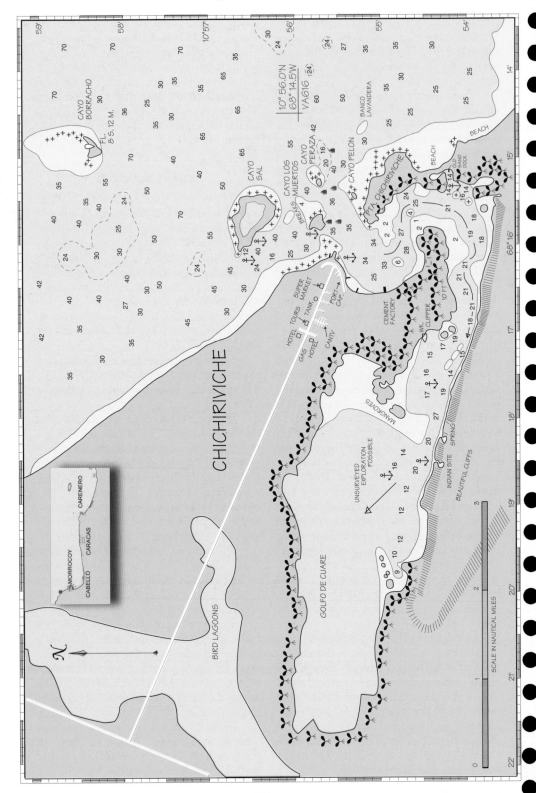

truck they are willing to use to run you a mile to the gas station where you can buy diesel. Before the gas station, is a Cantv where you can make overseas calls. Tucacas has several supermarkets and liquor stores, many of which will deliver to the dinghy dock. A large, local market close to the docks opens on Tuesday mornings. There are about a dozen good, simple restaurants. These get very lively and full on weekends. Both Panaderia Reina Del Mar and Luncheria La Entrada in Avenida Libertador are good places, simple and inexpensive to eat at.

Marina Puerto Varadero (0414 481 5123) is in Tucacas on the sea side of the bridge. (Check your charts for the approach, we do not show it.) It has floating docks for 45 boats but is shallow (maximum draft 5.5 feet). It is run by Domenico Spinalli, and has a marine store, grocery and restaurant that open on weekends.

Passages between Cayo Sombrero and Chichiriviche

When heading north, head over towards the small sand Cayo Nuevo to avoid the shoals at the northern end of Cayo Sombrero, then, when past Cayo Sombrero, head northeast till you clear all the shoals north of Cayo Nuevo (about half a mile, you are clear of them by 10°54'N). You can now head for the western side of Cayo Borracho till you see the entrance channel into Chichiriviche. The danger to avoid here is Banco Lavandera, often visible in breaking seas.

If heading south from Chichiriviche, stay offshore enough to clear Banco Lavandera. As you approach Cayo Sombrero look for the small sand Cayo Nuevo (New Cay). Stick to the Cayo Nuevo side of the channel to keep in the deep water. Once past the shoal area, eyeball your way up to the beach on Cayo Sombrero.

CHICHIRIVICHE

Chichiriviche is about as far west as most people cruise in Venezuela. Farther west are the oil fields of Maracaibo, which is no place for a yacht. Those heading west usually follow the island chain out to Aruba before heading on toward Cartagena.

Chichiriviche and Morrocoy national park offer excellent cruising, with small islands of beaches and palms, huge mangrove areas, and the Golfo de Cuare.

Some people sailing from Bonaire to the Eastern Caribbean bypass this area because they can lay Puerto Cabello, which is farther east, on one tack. If you have extra time, a visit to Chichiriviche and the Morrocoy national park is a good way to use it. Getting back to Puerto Cabello is not hard, and you can most often make it in one fast, easy tack.

It is usually an easy reach between Chichiriviche and Bonaire in either direction. However, for those who are dogged by ill winds, a southerly or northerly is possible.

Navigation

The whole area offshore of Chichiriviche is of mixed depths, mainly from 30 to 60 feet. Sometimes this area is calm, but a combination of uncomfortable swells and honking trades will produce conditions to delight the windsurfer and convert the pocket cruiser into a semi-submersible. If possible, avoid areas in the open ocean with charted depths of 24 feet or less, as we noted considerable shoaling on some of them.

The easiest approach to Chichiriviche is from the east, entering the ship channel, passing just south of Cayo Peraza. We have left in the positions of the channel buoys hoping they will be in place, but they are often missing. If coming from the north, give the northern and western side of Cayo Borracho a wide clearance. The reef system going north from Cayo Borracho is the best part of a mile long.

From the north, you can also enter inside the islands in good light. Pass fairly close to the western side of Cayo Sal (Salt Cay), then hug the western side of Cayo Los Muertos (Dead Mens' Cay) before joining the ship channel.

You can anchor anywhere off town, but in a brisk easterly wind, a surge does enter. One of the calmest anchorages for easy access to the town is off Cayo Los Muertos.

Lanceros run tourists all around the area in fast pirogues. They are usually happy to act as water taxis and can be helpful for getting to town from Cayo Sal. They also make trips into Golfo de Cuare, should you not wish to take your yacht in.

In bad weather, you could not ask for a safer anchorage than the old sand dock or Golfo de Cuare.

Regulations

Chichiriviche comes under the jurisdiction of Puerto Cabello, which is a port of entry. There is no customs or immigration in Chichiriviche. The port captain (VHF: 16) does not want to be bothered by yachts, but if you arrive from abroad, he may give you permission to spend a day or two on your way to Puerto Cabello at his discretion. The port captain's office is in the blue-and-white building on the road immediately facing the dock. If you are leaving Venezuela from Chichiriviche, get your clearance at Puerto Cabello before you come here. No need to check here.

Ashore

Chichiriviche has a large cement factory which brings in ships from all over the region. It is a fishing port with an active fishing fleet of open boats. Nowadays, it is becoming a tourist destination, because it is only 90 miles from Caracas and is the gateway to several pretty islands and Morrocoy national park.

You can beach your dinghy anywhere, or tie it to the unfinished main dock or the other small docks. Do not dinghy close to shore on the south side of the main dock, as a reef comes a fair way out. The main dock is built for lanceros and fishing boats, and it is in shoal water.

Most shops are strung along the dusty Avenida Zamora, the main road leading out of town, which is a little north of the main dock (see our sketch chart). This rather ugly street has recently been quite crowded with tourists, many of whom are Italian. You will find most essentials here, but the place to aim for is Gelateria Roma which has the most delicious ice creams you can imagine. This is close to the waterfront, about 100 meters up the road. They open from 1600 to midnight.

The seafront has lots of small restaurants; a good inexpensive one is Brisas del Mar, owned by Nelida Cumare. She serves excellent local food, including fish, and opens for both lunch and dinner (0259 741-5867). While here, you need to take the two-kilometer walk out of town on the main road to Tucacas. Here you get a great view of a huge lagoon that is part of the national park. Flamingos and ibis are abundant, and the dark red ones are spectacular. People often make their way up here before dawn, when the flamingos fly from one side to the other.

CAYO SAL AND CAYO LOS MUERTOS

Cayo Sal and Cayo Los Muertos are both delightful islands with sandy beaches and coconut palms. They are popular on weekends and holidays, and Cayo Sal has a restaurant that opens when things get busy.

Indian caves, Golfo de Cuare

When passing between Chichiriviche and Cayo Los Muertos, stay close to the island to avoid the shoals that extend out from the Chichiriviche side. Anchor toward the northern end of the west side in the calmest spot.

In Cayo Sal, there is a good anchorage off the southwest coast in 35 feet of water, or you can anchor right at the western end, where the water is 12 feet deep.

GOLFO DE CUARE

Golfo de Cuare is a wildlife refuge and a marvelous place to spend a day or two exploring, bird watching, and fishing. There are spectacular cliffs sculpted into caves, caverns, walls, and steep valleys along much of the southern shore. Once, the whole area was underwater and the cliffs are made of limestone from old coral formations. About seven million years ago, tectonic activity uplifted them to their present position. Acids, borne by rain, dissolved parts of the limestone, causing whole areas to fall away until they reached their present shapes. Much of the cliff bottom has been eaten away by sea action, so there are low overhangs at sea level. These make a cheerful chuckling noise in small waves. The cliffs are covered in part by trees, vines, and shrubs, mainly of the dry forest type. The whole area is decorated by white frangipani flowers. Among the trees are many birds, much more easily heard than seen. Hawks glide overhead, swallows flit out over the gulf, and you may catch glimpses of woodpeckers and other brightly colored birds flying close to shore.

Navigation

Despite the large shoals, access to the gulf is easy, and you can see all the shoals in good light. If you make a mistake, most of the bottom is mud. The entrance channel is much wider than it looks on our small-scale sketch chart. Pass close by the long shoal that stretches southwest from Punta Chichiriviche, then head slightly east of center channel to avoid the four-foot patch. It is a little harder to see than the other shoals.

Stay in the middle of the channel, avoiding the shoals marked on our sketch chart. Electric cables used to run across the entrance of the gulf where we show them. I do not think they are to be replaced, but if they are, you used to have at least 60 feet under the high end.

The easiest and most interesting way up the gulf is to follow the southern shore. Stay about 100 yards off, just outside the shallows. You will pass a series of reefs to starboard, but the passage is amply wide. Farther up, you pass another shoal to starboard, which comes all the way over from the northern shore.

Ashore

You can anchor anywhere in the gulf, but the most interesting anchorage is off the Indian site. Here, the cliffs are at their most dramatic. Ashore there is a small jetty (hard to see) and a notice outlining the history. The cave was used as a burial ground by the Caquetios, who lived here about 3400 BC. There are quite a few rock carvings, and if you walk back behind the jetty, you will find yourself in a crater with sheer cliff sides some 200 feet high. Take bug spray. Look on the mangrove trees at the entrance for mangrove crabs and exotic spiders.

There is another wonderful grotto just a short distance east of the Indian site that you can dinghy right into, with shallow water suitable for lying in. This, too, has religious significance, judging by all the little statues and candles placed on the rocks. There is a little freshwater spring that comes out of the rocks behind a mangrove tree.

On the northern shore of the gulf, just northwest of two little islands, is a large wreck with a clipper bow, apparently once a square-rigged ship.

There is another excellent anchorage off the old sand dock. This was used for shipping out sand mined from the beach, an activity that is now banned. From here, it is just a few steps to the windward beach where you can walk for miles. There is also excellent dinghy exploration in several little mangrove lagoons. In the deep ones, go slowly without creating a wash, because sometimes there are people up to their necks in water picking oysters off the mangroves.

Venezuela's Offshore Islands

AREA 7

Harry Terhorst photo

Venezuela's Offshore Islands

*V*enezuela's offshore islands are a cruiser's dream ~ remote, low-lying islands surrounded by coral with perfect cyan and turquoise water and spectacular beaches. For most of them, you will have to take everything you need with you. But Margarita or the mainland is only a 12- to 24-hour sail away, and it is the very lack of anything that makes these islands so appealing. The landscape is mainly desert, but with a lovely variety of beach and desert plants. Those who now sit in the Eastern Caribbean, anchors dug so well into the sand that tendrils of weed threaten to wrap around their keel, and who write complaining letters to Compass about the poor anchoring abilities of bareboaters and increasing regulations, should get serious about cruising and visit these islands.

We have already covered Los Testigos in our section Eastern Venezuela, so here we will cover the others: Blanquilla, Tortuga, Los Roques, and Las Aves. There is also Ochilla, which is reserved for the military.

We suspect any shells they have on the beach there may not be the kind you want to pick up, and it is out of bounds, and so it is not included.

PASSAGES BETWEEN MARGARITA, BLANQUILLA, TORTUGA AND PUERTO LA CRUZ.

The current in these passages is variable, and though it can be strong, it is sometimes half a knot or less. You occasionally get a reverse easterly setting current between Tortuga and Margarita. This reverse current is generally weak.

The shortest distance between Margarita and Blanquilla is from Robledal (50

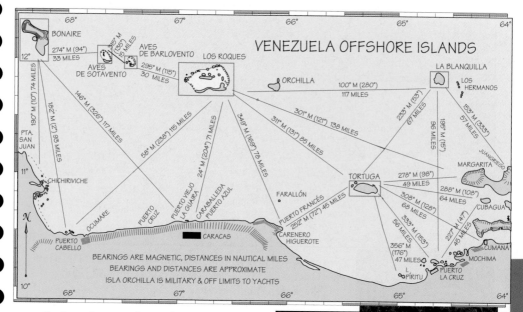

VENEZUELA OFFSHORE ISLANDS

BEARINGS ARE MAGNETIC, DISTANCES IN NAUTICAL MILES
BEARINGS AND DISTANCES ARE APPROXIMATE
ISLA ORCHILLA IS MILITARY & OFF LIMITS TO YACHTS

miles), and it can be a pleasant reach in either direction. There is also no problem sailing from Juangriego or Porlamar, though you may want to do it overnight. From Robledal, you can make either Blanquilla or Tortuga as a day-sail, but be prepared to use your engine if the wind drops.

Blanquilla is low and cannot be seen until you are within a few miles, but it is easy to see Los Hermanos Rocks. They are about six miles east of Blanquilla and cover about six miles in a southerly direction. The largest one is 600 feet high and is easily seen from afar.

Tortuga is low-lying, and you cannot see it until you are within six or seven miles.

Tortuga is also only about 60 miles from Puerto la Cruz, so you can also make that in a day with luck. You can cut about 10 miles off this distance by overnighting in Islas de Píritu on your way. Tortuga is also well placed between Puerto la Cruz and Carenero and makes a good stopping place between these two ports.

Blanquilla

Blanquilla is a delightful island, about 50 miles north of Margarita, well off the beaten track. It is low-lying, only about 50 feet high. There are spectacular beaches, clear water, and wonderful snorkeling. It would be easy to sit here a week or

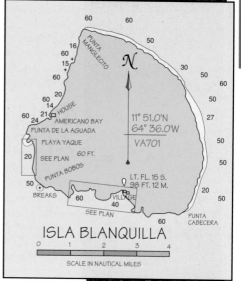

ISLA BLANQUILLA

11° 51.0'N
64° 36.0'W

VA701

SCALE IN NAUTICAL MILES

Venezuela's offshore islands

231

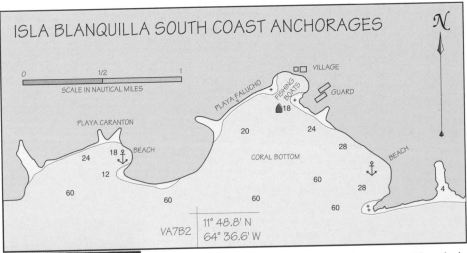

ISLA BLANQUILLA SOUTH COAST ANCHORAGES

SCALE IN NAUTICAL MILES
0   1/2   1

VILLAGE
PLAYA FALUCHO
FISHING BOATS
GUARD
18
PLAYA CARANTON
20
24
BEACH
28
24   18   BEACH
CORAL BOTTOM
12
60
BEACH
60
60   28   4
60   60
60

VA7B2   11° 48.8' N   64° 36.6' W

two, enjoying the water and watching the sunsets. The whole area is a national park, and spearfishing is not allowed.

There is a small settlement around Playa Falucho with a few fishermen and a small garrison of the national guard. Wherever you anchor, expect the national guard to visit at some time to check your papers. If this is your first stop in Venezuela, you should check with them. In emergencies, you could possibly find medical assistance and beg a little water. There is an airstrip by the village and a lighthouse that flashes every 15 seconds.

SOUTH COAST ANCHORAGES

The village anchorage is a sandy spot right at the head of Playa Falucho. The surrounding bay has a coral bottom 18 feet or more deep. The sandy patch is tiny and rather shallow. You can stop here for a short while, but if you stay long, you will be in the way of the fishermen. A more secluded spot, still within reach of the village, is just inside the headland at the eastern end of the bay. Most of the bottom is coral, but you can find a patch of sand just in front of the beach.

Snorkeling is good here, and just around the headland is an interesting fjord that can be explored by dinghy.

If you feel like walking, there is a road of sorts, which goes over to Americano Bay.

PLAYA CARANTON

There is a good little anchorage round the headland off Playa Caranton. It offers small fjords for dinghy exploration and good snorkeling.

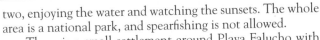

PLAYA YAQUE ANCHORAGE

Playa Yaque is in the lee of the island. It is lovely, with gorgeous white beaches interspersed with rocks. There is plenty of coral, and the snorkeling is excellent.

When approaching from the east, beware of the little rock that breaks just below the surface about a hundred yards offshore and a little to the east of Punta Bobos.

The seabed off the beaches is a mixture of sand and coral. There are many coral heads that stick up within four to six feet of the surface, but these are mainly within a hundred yards of the shore.

The north end of Playa Yaque terminates in a strange outcropping of sharp-pointed rocks. The most protected anchorage is inside this point, between it and the big flat rock that sticks out from the shore below the small ruins. Enter in good light and stay over the sand bottom. Unfortunately, more than two boats are a crowd.

Farther down, the prettiest anchorage is off the best beach, which is marked by a clump of palms in the middle. You have to look carefully to make sure you are anchored on a patch of sand, as much of the bottom is coral.

Ashore

You can enjoy walking over the flat, dry land. The ground is covered with thousands of pretty flowering cactuses. These plants, which look so pretty in a pot, take on a different complexion when embedded in your foot. Stout footwear is recommended.

There is a great dinghy trip to Americano Bay. As you enter, there are cliffs on each side and a deserted beach at the head. On the south side is a deep cave that goes way under the rock. On the north is a spectacular natural rock arch.

The bay is named after the American, Mr. Blankenship, who built the little house here, long before anyone was using the island. He used to land his plane near the house. It is an ideal "away from it all" spot.

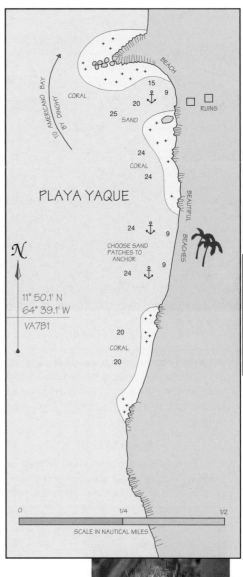

PLAYA YAQUE

11° 50.1' N
64° 39.1' W
VA7B1

SCALE IN NAUTICAL MILES

Venezuela's offshore islands

233

Playa Caldera

Isla Tortuga

Isla Tortuga is gorgeous. It is a low and dry island with sensational beaches, brilliant water colors, good snorkeling, and enough anchorages to keep you happy for a week or more.

Navigation

Tortuga and its associated islands are steep-to within half a mile, so you can approach from any direction. The only place that may give trouble is Los Palanquinos, rocks that are only a few feet high and difficult to see in some light conditions. If you are approaching from the north, you can gauge your position by taking bearings on Cayo Herradura. If you are approaching Punta Delgada from the north, you can usually distinguish it from the rest of the coast by dark green mangrove trees, which stand out. It is sensible to approach Tortuga by day. If

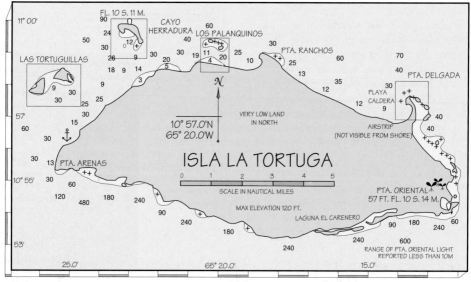

234

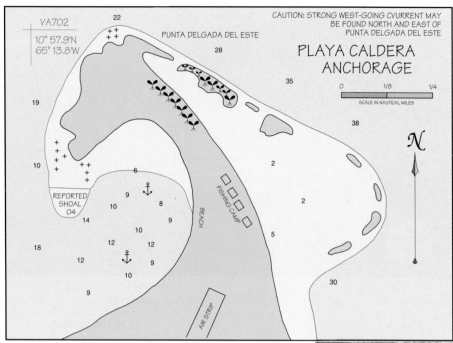

you must come in after dark, the best approach is around Cayo Herradura from the north, because of the conspicuous lighthouse (assuming it is working).

You can sail along either the north or the south side of Tortuga. The north side is best navigated when the light is not straight ahead, so you can see your way past Los Palanquinos. You can stay fairly close to shore, but there are a few reefs and shoals, especially east of Punta Ranchos and along the shore off Los Palanquinos and Cayo Herradura.

There are excellent anchorages in Tortuga for much of the time. However, northerly swells can make things pretty uncomfortable in most places and untenable in Playa Caldera. During the month of May, there are often southerly winds for some hours. This can make Cayo Herradura and Las Tortuguillas uncomfortable, though not generally untenable.

PLAYA CALDERA

Playa Caldera (Cauldron Beach) is an outstanding half-moon beach of white sand over a mile long. Around noon, the whole anchorage feels bleached and baked, heat shimmers, and the houses look timeless and unreal. Distances become hard to judge.

The fishermen's shacks ashore are used seasonally. A rough airstrip is used on weekends by people from Caracas who come in small planes to enjoy the beach, and by the occasional adventurous tourist. I am told that after a day's boozing and sunning, some pilots like to show off to their friends with low-level aerobatics. I do not know whether this is true, but

235

LOS PALANQUINOS

ODD CORAL
HEADS
POSSIBLE

(PA) ABOUT
2 FT.

SOMETIMES
SHOWS

N

10° 59.1'N
65° 20.0'W
VA703

TORTUGA

0   1/4   1/2
SCALE IN NAUTICAL MILES

Above: Los Palanquinos

Opposite:
Playa Herradura

we did find the wreck of a plane on the other end of the island.

Navigation

I used to eyeball my way pretty close to Punta Delgada. The reef does not extend far from the point, but I have been told the sand-and weed-bottom has shoaled. So it is probably best to stay a couple of hundred yards off the point.

Once you are right in the middle of the bay, find the best anchorage by feeling your way up into the northern corner, and anchor in eight to nine feet.

Ashore

The beach here is stupendous, with dunes on the south side that are decorated by a variety of plants so tastefully arranged that a landscape gardener could learn a thing or two. On the windward beach, you can walk for miles. A large lagoon to the east of Punta Delgada is formed by a group of small islands. It is very shallow, and you can wade out along much of it. The fishermen bring boats in at the south end, where the water is deeper.

LOS PALANQUINOS

Los Palanquinos is a mile beyond Punta Ranchos. It is an offshore reef with a few rocks sticking out. In moderate trades, the anchorage here is well protected with some good

snorkeling, and it is within easy reach of the shore for a walk. In really strong winter winds, it might be untenable.

Navigation

This reef is hard to spot in some conditions, but easy enough to see when approaching along the coast in good light. If you are approaching from the north, you can come around either side of the reef, but stay half a mile away from it. There is plenty of room to anchor between the reef and the shore, out of most of the northerly surge. The anchorage is weed and grass. Avoid the shoal area that extends from the Tortuga side.

The snorkeling here is well worthwhile. There are plenty of small barracudas out on the reef. Dinghy over to the Tortuga side for great walks, but if you plan to go far inland, take a compass and some liquid to drink.

CAYO HERRADURA

Cayo Herradura (Horseshoe Cay) is the most favored of the Tortuga anchorages. It is a mile-long island made up for the most part of fine white sand. The island is quite popular on weekends with powerboats from the mainland. At the north end there is a fishing camp, which is occupied for most of the year.

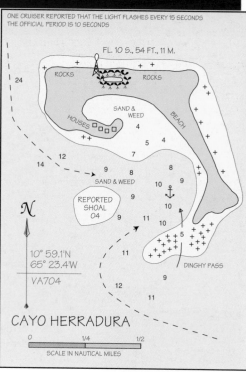

ONE CRUISER REPORTED THAT THE LIGHT FLASHES EVERY 15 SECONDS THE OFFICIAL PERIOD IS 10 SECONDS

FL. 10 S., 54 FT., 11 M.

ROCKS

ROCKS

SAND & WEED

HOUSES

BEACH

24

12

14

9

8

SAND & WEED

REPORTED SHOAL 04

9

10

10

11

11

11

12

10

9

8

5

4

4

7

9

10

9

10

5

DINGHY PASS

9

11

10° 59.1'N
65° 23.4'W

VA704

CAYO HERRADURA

0   1/4   1/2

SCALE IN NAUTICAL MILES

Venezuela's offshore islands

Navigation

Approach Herradura from either end, but not in the middle, where we show the reported shoal. The reef off the southern end of the island extends a quarter of a mile from the beach at most, not the three-quarters of a mile marked on some charts. You can approach from the southwest, but give this reef a fair clearance. It is usually quite visible, but it is sometimes hard to discern

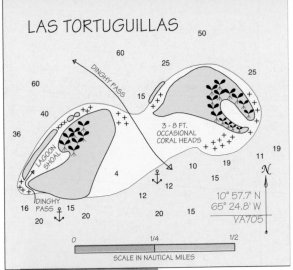

LAS TORTUGUILLAS

```
                                              50
                     60
                             25
   60                                              25
                                 15    +
   40              ++ +          + +
36                 ++            + +
                   xx x            3 - 8 FT.
              O O O               OCCASIONAL
              ×××                 CORAL HEADS   +  + 19
                           4              19
                                   10   19       11
                                  12    15
   DINGHY             12                         10° 57.7' N
16 PASS    15                20    15            65° 24.8' W
   20      20                                    VA705

        0              1/4              1/2
        ████████████████████████████████
              SCALE IN NAUTICAL MILES
```

DINGHY PASS

LAGOON SHOAL

Las Tortuguillas. The lagoon on the western side is clearly visible.

from the rest of the bottom, which is sand and weed. Most of the bottom here is 10-12 feet deep with the odd patch about 8.5 feet deep. Boats drawing over eight feet might prefer to approach around the north of the island, where they can stay in deeper water. You can approach the beach quite closely and anchor in 9 or 10 feet. The northern half of the bay is shoal and should be avoided. There is a red-and-white lighthouse on Herradura, which flashes every 10 seconds.

LAS TORTUGUILLAS

Las Tortuguillas (The Little Turtles) are two lovely, deserted islands with phenomenal beaches and fair snorkeling reefs.

Navigation

Protection from the east comes from Tortuga, and there is a two-mile fetch, so you can get a chop in here. Some people anchor between the islands, edging in gently as far as possible. Remember that this is a lee shore. I have seen centerboard yachts tuck up behind the reef off the western island and still roll. A preferable anchorage, where the water is deeper, is off the southern side of the western island. If the conditions are not suitable for overnight anchorage, come and enjoy it by day.

Ashore

Take the dinghy into the lagoon behind the western island. The approach is right along the beach. The water inside is very shallow and warm. It is a great place to lie suspended with a face mask watching the little fishes below or to laze on the beach or examine the animal and plant communities ashore. There are hermit and soldier crabs and lots of birds. Red mangroves, saltwort, bay cedar, and joewood dominate the plant community.

ANCHORAGE NORTH OF PUNTA ARENAS

You can anchor anywhere along the west coast north from Punta Arenas. This is not a good anchorage in the winter, when the wind comes from the northeast.

LAGUNA EL CARENERO

Some yachtspeople visit Laguna El Carenero (The Carenage Lagoon) on Tortuga's south coast. It is a good anchorage for powerboats, multihulls, and centerboarders. I don't consider this a good anchorage for most keel yachts, because the entrance is tricky and the depths are marginal. There is a maximum of six feet at the entrance at low water. One boat has been wrecked here, and others have had close calls. I have not yet charted it, but for shallow-draft yachts, we include an aerial photo, which should be adequate.

The entrance to Laguna el Carenero is clearly visible, but the water is shallow.

Los Roques

I can think of few places where I have had as much pleasure just sailing as among Los Roques. Stiff breezes, a flat sea, and ever-changing water colors make it sheer bliss. Everything is so clear that you can often negotiate difficult reef passages under sail and tack between reefs right up to anchor.

Los Roques is an unbelievable cruising area made of about 14 by 25 miles of protected, reef-studded water, dotted with pretty little islands. The shallow reef areas reflect so much light that the clouds sometimes turn a green color, and whole areas of reef seem to give off a greenish glow. Part of the attraction is that it is poorly enough charted that it is easy to find anchorages on your own and get the feeling that you are really out there on the edge, exploring.

In many places the anchorages are from 40 to 50 feet deep. There is no problem anchoring in such areas ~ the holding is often excellent, but you do need to come with enough anchor rode. Unless you have a reliable windlass, I would suggest anchoring with rope.

It is best to visit Los Roques in the spring and summer, rather than in the winter. Summer winds are breezy and pleasant. Winter winds can sometimes turn the whole place into a kind of tropical roaring forties. While cruising is not a problem at this time of year, it is not as pleasurable. Northeasterly winds and northerly swells can eliminate many good snorkeling areas, make dinghy exploration difficult, and create rolly anchorages.

If you want to get the most out of Los Roques, I recommend temporarily rigging a few ratlines, just enough to get your feet about six feet above deck level. While this is not strictly necessary for navigation, it does make it a lot easier when exploring poorly charted areas, and apart from that, you are going to love the way the view opens from just a few feet up.

For nature lovers, there are some 80 species of birds that either live here or are migratory species passing through.

Los Roques are not as remote as before. The main island has foodstores, restaurants, and souvenir shops (but it is still a good idea to come with most things you will need).

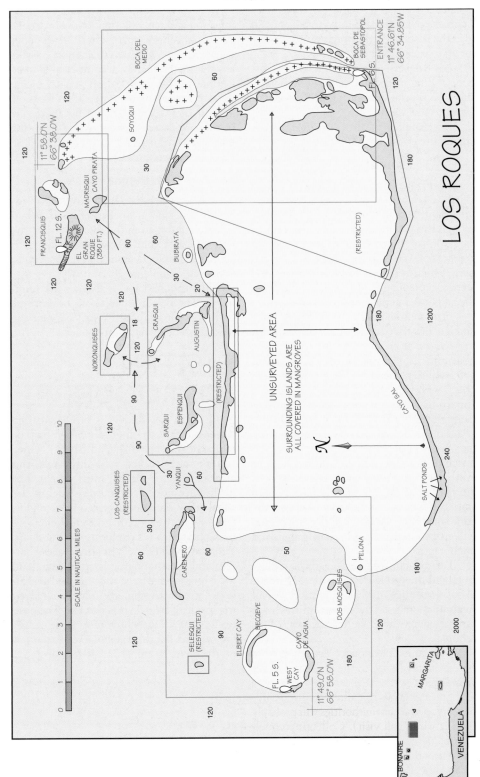

LOS ROQUES

SCALE IN NAUTICAL MILES
0 1 2 3 4 5 6 7 8 9 10

Tourists pour in by day to go to beaches all over the islands. Bright beach sunshades get set up to welcome them.

Los Roques is reputed to have the best bone fishing in the world, and aficionados stay in a special club on Gran Roque that caters to this sport.

Los Roques is also considered safe among the cruising community.

Regulations

Los Roques is a national park, and Jesus Duran (0416 614-2297) is the current super-intendant. You are limited to a 15-day stay, though this can be extended to a second 15 days. One of the reasons for this restriction is that some overseas yachts have chartered here, which is strictly forbidden. The legal Venezuelan tour operators learn about these illegal boats and put pressure on the park.

You will be charged a fee; these may change, but they have been stable now for some years, at about 2$US per foot for the boat and 12$US per person. On arrival, you have to proceed to El Gran Roque and check with (in this order) the coast guard, Inparques, the national guard and Los Roques Authority. Los Roques Authority (Autoridad Unica) collects the $2 per foot fee. You will find the first three along the beach to the west of town, and Los Roques Authority at the airport, where the fees are paid. You can identify the coast guard station by the big Venezuelan flag and the park authorities by the park flag. Inparques will give you a list of the currently approved anchorages.

Part of your fee goes to garbage collection, and the garbage scow collects garbage about three times a week from yachts in all main anchorages. The exception to this is Gran Roque, where there are garbage bins ashore.

You cannot clear out of Venezuela from here; you have to go to the mainland to get clearance.

Spearfishing is not allowed (if you carry a speargun, the park authorities will probably hold it while you visit). Collecting conch is forbidden. There must be no dumping of garbage or discharging oil. You can fish with a hand line. Permits may be necessary for us-ing a rod and reel; ask Inparques for details. You should check with the authorities about where you are permitted to anchor. As with any marine park, they need to be able to be flexible so they can seal off areas showing signs of stress. The restricted areas we show are still likely to be restricted, but there may be more restricted areas as well. Anchoring must always be on sand, never on coral. Use moorings where provided.

Navigation

Unless you have a high-powered speed-boat, Los Roques is an overnight sail. When you are coming from the south or west, the light at Isla Orchilla is a great help. It is about 436 feet high, flashes every 13 seconds, and has a 20-mile range.

Lighthouses on Los Roques are unreliable. The one most likely to be working is the one at El Gran Roque, because the officials notice when it goes out.

EASTERN LOS ROQUES

Eastern Los Roques is protected from the east by a long outer reef called Bajo de la Cabecera (Head-shaped Shoal). Once you are safely tucked behind the reef, this area is navigator-friendly in good light. The navigable water is deep and very blue and the shoal areas jump out as brown reefs or glow the color of the sand that covers them. This is the best area for exploring off the chart. You find some of the best anchorages yourself, and the snorkeling is often excellent. Most charts have large areas marked as shallow, dotted with small reefs drawn all along the inside of Bajo de la Cabecera. The positions of the squiggly little reefs are generally pretty good, but the water marked as shallow on the chart is often 12 to 40 feet deep.

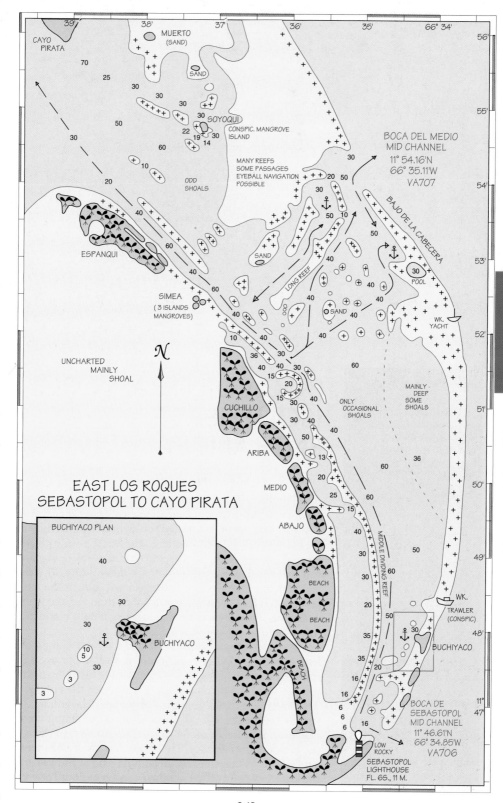

**EAST LOS ROQUES
SEBASTOPOL TO CAYO PIRATA**

CAYO PIRATA

MUERTO
(SAND)

SAND

SOYOQUI

CONSPIC. MANGROVE
ISLAND

MANY REEFS
SOME PASSAGES
EYEBALL NAVIGATION
POSSIBLE

ODD
SHOALS

ESPANQUI

SAND

SIMEA
(3 ISLANDS
MANGROVES)

LONG REEF

BOCA DEL MEDIO
MID CHANNEL
11° 54.16'N
66° 35.11'W
VA707

BAJO DE LA CABECERA

POOL

WK.
YACHT

UNCHARTED
MAINLY
SHOAL

N

SAND

ONLY
OCCASIONAL
SHOALS

MAINLY
DEEP
SOME
SHOALS

CUCHILLO

ARIBA

MEDIO

ABAJO

BUCHIYACO PLAN

BUCHIYACO

BEACH

BEACH

BEACH

MIDDLE DIVIDING REEF

WK.
TRAWLER
(CONSPIC)

BUCHIYACO

BOCA DE
SEBASTOPOL
MID CHANNEL
11° 46.61'N
66° 34.85'W
VA706

LOW
ROCKY

SEBASTOPOL
LIGHTHOUSE
FL. 6S., 11 M.

Looking south to Boca de Sebastopol. Both the Bajo de la Cabecera outer reef and the middle dividing reef show up clearly.

BOCA DE SEBASTOPOL (SOUTHEAST ENTRANCE)

Navigation

The Boca de Sebastopol entrance is convenient if you are approaching from the south. It is an all-weather entrance, if somewhat hairy in big swells. You do need enough light to see the reefs and shallow patches, though these are clearly demarcated. From the southeast, the land is low-lying, and you will not see it until the last six miles. Once in view, you probably can pick out the lighthouse against the trees behind it. It looks very conventional, with its red and white stripes, an illusion wrought of modern materials; it is in fact lightweight and made of fiberglass.

If you have been carried north and are approaching more from the east, another conspicuous feature is the wrecked trawler just north of Buchiyaco. Steer for the lighthouse until you get about a mile off and can begin to see the entrance. The land that extends from the lighthouse to the entrance is very low and rocky, not easy to see until you are almost there. However, it is usually easier to see than the reef on the opposite side of the entrance. The entrance is about a quarter of a mile wide. When you can see both the end of the reef and the low rocky point off the lighthouse, enter midway between them. When you are past the entrance, the sea begins to subside, but there will still be some leftover swells. Look for the middle dividing reef that separates the two channels, and aim for the end of it. When you reach it, stay on the eastern side and follow it closely northwards. The depth at the entrance is 20 feet, and soon after you get in, it shoals to about 16 feet. Then it gets deeper again, and you find yourself in a wonderful area of very deep blue water, 30-60 feet deep, and dotted with occasional shoals.

SEBASTOPOL NORTHWARDS

The clearest and easiest route is to sail northwards, keeping the middle dividing reef close on your port side all the way to Espenqui. From here you can head for Gran Roque. Up to Cuchillo you will see over the reef to the inside deepwater passage. This passage stops at Cuchillo, but the reef continues to Espanqui. This reef is very easy to see and is continuous except for a few cuts into the inner passage near Cuchillo and Ariba. Hug the reef, passing inside any off-lying shoals along the way to Espenqui. This will give you the best and easiest passage in water mainly 40-60 feet deep. Unless the wind is against you, you can sail the whole way. You may notice this does not match most charts which show a detour outside a second set of reefs after Cuchillo. As far as we can see, this is bad charting; use our sketch chart instead. You can also follow the route shown on other charts, but it is less clear, and you have to dodge more reefs.

There is a good anchorage in the lee of Buchiyaco. There is a broad area of very shoal water extending from the reef. Behind that is a band of deep water, then a few shoals with 3 to 10 feet of water over them. Eyeball your way in, avoiding the shoal spots, and anchor anywhere in the lee of the island. If it is blowing hard, you can get a little lee from the mangroves. Holding is good in 30 feet of water.

You can also anchor anywhere along the reef, though if big waves are breaking over the top, it could get uncomfortable. I would recommend looking for areas with depths of 30-40 feet to anchor in. The holding is often good in sand. Some people like to anchor "hanging off" the shallow areas ~ taking an anchor into the really shallow water. There are two potential problems with this. One is that the very shallow water is usually the top of a reef bank and consists of hard, dead coral covered by a minimum of sand. The other is that often these shoal areas do have corals or sponges growing on them, and these are not always easy to see from a dinghy. So if you do anchor this way, use a mask and put the anchor down clear of any living creatures.

THE INSIDE PASSAGE WEST OF THE MIDDLE DIVIDING REEF

This long, completely protected body of water is a great place just to explore under sail. This is all you can do, because anchoring and fishing are forbidden here. Unless you are shoal-draft, I would not recommend approaching this area from the southern (Sebastopol) end. There is a bar at the entrance, which is downwind in rough seas and only about seven feet deep at mid-tide, which does not seem like an adequate safety margin for most keel boats. Even shoal boats would be better off trying this channel on their way out before attempting the downwind and down-sea entrance.

You can access the center channel through any of the three breaks opposite the islands of Ariba and Cuchillo. Enter one of these and eyeball your way down. You do have to steer round a few reefs (see our sketch chart), but this is easy in good light. There is an absolute minimum depth of 13 feet in the channel, but most of it is 20-40 feet deep. The passage goes right up to the north end of Cuchillo, but this is a cul-de-sac with little room to turn round in under sail.

Venezuela's offshore islands

BOCA DEL MEDIO AND NEARBY ANCHORAGES

Opposite: El Gran Roque. Francisquis are visible to the top left.

Looking south from Long Reef (just visible right front). Notice the shoals lie in deep water and are easy to see.

Boca del Medio is an easy exit and not a bad entrance for more experienced reef navigators when conditions are reasonable and the light is right. Use your GPS to get you close to the entrance and eyeball your way in. Once inside, swing round the reef to the south until you are out of the seas. Getting back to the main channel is discussed below.

Navigating this area is strictly by eye, and you should only do it when the light is acceptable. The positions of sand islands may be unreliable as these come and go. South of the reef we have called Long Reef on our chart, the reefs tend to be discreet so you do not have to worry about getting caught in a cul-de-sac. You can easily explore this area under sail with a good lookout.

You can choose your own passages between the reefs. The reef we have marked as Long Reef can be used as a highway ~ just follow it up or down. Another easy way through the reefs to or from the main channel begins just west of the northern cut in the reef opposite Cuchillo. From here, a course of about 65° magnetic takes you pretty much out between shoals to the outer reef.

There is a delightful anchorage inside the outer reef, just beside a deep pool surrounded by reef. The anchorage is 49 feet deep, but the holding is good. You can swim or dinghy through to the pool. The water is clear, and the snorkeling is excellent. Wherever there are patches of reef, you find healthy corals, sponges, very tame parrotfish and doctorfishes, clams, and pencil clams. This is also true on the reef outside the pool. More ambitious people might want to work their way down toward the entrance, where the snorkeling is even better.

There is an area for excellent snorkeling right opposite Boca del Medio, behind the next reefs. We show the two

eastern entrances on our chart, but the southern one is only 10 feet deep, and both are subject to rough seas, as they are opposite Boca del Medio. It is safer to approach down the northern side of Long Reef. Although the water is quite deep, you need to send a snorkeler over before dropping your hook to make sure it is not in coral, as even the sand bottom here has some corals growing on it. There is lots of coral here, nearly all of it alive, and there are hundreds of colorful reef fish, including tame groupers.

We mention these two anchorages, but one of the delights of this area is that it is not terribly well charted, and there are excellent anchoring and exploring possibilities. You can find and choose your own anchorage just about anywhere between the reefs, as long as it is outside the restricted area.

The reef north of Boca del Medio also has many anchoring possibilities. A good starting point is Soyoqui, a distinctive, small, mangrove-covered island that you can see from afar. Soyoqui has many anchoring possibilities because there is a channel all around, and you can choose your spot to suit the conditions. It is easy to approach from Cayo Pirata or from the channel off Espenqui. From here you can explore outwards and find your own spot.

NORTHEAST LOS ROQUES

There are several islands here and many good anchorages. Among them is the main island, El Gran Roque. With hills about 380 feet, it is the only island in the group to attain any height.

EL GRAN ROQUE

With its 380-foot hills, El Gran Roque stands out like a beacon across the other flat islands. A very easy way to come in to Los Roques is to approach from the north. Just sail in round the west of El Gran Roque. It is impossible to mistake this island for any other in the group.

The other logical way to come in this area is by the northeast channel, between Fransiquies and Nordisqui. This is no problem, provided you have correctly identified the islands.

Once you reach El Gran Roque, anchor off the town just south of the dock. There is a convenient anchoring shelf some 150 feet wide with depths of 10 to 13 feet. Outside this, the depths plummet and inside, they shoal rapidly.

Los Roques airport - Harry Terhorst photo

Communications

La Chuchera Restaurant offers an internet service for yachting customers who use their restaurant. They open 0900-2230. They will also help with phone rentals, sending faxes, and general advice.

Services

Los Roques is dry; best come with plenty of water. However, you can normally get water here. Elis and Mari (0414 249-1201) have been delivering water alongside to yachts, and Mari does laundry. If for any reason that is not happening, check out the dive shop, if they cannot help out themselves with a few jerry jugs, they will know someone who can. Fuel is sometimes available also, though if it comes over by boat, there is no guarantee on purity.

Flights to Caracas can be arranged from one of the airline offices.

Ashore

This is the only island with a village on it, and it also has the main airport. There are no cars, and the streets are sand. Most of the houses were built as holiday homes for Venezuelans, and they are simple but pleasant. Los Roques has become a major day-tour destination for tourists, many of who fan off to the surrounding islands.

Salazar and Agusto are among the three food stores (abastos) that get supplied from the mainland about once a week. Fresh produce can sometimes be slim pickings on the weekends. It is probably still best to arrive in Los Roques with most things you need, but there is plenty to top up on. You will also find plenty of souvenir shops, which are often open in the cool of the evening, when the town gets quite social.

There are now several small restaurants in town. Pedro Diaz has proved very helpful to visiting yachts at his La Chuchera restaurant ($B-D, 0237 221-1417). This is a red-and-blue house on the main square, Plaza Bolivar. Pedro opens 0900-2230 and serves local fish, good meat, salads, pizzas, and more. You can get breakfast, lunch, and dinner here, at almost any time of day. No reservations are required unless you are a big group (15 people or so). You can also rent a phone, email, or send a fax here.

While you are here, follow the well marked trail up the hill to the oldest of the three lighthouses. Take your camera for a brightly colored all-round view.

Water Sports

There is good diving and excellent diving in Los Roques. The good diving can be had by snorkeling anywhere that is deep enough and if it looks promising, go back for the tanks. One fine spot is off the northwestern point of El Gran Roque. The excellent diving is all along the south side of Los Roques, where there is a dramatic dropoff. The best way to get there is to dive with the local dive shop, Sesto Continente Dive Resort (VHF: 16). As it is a fair distance, they usually run a two-tank dive with a break for lunch. The manager is helpful and speaks English. He also rents and fills tanks.

FRANCISQUIS

These islands and their fringe reefs form a completely protected anchoring lagoon with lots of space. Powdery beaches, good snorkeling, and proximity to El Gran Roque make this a favorite. There are one or two habitations, but not enough to spoil it.

Navigation

Enter from the south, eyeballing your way between the shoals. There is about 14 feet of water over the entrance channel. Once inside, there are a couple more reefs to dodge, and after that, most of the lagoon is 40 feet deep with several good anchorages. For breeze and an open aspect, the best is off the reef at the northern end of the lagoon. For beaches, you can choose between the two eastern islands. The southern one is longer, prettier, and has easy anchoring in 12 feet of water. This is probably why it is used by many day-charter boats and why many cruising people go to the northern one. You can also carry about six and half feet through the narrow cut into the mangrove-lined lagoon between the two

Looking east over the two eastern Francisquis across the northeast channel to Nordisqui

Cayo Madrisqui - Harry Terhorst photo

eastern islands. Once inside, the water is 10 to 12 feet deep. Some Venezuelans keep their boats here.

Water Sports

There is splendid snorkeling on the eastern side of the two eastern islands. While ashore, look for a bird that looks like a great blue heron, except it is white. It is a variant of the great blue, and this is one of the places you see it.

CAYO PIRATA AND CAYO MADRISQUI

These islands are joined by a sandbar at their southern ends. You can anchor between them on the northern side. The water is 60 or 70 feet deep, but you can edge gently into the shore until the depth gets to be 25 feet before dropping your hook. If you are staying long, a line ashore and an anchor in the deep water would be the best way to secure your boat. The holding is not great. Ashore there is a fishing camp where you can buy lobster during the season.

Cayo Madrisqui (Namusqui on some charts) has a pristine beach, though there are a few houses here. The water off the northern end of this beach is very shoal, but you can eyeball your way into the southern end between the shallow water and a reef. Anchor where the water is about nine feet deep. Being close to Gran Roque, this beach becomes a very popular tourist beach by day.

MUERTO

Muerto is a sandbar and a pleasant place to lie out and play in the shallow water. The water tends to be too deep or too shallow. Place one anchor in the shallow water and another in deep to keep you from swinging aground.

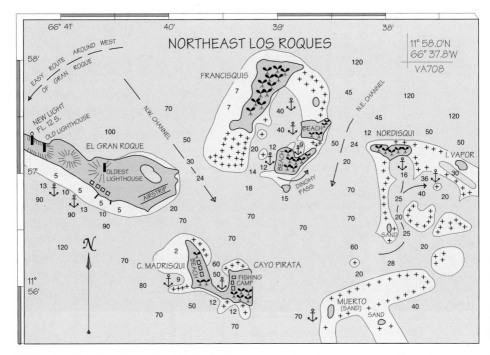

ISLA VAPOR AND NORDISQUI

There are quite delightful anchorages tucked up in the reefs by these islands. Start at Muerto, follow the reef it lies on eastwards. You have to dodge one side or the other of one little reef that might get in your way if you are under sail. When you get to the long reef that extends south of Nordisqui, follow it up on the eastern side, sailing between it and the next reef. If you want to be close to the shore, anchor off Nordisqui. If you like being in the open, anchor off Isla Vapor. Isla Vapor is a small island covered in seaside purslane, which is almost as good as grass to lie on. The island is inhabited by hundreds of terns. They will resent your presence if you go to the eastern side of the island, but if you stay near the beach, they will leave you alone.

Between Isla Vapor and the anchorage is a pool of deep blue water some 30 feet deep surrounded by reef. The water colors are incredible here, as they change from pale green to dark blue. The water in the shallows is warm enough to lie in all day. There is good snorkeling on the reef patches both inside the pool and out between the reefs.

ANCHORAGES IN NORTH-CENTRAL LOS ROQUES

This whole area is dotted with little islands, most of which have delightful anchorages. Usually the next island is no more than a couple of miles away. Since sailing is such fun in Los Roques, I recommend darting from one area to another rather than exploring systematically.

NORONSQUIS

Three little islands and a barrier reef create a lustrous blue lagoon of deep water surrounded by several unblemished little beaches. On the north shore of the westernmost island is the conspicuous wreck of a Venezuelan navy vessel that was being used to ferry supplies. It was anchored in Gran Roque when its mooring line parted. It somehow caught fire after grounding,

Looking southeast at Noronsquis. The wreck shows up clearly in the foreground.

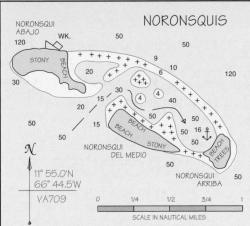

NORONSQUIS

NORONSQUI ABAJO
120
WK.
STONY
30
50
50
NORONSQUI DEL MEDIO
BEACH
STONY
BEACH
20
15
30
15
20
9
10
6
50
50
40
50
50
50
16
50
50
120
BEACH TREES
NORONSQUI ARRIBA
50

N
11° 55.0'N
66° 44.5'W
VA709

0   1/4   1/2   3/4   1
SCALE IN NAUTICAL MILES

which added to its problems, and it is still sitting on the shore.

Navigation

Sail to the south side of the island group and enter midway between Noronsqui Abajo and Noronsqui del Medio. Depth over the bar is about 15 feet. Inside, the lagoon is mostly about 50 feet deep. Stay in deep water, closely following the reef along the north shore of Noronsqui del Medio to avoid the two four-foot reefs in the middle. The calmest anchorage is off the tiny beach on the west side of Noronsqui Arriba. The water is deep and you can take a line ashore or into the shallows.

There are great beaches to explore and the snorkeling is good, though much of the coral inside is bleached. When snorkeling look out for the huge midnight and rainbow parrotfish along the north shore of Noronsqui del Medio. Weather permitting, you can dinghy out through the six-foot break in the reef for advanced snorkeling on the outside.

CRASQUI

Crasqui has a picture-perfect beach that seems to go on forever. While there is no snorkeling on the lee side of the island, aficionados can dinghy to the windward side, where the snorkeling is good. This is a very popular anchorage with Venezuelans and will be crowded on weekends, though there is plenty of space. A hotel and restaurant opened here for awhile, but it has been closed by Inparques in an effort to preserve the natural state of the island.

Navigation

If you are approaching from the north, pass to the west of the sand cay to the northwest of Crasqui. Anchor anywhere along the beach. If you are approaching the beach at the north end, you have to ease your way in

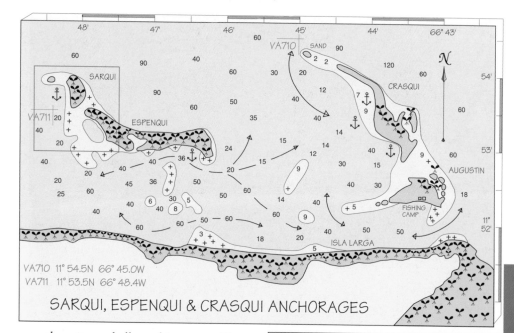

SARQUI, ESPENQUI & CRASQUI ANCHORAGES

VA710 11° 54.5N 66° 45.0W
VA711 11° 53.5N 66° 48.4W

gently, as it gets shallow a fair way out. There is deeper water down at the south end.

If you are leaving to sail south and east round the south end of Augustin, note that there is a long shoal that ends in a reef extending to the west of Augustin. You may find eight feet of water cutting inside the shoal, but it is hard to read the depths and not worth it. When you pass between Augustin and Isla Larga, you have to sail closer to Isla Larga to avoid the reef off Augustin. It is best to do this in good light. There is plenty of room for most modern yachts to tack through under sail. Give the eastern side of Augustin good clearance.

If approaching southwest round the south side of Espenqui, avoid the reef halfway between Augustin and Espensqui.

ESPENQUI

Most charts do not give details on this area, but you should find our sketch chart adequate. There are several shoals between Espenqui and Isla Larga. The easiest route is to follow the southern coast of Espenqui. However, the shoals are easy to avoid in good light, and you can pick your own route between them. The minimum depth in any passage between two shoals is 15 feet.

There is a good little getaway anchorage

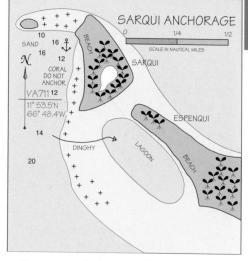

in Espenqui tucked up into the eastern end of the south coast. Lots of birds live here, and snorkeling is worthwhile around the eastern end of the island.

SARQUI

Sarqui has a superb, if somewhat small, anchorage. Three moorings are available. If you are approaching from the south, give a good clearance to all the reefs that extend south of Sarqui and west of Espenqui. The anchorage is right at the northern end of

Venezuela's offshore islands

Los Roques

the island, protected by the reef that extends eastwards from Sarqui to a small island. You can anchor here in sand in 10-16 feet of water. Do not anchor south of the sandy area, as you will be on coral, which is not allowed.

This is a great place to sit and watch all the birds in action and to go for a snorkel. Snorkeling is good both over the coral in the bay and out around the north and east side of Sarqui. There is also good dinghy exploration into the lagoon at the north end of Espenqui, where there is a delightful beach and bathing pool.

LOS CANQUISES AND SELENSQUI

These islands are restricted areas, and anchoring is not allowed. Los Canquises is full of birds and during the winter from January to March, flamingos are seen here. Dinghy exploration is allowed, but the passage across can be rough. If you do visit, do not disturb the birds.

ANCHORAGES IN WESTERN LOS ROQUES

There are delightful anchorages in western Los Roques. This is far from El Gran Roque, so there are often only a few boats around.

Above: saltponds at Los Canquises

Opposite: Crasqui

255

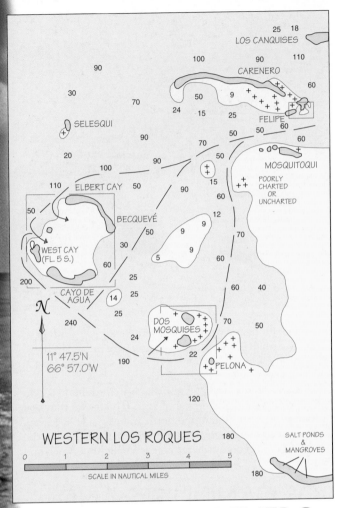

WESTERN LOS ROQUES

LOS CANQUISES
CARENERO
SELESQUI
FELIPE
MOSQUITOQUI
POORLY CHARTED OR UNCHARTED
ELBERT CAY
BECQUEVÉ
WEST CAY (FL. 5 S.)
CAYO DE AGUA
DOS MOSQUISES
PELONA
SALT PONDS & MANGROVES

11° 47.5'N
66° 57.0'W

SCALE IN NAUTICAL MILES
0 1 2 3 4 5

ISLANDS AT EASTERN END OF CARENERO

CAYO REMANSO
DINGHY EXPLORATION
FELIPE
VA712
11° 53.0'N
66° 50.5'W

SCALE IN NAUTICAL MILES
0   1/8   1/4

ISLA CARENERO

Cayo Remanso and Felipe are two small mangrove islands at the eastern end of Carenero. Between them is a perfect lagoon anchorage. Approach from the south and eyeball your way in. There is a four-foot shoal in the middle of the entrance. The deepest and clearest route is to the east of the shoal.

Once inside, you will have a beach backed by mangroves on the eastern side and a lovely open vista across miles of blue and turquoise water to the west. The seabed in the lagoon is sand, and you can easily see the 20 feet to the bottom. Six moorings are available.

The snorkeling is excellent as you fol-

256

low the reef out of the bay to the northeast. There are more than enough fish to make up for the fact that much of the coral is bleached. Or you can take the dinghy over to Carenero for a long walk.

This anchorage is very popular with yachts, and fishing boats often come in here for repairs.

DOS MOSQUISES

Dos Mosquises are two pretty islands sheltered by a protective barrier reef. This was where the Amerindians chose to live when they inhabited this area. They arrived in huge dugout canoes that carried 50 people and stayed for the fish, conch, lobster, and turtles. Dos Mosquises was a good choice, conveniently close to Cayo de Agua for water, and the nearest island to the mainland. They were close to the natural salt ponds, which enabled them to salt their fish, and there are plenty of mangrove trees close by, which could be used for making fires and building.

Nowadays Mosquises Sur houses a small research and fisheries station. On the fisheries side, they take turtle eggs, hatch the turtles, keep them until they are one year old, and then let them go. Many people come here to do research on all aspects of the area. It is a good place to come for natural history information, but what you find will depend on who is there at the time.

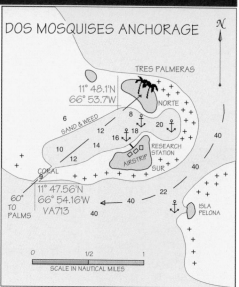

Navigation

Enter Dos Mosquises from the south (if coming from the north, you can pass between Isla Pelona and Dos Mosquises to get to the south side). The entrance is a little worrisome as you have to cross an area of reef. While this is about nine feet deep at low water, it is impossible to tell if one coral head is sticking up more than the others and coral does grow. Therefore, if you have 6- to 7-foot draft, I would suggest crossing the bar at high water, which will give a safety margin. The best angle of approach is with the palms on Tres Palmeras, bearing about 60° magnetic. Once over the reef, there is plenty of water inside,

Venezuela's offshore islands

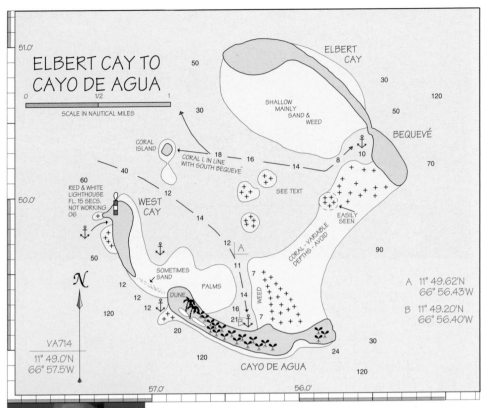

ELBERT CAY TO CAYO DE AGUA

SCALE IN NAUTICAL MILES

0   1/2   1

51.0'

50

ELBERT CAY

30

120

SHALLOW
MAINLY
SAND &
WEED

50

BEQUEVÉ

CORAL
ISLAND

CORAL I. IN LINE
WITH SOUTH BEQUEVE

30

18

16

14

8

10

70

40

60
RED & WHITE
LIGHTHOUSE
FL. 15 SECS.
NOT WORKING
06

50.0'

12

WEST
CAY

14

SEE TEXT

EASILY
SEEN

CORAL - VARIABLE
DEPTHS - AVOID

90

50

SOMETIMES
SAND

PALMS

12

A

11

12

14

16

21

7

WEED

7

A 11° 49.62'N
66° 56.43'W

B 11° 49.20'N
66° 56.40'W

N

12

12

12

120

DUNE

20

120

24

30

CAYO DE AGUA

120

VA714
11° 49.0'N
66° 57.5'W

57.0'

56.0'

with depths from 12 to 25 feet. You can go past the islands and anchor in the lagoon. It gets much shallower towards Tres Palmeras (Mosquises Norte), though you can edge in towards the beach at the eastern end.

Ashore

The research station welcomes visitors. Tres Palmeras is deserted, with a fabulous beach. There is good snorkeling on the reefs all around, which is particularly excellent along the outer part of the reef, south of the south island.

ELBERT CAY TO CAYO DE AGUA

This little archipelago consists of four islands: Elbert Cay, Bequevé, West Cay, and Cayo de Agua, along with many reefs. It is a delightful area with good island exploring, fine snorkeling, and excellent fishing.

Navigation

While the outer edges of the archipelago are deep, the water between the islands is rather shallow with lots of coral. To make things worse, it is littered with grass beds, which makes it harder to read. Nonetheless, if you follow the main

Cayo de Agua has a typical Venezuelan lighthouse, a red-and-white striped structure. These lighthouses are now made of fiberglass and shipped out to the location in sections, where they can be rapidly assembled.

routes into the anchorages as shown on our chart, you should not have a problem.

BEQUEVE

Bequevé and Elbert Cay are currently joined by a sand dune and will probably stay that way. The only anchorage is close to where the two islands join. It is a good anchorage and well protected from trade winds. You do need to arrive in good light. Enter between Elbert Cay and the little coral island. Head southeasterly until you are on a line between the coral island and the southern tip of Bequevé, and then keep on this line. You should be able to make out the shoal we have marked "easily seen" on our sketch chart. Eyeball your way up into the anchorage. The entrance is quite narrow, with a reef to the south and shallow grass and sand to the north. At this point it is only about eight to nine feet deep. Once inside, the water gets a little deeper, and there is plenty of room to anchor.

Ashore there are miles of fabulous, sandy island to explore, with beachfront that will please the fussiest beach lover. When that tires, there is snorkeling on all the reefs around.

CAYO DE AGUA

Cayo de Agua has two anchorages, one on the north

Where Cayo de Agua is closest to West Cay. It is sometimes joined with a sandspit, and at other times there is a shallow sandbar. In this photo, the spit is awash. - Harry Terhorst photo

side and the other on the west. The northern anchorage is much larger and better protected, except in howling northeasters. Enter between the coral island and West Cay and head for the northeastern point of Cayo de Agua. After that, just eyeball your way between the reefs. The eastern reef is flanked by a long, shallow weed bank to its west. Treat this as part of the reef. The entrance is narrow, but once inside, the water gets deeper and a large anchoring area opens up. The calmest water is close to the beach and the reef at the eastern corner.

Having said that, Dick and Tricia Marx on Geramar did not find eyeballing as easy as I did and kindly sent me the waypoints A and B, shown on my sketch chart. A is the entrance to the bay, and B is the anchorage. They point out that the anchorage has two very easily sighted landmarks: a lone palm tree, clearly visible (several hundred yards from the group of palm trees further west), and a path of clear white sand going up a dune just east of this palm tree (like a white stripe set on a grayish dune), a transit with the western end of Elbert Cay to the palm tree/white sand path, bearing about 190° magnetic gets you in.

While it is possible to eyeball your way between this anchorage and Bequevé, I would not recommend it, as you have to pass over many banks of coral 8-12 foot deep, and one never knows where the extra- tall coral head is.

The anchorage on the western side of Cayo de Agua is good but only has room for two boats. It is right at the western end of Cayo de Agua, where it is closest to West Cay. Sometimes it is joined with a sand spit, and at other times there is a shallow sandbar.

The water is clear, and the approach is easy. Just avoid any small coral heads and the reef to the south, which provides the protection. To get out of the swell, edge as closely as possible in to the beach. The water shelves gradually from about 12 feet, so this is no problem.

This island, and in particular this beach, has become one of the popular day-tour destinations. So if you do use this anchorage, you can expect some company during the day. The northern anchorage is much more secluded.

A very small anchorage is under the lighthouse at West Cay. This is a one-boat anchorage where you have to use one anchor in the shallows (or on the beach) and another to

hold your stern as there is no swinging room.

My last report was that the lighthouse was not working. I notice also that in my last guide, I had the lighthouse flashing every 5 seconds, and I have now corrected this to the information given on the government lighthouse site, which has it flashing every 15 seconds. On the other hand, looking at the photo and the background on the government site photo, I suspect they might have the wrong lighthouse posted. I suggest you don't even think of sailing around Los Roques at night.

Ashore

Cayo de Agua is a delightful island of tall sand dunes, a palm grove, mangrove trees, lagoons and water holes. The bird watching is tremendous with all manner of terns, pelicans, herons, oystercatchers and wading birds in the lagoon behind and along the shores. Terns nest here, so be careful not to disturb them.

Since you are now at the western edge of Los Roques, this also makes a great place to spend a few days before heading on to Los Aves.

You will notice lots of water holes dug in the ground in the area of the palms. Cayo de Agua got its name because there is lots of fresh water a few feet down, and it has proved an invaluable supply to the Amerindians, fishermen, and the occasional desperate yachtsperson. I was amazed to come here at the end of a very dry season and still find water that was only a tiny bit brackish in the holes.

Water Sports

Snorkeling and diving on the south coast of Cayo de Agua are excellent, because of the bright sand bottom and lots of thick coral patches. It falls off downhill steeply, but without a dramatic wall. It is a pretty area of coral gardens where the coral is alive and well and fish are bright and tame.

Trolling or hand-lining from the dinghy here will usually be rewarded with a fish big enough for dinner.

If you are anchored on the northern side, the snorkeling is good in places on the reefs all around. Hand-line fishing is also very good in the region of the coral island.

Aves de Barlovento

Islas de Aves are two separate little island archipelagos, separated by about 10 miles of deep water. They got their name from the large number of birds that make them their home. They are conveniently placed en route to Bonaire and should not be missed.

The birds live in the dense mangrove forests on the larger islands. You can anchor near these but also out on the reef in isolated splendor. On both groups you will find some good little beaches, though they are not as plentiful as in Los Roques.

Aves de Barlovento has a horseshoe reef that gives protection to two islands and a few smaller cays. The bird life on the southern island has to be seen to be believed. From afar, you can see birds by the hundreds perched in the trees. The majority are various species of booby, but there are also other seabirds and herons. Close-to, they set up a wonderful chorus as they argue over branch rights and feed their young.

Above: Boobies on Isla Sur

P.265: Ashore on Isla Sur

Navigation

Aves de Barlovento is relatively easy to navigate. For the most part, the water is either very deep or very shallow. The charting is not all that accurate and there are some shoals that are not marked. If you always keep a good lookout, sail when the light is reasonable and avoid anything that looks shallow, you should be alright.

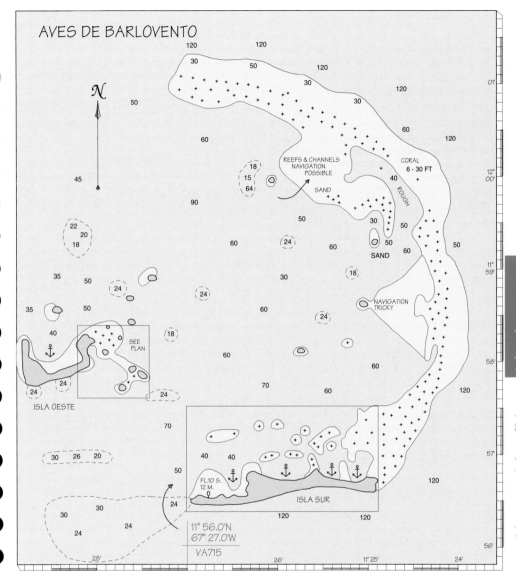

ISLA SUR

Navigation

It is easiest to approach from the southern side as Isla Sur, the barrier island in the south, has 40-foot-tall mangrove trees, which makes it clearly visible.

The places we have marked shoaling on our sketch charts are living coral and considerably shallower than the charts show. It is best to avoid them, either by eyeballing your way round or making a sweep out toward the

little island of sand and seaside plants.

Fishing boats often anchor in the first bay just east of the lighthouse. This anchorage is exposed and can be rolly. It is much better to carry on to the east, where there are three different bays behind the reefs that are reasonably well protected from all directions. It is easy to find your way through in reasonable light conditions, and you can enter the first one even in poor light, provided you can make out the very shallow reefs. While you can pick your own route through the reefs, I suggest you use those shown on our sketch chart for the first time.

The first protected bay is half a mile long, though it does have a five-foot shoal in the middle, which is a little hard to see. It is quite an experience to be anchored here, with the noise and sight of hundreds, maybe thousands, of boobies in the trees ashore. The water is deep almost all the way to the mangrove trees. However, I would not anchor too close in, as you will probably get splattered by defecating birds and bitten by bugs. You should be fine on the north side of the anchorage and still close enough to see and hear the boobies.

If you leave this bay and follow the reef round, you come to the middle bay. The entrance is narrow, but there is 14 feet of water over it. Depths in the bay are 20 to 30 feet, and you can anchor anywhere off the reefs. This bay also has mangrove trees and birds, but the action is not quite as intense as in the first one.

The easternmost bay is probably the prettiest of the three. You have to wind your way down a narrow reef channel out toward the eastern end of the island. This end of the island is low, with only one or two small mangroves by the water's edge. You don't see so many birds, but you still get a few wading visitors along the shore. Access

to the island here for a walk is easy via the beach. There is a dinghy pass through into the middle bay along the shore.

Close to Isla Sur, temporary anchorage is also available off the little island of sand and seaside plants. I would anchor on the south side in about 45 feet of water. There is good snorkeling and interesting exploration.

Ashore

You can get ashore onto Isla Sur at the place marked on our chart from the first bay and from the beach in the eastern bay. The island is very colorful, with big patches of southern glasswort, seaside purslane, and saltwort all in different shades of green. According to our Venezuelan book on Los Roques, saltwort is known as fisherman's tobacco, as it can be dried and smoked. Heaven knows what it does to your lungs.

This is an extraordinary place to watch birds. Many species use this island, but boobies predominate, and with a pair of binoculars you can watch the fluffy white chicks. (You can also walk up to them, but this is not recommended, as in the long term it could affect where they nest). It is a great place to look at the red-footed booby, as its feet are quite visible in the branches.

There are small pools with crabs, and

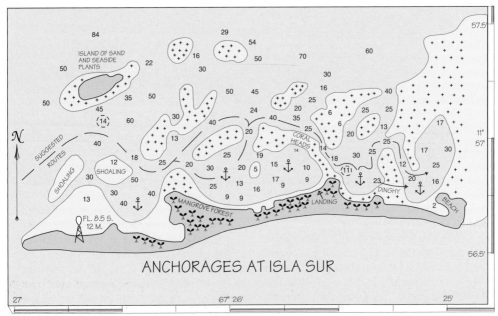

ANCHORAGES AT ISLA SUR

you will also see many hermit crabs in the grasses and bushes.

Water sports

The snorkeling is good on the reefs. Some spots are excellent, others drab. You have plenty to choose from.

Sometime toward dusk, get out the hand-line or troll round the bay. The fishing is excellent, and the odds are you can leave that can of corned beef in the locker.

ISLA OESTE ANCHORAGE

There is a good anchorage at the eastern end of the Isla Oeste. If you are approaching from Isla Sur, pass south and west of all the little islands just off Isla Oeste. The anchorage is off the beach right up at the eastern end of the island. The water is very deep, and the best way to anchor is bow- or stern-to the shore. There is only room for about two boats in comfort. You are protected from all directions except the south. If you wish to head out eastwards, note that the 60-foot channel shown on some charts between Isla Oeste and its offshore islands does not exist. Either the parrotfish have been very busy or the cartographer had a bad morning back in 1870 or whenever it was surveyed. A bank of sand and coral goes all the way across. You can get about 18 feet of water through here, if you avoid the coral heads.

The bay on the northern shore looks inviting, but it is full of coral and not a good place to anchor.

Ashore

This is a delightful spot with a pleasant beach, plenty of islands for dinghy exploration, and lots of snorkeling. Start with the reef right off the south end of the beach. The fishing is superb, so you shouldn't go hungry.

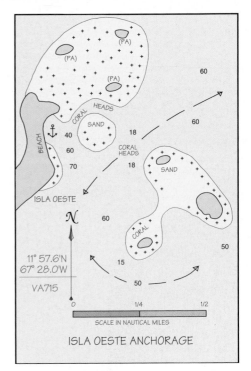

ISLA OESTE ANCHORAGE

OUT ON THE REEF

Being anchored out on the reef is wonderful in fine weather, with reasonable breezes. If the wind is howling from the northeast, it is possible but uncomfortable. You will find most anchoring spots in 20-40, or more, feet of water, and these will have the best holding.

You have to eyeball your way out and choose your spot. Note that there is a break in the reef about a third of the way down. This is not deep enough to pass through, but it does let waves in, which is worth keeping in mind when choosing your spot. The two little islands just close to this break are fun to explore, with good snorkeling, but the water is about 60 feet deep. There is a whole area to the northwest of this where you can get right among the reefs. Follow up inside the reefs to the northernmost little island. Eyeball your way in from here. There are deep passages between the reefs.

Aves de Sotavento

View from Islas
Palmeras

Aves de Sotavento lie about 10 miles west and a little
north of Aves de Barlovento. It has some delightful islands and
reefs, but navigation and anchoring are a little problematic,
because there are much larger areas of shallow water, and the
most protected harbor has a shoal approach that could be
difficult if large swells are running. Most yachts anchor in the
lee of the three pretty little islands. This is perfect in good
conditions but uncomfortable in a northerly swell. The alternative is to go to the windward side of the small islands and
anchor somewhere out on the barrier reef. This is fine if the
wind is not blowing too hard, but in a howling trade wind, you
are going to get some chop and roll. In short, it is best to visit
Aves de Sotavento in the spring or summer, when there are
no northerly swells and the winds are not too strong.

Navigation

You can approach around the northern or southern end.
The northern end is easier, because you stay in very deep water
to the first anchorages. The Saki Saki light flashes every seven
seconds, which is close to Barlovento's (10 seconds). I would
suggest staying well away from this area at night.

Regulations

There is a coast guard station on Isla Larga. Call them
on the radio when you arrive (VHF: 16) and they will come
and check you in. They also check you in for Barlovento, so

267

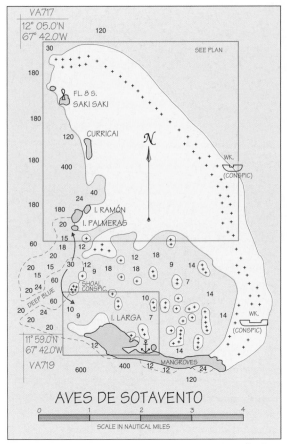

FL. 8 S.
SAKI SAKI

CURRICAI

N

WK.
(CONSPIC)

I. RAMÓN
I. PALMERAS

SHOAL
CONSPIC.

DEEP BLUE

I. LARGA

WK.
(CONSPIC)

11° 59.0'N
67° 42.0'W
VA719

MANGROVES

AVES DE SOTAVENTO

SCALE IN NAUTICAL MILES

for anchoring. The shelves on which one can anchor are mainly coral with patches of sand. This presents a headache for those anchoring on rope, as it will quickly get twisted around coral heads and chafe. Those with chain will have no problem, but the coral will. A sweeping chain can cut in seconds through structures that have taken centuries to build. If you anchor on chain, snorkel on your anchor and minimize damage in any way you can. A second anchor helps, as it stops the boat swinging from side to side. If you are anchoring on rope, think about putting a buoy about 20 feet from the anchor to keep the rode lifted above the coral. Again, two anchors will help.

ISLA PALMERAS

Isla Palmeras has two little sister islands, Isla Ramón to the east and another to the south. There are several good anchorages, depending on the conditions. There is a good little anchorage between Isla Palmeras and Isla Ramón. Approach from the Isla Palmeras side and ease in gently, as the water keeps getting shallower. You can find good anchorage in 10-12 feet of water, with only a couple of coral heads to avoid.

You can anchor in the lee of Isla Palmeras. This presents the same coral and sand problem as in Saki Saki and Curricai, though here the patches of sand tend to be greater and the patches of coral smaller.

There is also an anchorage on the south side of the little island to the south of Isla Palmeras. This is generally sand or sand and weed, with only a few coral heads, which can be avoided. It gives good shelter from the northeast, but if the wind blows hard from the east or southeast, there will be a chop. If you do anchor here, snorkel on the little reef right off the small southern island. It looks like very little from the boat, but it seems to house an astonishingly large number of

if you are coming from this direction, call in and see them.

Commercial fishing and the taking of any turtles or conch are forbidden.

NORTHERN ANCHORAGES

Most people stay on the west side of the reefs and anchor in the lee of the little islands.

SAKI SAKI AND CURRICAI

These two islands are photogenic, with powdery beaches, lovely water colors, and good snorkeling. The approach from the west is in deep water and presents no problems. However, both share the same problem colorful fish. From your yacht, you will probably see a lovely looking deep lagoon just to the east of Isla Palmeras. We sounded nine feet of water through the most obvious-looking cut toward high water. But it is narrow, and the lagoon would not be all that well protected in a strong wind.

EAST OF THE ISLANDS

The northern part of Aves de Sotavento is much deeper than the southern part. Once you pass into the reef system, there is a huge area between the islands and the barrier reef.

P256- Palmeras sunset

P257 - red footed booby

Venezuela's offshore islands

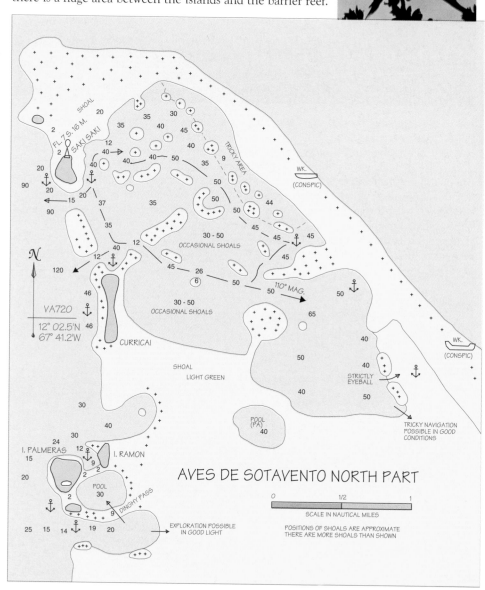

AVES DE SOTAVENTO NORTH PART

SCALE IN NAUTICAL MILES

0   1/2   1

EXPLORATION POSSIBLE IN GOOD LIGHT

POSITIONS OF SHOALS ARE APPROXIMATE THERE ARE MORE SHOALS THAN SHOWN

It is easily accessible though two cuts. One is just south of Saki Saki, with about 15 feet in the channel, and the other is just north of Curricai, with about 12 feet in the channel. Once inside, you often have 40-50 feet of water, which is deep blue and easy to tell from the many reefs. You have to be prepared to anchor in these depths, as shallower water that is not part of a reef can be hard to find. We have shown most main reefs and passages on our sketch chart, but it should be emphasized that this area is strictly a matter of eyeball navigation in good light. You can anchor anywhere inside that seems reasonable for the conditions. You get the most protection at the outer reef, but it is still not that calm in windy conditions. This is a good place to be if big northerly swells start rolling in.

The easiest access to the outer reef is

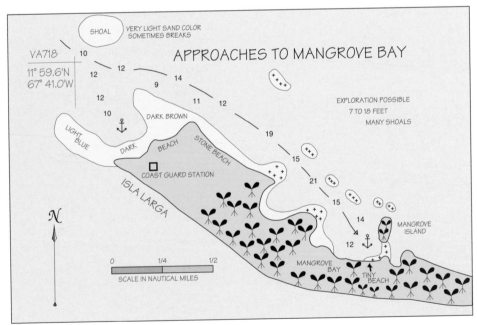

APPROACHES TO MANGROVE BAY

VA718
11° 59.6'N
67° 41.0'W

SHOAL VERY LIGHT SAND COLOR SOMETIMES BREAKS

EXPLORATION POSSIBLE
7 TO 18 FEET
MANY SHOALS

LIGHT BLUE
DARK
BEACH
DARK BROWN
STONE BEACH
COAST GUARD STATION
ISLA LARGA
MANGROVE ISLAND
MANGROVE BAY
TINY BEACH

N

SCALE IN NAUTICAL MILES
0   1/4   1/2

from Curricai. Enter through the pass, and then take the passage to get you just east of Curricai. From here, if you head about 110° magnetic, you have an almost straight-shot out to the reef with just minor adjustments to avoid shoals along the route.

Nearly all the reefs provide excellent snorkeling.

ISLA LARGA

The Dutch once settled Isla Larga and mined guano. The ruins of three old forts are all that remain of their reign. Isla Larga, like Isla Agua in Los Roques, has water just beneath the sand. There are plenty of birds here, but not in the same extraordinary numbers that are found in Aves de Barlovento. The coast guard station is at the western end of the island.

MANGROVE BAY

Mangrove Bay is the most protected anchorage in Aves de Sotavento, though the access is a little shallow. If you are coming from Isla Palmeras, get into the dark blue water and follow it south until you see the shoal about half a mile north of the coast guard station. The shoal shows up clearly as very light-colored water. Enter south of this shoal and head for the easternmost point of Isla Larga. Depths will be mainly 10-12 feet. When you get near the island, follow it round into the anchorage. Shortly before the anchorage, pass close to the two obvious reefs extending from the two points of land. This avoids other, harder-to-see reefs farther out. You get good protection in the southern corner of the bay, but enough breeze to keep bugs away. This is a comfortable place to hang out, and you can explore the island by dinghy. There are lots of reefs around for snorkeling.

Venezuela's offshore islands